STRUCTURED COMPUTER ORGANIZATION

STRUCTURED COMPUTER ORGANIZATION

Harsh Marwah

ANMOL PUBLICATIONS PVT. LTD.
NEW DELHI-110 002 (INDIA)

ANMOL PUBLICATIONS PVT. LTD.
Regd. Office: 4360/4, Ansari Road, Daryaganj,
New Delhi-110002 (India)
Tel.: 23278000, 23261597, 23286875, 23255577
Fax: 91-11-23280289
Email: anmolpub@gmail.com
Visit us at: www.anmolpublications.com

Branch Office: No. 1015, Ist Main Road, BSK IIIrd Stage
IIIrd Phase, IIIrd Block, Bangalore-560 085 (India)
Tel.: 080-41723429 • Fax: 080-26723604
Email: anmolpublicationsbangalore@gmail.com

Structured Computer Organization

First Edition, 2011

ISBN 978-81-261-4580-5

PRINTED IN INDIA

Printed at Mehra Offset Press, Delhi.

Contents

	Preface	*vii*
1.	Introduction	1
2.	Digital Computer Generation	30
3.	Central Processing Unit	63
4.	Floating Point Arithmetic Operations	100
5.	Control Unit	171
6.	Hardwire and Micro Programmed Control	191
7.	Memory	225
8.	Storage Devices	266
	Index	278

Preface

Structured Computer Organisation is a widely adopted textbook on Computer Science that covers the fundamental concepts based on the principle that a computer can be regarded as a hierarchy of levels, each one performing some well-defined functions. Intended for students offering course on Computer Organizations and Architecture in Computer Science, IT courses, Electrical/Electronics Engineering and MCA.

The book takes a modern structured, layered approach to understanding computer systems. It's highly accessible and been thoroughly updated to reflect today's most critical new technologies. The book includes detailed coverage at the digital logic and micro-architecture levels, instruction set level, and operating system machine level, and contains a complete and updated information on parallel computer architecture. The book is required for all computer professionals and engineers who need an overview or introduction to computer architecture.

Author

Chapter 1

Introduction

NUMBER REPRESENTATION

CONCEPT

When working with any kind of digital electronics in which numbers are being represented, it is important to understand the different ways numbers are represented in these systems. Almost without fail, numbers are represented by two voltage levels which can represent a one or a zero (an interesting exception to this rule is the new memory device recently announced by Intel which uses one of four possible voltage levels, thereby increasing the amount of information that can be stored in a given space). The number system based on ones and zeroes is called the *bi*nary system (because there are only two possible digits). Before discussing the binary system, a review of the *dec*imal (ten possible digits) system is in order, because many of the concepts of the binary system will be easier to understand when introduced alongside their decimal counterpart. You should all have some familiarity with the decimal system. For instance, to represent the positive integer one hundred and twenty-five as a decimal number, we can write (with the postivie sign implied). The subscript 10 denotes the number as a base 10 (decimal) number.

$$125_{10} = 1*100 + 2*10 + 5*1 = 1*10^2 + 2*10^1 + 5*10^0$$

The rightmost digit is multiplied by 10^0, the next digit to the left is multiplied by 10^1, and so on. Each digit to the left has a multiplier that is 10 times the previous digit. Hopefully this is all a review.

Some observations:

- To multiply a number by 10 you can simply shift it to the left by one digit, and fill in the rightmost digit with a 0 (moving the decimal place one to the right). To divide a number by 10, simply shift the number to the right by one digit (moving the decimal place one to the left).
- To see how many digits a number needs, you can simply take the logarithm (base 10) of the absolute value of the number, and add 1 to it. The integer part of the result is the number of digits. For instance, $\log_{10}(33) + 1 = 2.5$. The integer part of that is 2, so 2 digits are needed.
- With n digits, 10^n unique numbers (from 0 to 10^n-1) can be represented. If n=3, 1000 (=10^3) numbers can be represented 0–999.
- Negative numbers are handled easily by simply putting a minus sign (–) in front of the number. This does lead, however, to the somewhat awkward situation where 0=–0. We will avoid this situation with binary representations, but with a little bit of effort.

Representing fractions is a simple extension of this idea. To wit,

$$25.43_{10} = 2*10 + 5*1 + 4*0.1 + 3*0.01 = 2*10^1 + 5*10^0 + 4*10^{-1} + 3*10^{-2}$$

The only pertinent observations here are:

- If there are m digits to the right of the decimal point, the smallest number that can be represented is 10^{-m}. For instance if m=4, the smallest number that can be represented is $0.0001=10^{-4}$.

BINARY REPRESENTATION OF POSITIVE INTEGERS

Binary representations of positive can be understood in the same way as their decimal counterparts.

For example:

$$86_{10} = 1*64 + 0*32 + 1*16 + 0*8 + 1*4 + 1*2 + 0*1$$

or

$$86_{10} = 1*2^6 + 0*2^5 + 1*2^4 + 0*2^3 + 1*2^2 + 1*2^1 + 0*2^0$$

or

$$86_{10} = 1010110_2$$

The subscript 2 denotes a binary number. Each digit in a binary number is called a bit. The number 1010110 is represented by 7 bits. Any number can be broken down this way, by finding all of the powers of 2 that add up to the number in question (in this case 2^6, 2^4, 2^2 and 2^1). You can see this is exactly analagous to the decimal deconstruction of the number 125 that was done earlier.

Likewise we can make a similar set of observations:

- To multiply a number by 2 you can simply shift it to the left by one digit, and fill in the rightmost digit with a 0. To divide a number by 2, simply shift the number to the right by one digit.
- To see how many digits a number needs, you can simply take the logarithm (base 2) of the number, and add 1 to it. The integer part of the result is the number of digits. For instance, $\log_2(86) + 1 = 7.426$. The integer part of that is 7, so 7 digits are needed.
- With n digits, 2^n unique numbers (from 0 to 2^n-1) can be represented. If n=8, 256 (=2^8) numbers can be represented 0-255.

SIGNED INTEGERS

- It was noted previously that we will not be using a minus sign (–) to represent negative numbers. We would like to represent our binary numbers with only two symbols, 0 and 1. There are a few ways to represent negative binary numbers. The simplest of these methods is called ones complement, where the sign of a binary number is changed by simply toggling each bit (0's become 1's and vice-versa). This has some difficulties, among them the fact that zero can be represented in two different ways (for an eight bit number these would be 0000 0000 and 1111 1111)., we will use a method called two's complement notation which avoids the pitfalls of one's complement, but which is a bit more complicated.

- To represent an n bit signed binary number the leftmost bit, has a special significance. The difference between a signed and an unsigned number is given in the table below for an 8 bit number.

Table. The Value of Bits in Signed and Unsigned Binary Numbers.

	Bit 7	Bit 6	Bit 5	Bit 4	Bit 3	Bit 2	Bit 1	Bit 0
Unsigned	$2^7 = 128$	$2^6 = 64$	$2^5 = 32$	$2^4 = 16$	$2^3 = 8$	$2^2 = 4$	$2^1 = 2$	$2^0 = 1$
Signed	$-(2^7) = -128$	$2^6 = 64$	$2^5 = 32$	$2^4 = 16$	$2^3 = 8$	$2^2 = 4$	$2^1 = 2$	$2^0 = 1$

- Let's look at how this changes the value of some binary numbers

Binary	Unsigned	Signed
0010 0011	35	35
1010 0011	163	–93
1111 1111	255	–1
1000 0000	128	–128

- If Bit 7 is not set (as in the first example) the representation of signed and unsigned numbers is the same. However, when Bit 7 is set, the number is always negative. For this reason Bit 7 is sometimes called the sign bit. Signed numbers are added in the same way as unsigned numbers, the only difference is in the way they are interpreted. This is important for designers of arithmetic circuitry because it means that numbers can be added by the same circuitry regardless of whether or not they are signed.
- To form a two's complement number that is negative you simply take the corresponding positive number, invert all the bits, and add 1. The example below illustrated this by forming the number negative 35 as a two's complement integer:
- $35_{10} = 0010\ 0011_2$

  invert → $1101\ 1100_2$

add 1 → $1101\ 1101_2$

- So 1101 1101 is our two's complement representation of –35. We can check this by adding up the contributions from the individual bits
- $1101\ 1101_2 = -128 + 64 + 0 + 16 + 8 + 4 + 0 + 1 = -35$.
- The same procedure (invert and add 1) is used to convert the negative number to its positive equivalent. If we want to know what what number is represented by 1111 1101, we apply the procedure again
- ? = $1111\ 1101_2$
  invert → $0000\ 0010_2$
  add 1 → $0000\ 0011_2$
- Since 0000 0011 represents the number 3, we know that 1111 1101 represents the number -3.

Positive Binary Fractions

- The representation of unsigned binary fractions proceeds in exactly the same way as decimal fractions.
  For example:
- $0.625_{10} = 1{*}0.5 + 0{*}0.25 + 1{*}0.125 = 1{*}\ 2^{-1} + 0{*}\ 2^{-2} + 1{*}\ 2^{-3} = 0.101_2$
- Each place to the right of the decimal point represents a negative power of 2, just as for decimals they represent a negative power of 10. Likewise, if there are m bits to the right of a decimal, the precision of the number is 2^{-m} (versus 10^{-m} for decimal). Though it is possible to represent numbers greater than one by having digits to the left of the decimal place we will restrict ourselves to numbers less than one. These are commonly used by Digital Signal Processors.
- The largest number that can be represented by such a representation is $1-2^{-m}$, the smallest number is 2^{-m}. For a fraction with 15 bits of resolution this gives a range of approximately 0.99997 to 3.05E–5.
- Note that this representationis easily extended to represent all positive numbers by having the digits

to the left of the decimal point represent the integer part, and the digits to the right representing the fractional part. Thus

- $6.625_{10} = 110.101_2$

Signed Binary Fractions

- Signed binary fractions are formed much like signed integers. We will work with a single digit to the left of the decimal point, and this will represent the number –1 (= $-(2^0)$). The rest of the representation of the fraction remains unchanged. Therefore this leftmost bit represents a sign bit just as with two's complement integers. If this bit is set, the number is negative, otherwise the number is positive. The largest positive number that can be represented is still $1-2^{-m}$ but the largest negative number is –1. The resolution is still $1-2^{-m}$.
- There is a terminology for naming the resolution of signed fractions. If there are m bits to the right of the decimal point, the number is said to be in *Qm* format. For a 16 bit number (15 bits to the right of the decimal point) this results in Q15 notation.

FIXED AND FLOATING POINT NUMBER REPRESENTATION

FLOATING POINT

One problem with the mantissa/base/exponent representation is that not all base-10 numbers can be expressed perfectly as a base-2 number. For example, 1/2 and 0.25 can be represented perfectly as base-2 values, while 1/3 and 0.1 produce infinitely repeating base-2 decimals. These values must be rounded to be stored in the floating-point format. With sufficient digits of precision, this generally is not a problem for computations. However, it does lead to some anomalies where algebraic rules do not appear to apply.

Consider the following example:

```
REAL*4 X,Y
X = 0.1
```

```
Y = 0
DO I=1,10
Y = Y + X
ENDDO
IF (Y .EQ. 1.0) THEN
PRINT *,'Algebra is truth'
ELSE
PRINT *,'Not here'
ENDIF
PRINT *,1.0-Y
END
```

At first glance, this appears simple enough. Mathematics tells us ten times 0.1 should be one. Unfortunately, because 0.1 cannot be represented exactly as a base-2 decimal, it must be rounded. It ends up being rounded down to the last bit. When ten of these slightly smaller numbers are added together, it does not quite add up to 1.0. When X and Y are REAL*4, the difference is about 10^{-7}, and when they are REAL*8, the difference is about 10^{-16}.

One possible method for comparing computed values to constants is to subtract the values and test to see how close the two values become.

For example, one can rewrite the test in the above code to be:

```
IF (ABS(1.0-Y).LT. 1E-6) THEN
PRINT *,'Close enough for government work'
ELSE
PRINT *,'Not even close'
ENDIF
```

The type of the variables in question and the expected error in the computation that produces Y determines the appropriate value used to declare that two values are close enough to be declared equal.

Another area where inexact representation becomes a problem is the fact that algebraic inverses do not hold with all floating-point numbers. For example, using REAL*4, the value (1.0/X) * X does not evaluate to 1.0 for 135 values of X from one to 1000. This can be a problem when computing the inverse of a matrix using LU-decomposition. LU-decomposition repeatedly does division, multiplication, addition, and subtraction. If you do the straightforward LU-decomposition on a matrix with integer coefficients that has an integer solution, there is a pretty good chance you won't get the exact solution when you run your algorithm. Discussing techniques for improving the accuracy of matrix inverse computation is best left to a numerical analysis text.

Floating-Point Formats

The examples of floating-point numbers shown on the previous page illustrated the most common general type of floating-point format, the one shown in the first line of the diagram below:

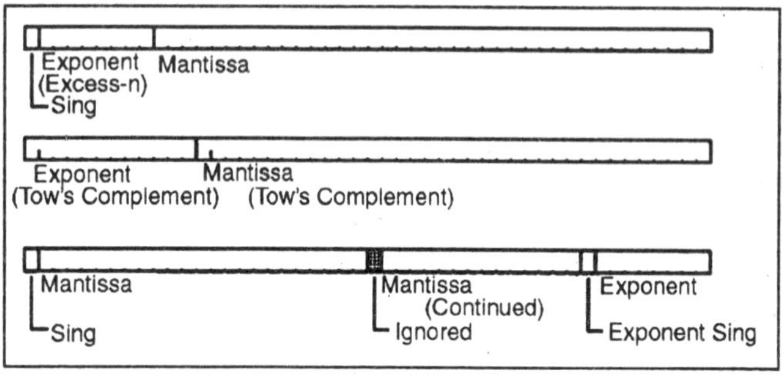

The format shown in the first line begins with a single sign bit, which is 0 if the number is positive, and 1 if the number is negative. Next is the exponent. If the exponent is eight bits long, as shown in the diagram, it is in excess-128 notation, so that the smallest exponent value, 00000000, stands for -128, and the largest exponent value, 11111111, stands for 127. Finally, we find the mantissa, which is an unsigned binary fraction.

If the mantissa is normalized, non-negative floating-point numbers can be compared by the same instructions as are used to compare integers. This format is particularly popular on computers that have hardware support for floating-point numbers. A number of variations on this format are used.

Of course, the length of the exponent field shown in the diagram is only one possibility. The second line in the diagram illustrates the kind of floating-point format used on computers such as the PDP-8 and the RECOMP II. Here, a floating-point number is simply represented by two signed binary numbers, the first, being the exponent, treated as an integer, and the second, being the mantissa, treated as a fraction, both represented in the ordinary format for signed fixed-point numbers used on the computer.

The third line of the diagram illustrates a kind of format which, with a number of variations, was found on most computers with a 24-bit word length. Computers with a 48-bit word length, on the other hand, typically had hardware floating-point, and used a floating-point format of the type given in the first line.

Why did these computers use such an unusual floating-point format? Typically, although these computers did not have hardware floating-point support, the way bigger computers with a 32-bit, 36-bit, 48-bit, or 64-bit word length did, they did come standard with hardware integer multiplication, unlike smaller computers with an 18-bit, 16-bit, or 12-bit word length.

In order to support floating-point arithmetic, the format of double-precision fixed-point numbers on most of these computers omitted the first bit of the second word of the number from the number itself, sometimes treating it as a second copy of the sign, so that fixed-point numbers could be treated as having the binary point on the right, making them integers, or on the left, after the sign, making them fractions on the interval [0,1), without having to adjust them by shifting them one place to the left after a multiplication.

A number of variations of each type of floating-point format exist, of course. When a floating-point format consists of a mantissa field followed by an exponent field, with no omitted bit, the choice of whether to consider the floating-point format as belonging to Group or Group is arbitrary.

This page, as currently constructed, has placed all the formats with no omitted mantissa bits in Group . My current thinking on this issue is now favouring moving those formats where the exponent is part of a partial word within a multiword format (that is, among those formats on this page, that of the Hewlett-Packard 2114/2115/2116, and that of the SDS 920/930/940/9300 and the SCC 600) in with Group. A Group format, as noted, tends to be used on an architecture for which the initial implementations supported floating-point in hardware. A Group format tends to be used where the word length is too long to use a full word for the exponent, and hardware multiplication features make it useful to align the beginning of the mantissa with the beginning of a word.

The Group format is most popular with machines with small word lengths and limited hardware arithmetic, but it was also used, as in the case of the Maniac and the Philco 2000, with architectures that started out with hardware floating-point as well. Also, in some cases, the floating point formats of different sizes for some machines belonged to different groups. When this happened, all the formats for any one architecture were placed within the discussion of one of the groups of formats included.

Particularly unsusual formats discussed below include the single precision floating-point format for the PDP-4, 7, 9 and 15, which can be thought of as a rearranged Group or Group format, and the double precision floating-point format of the ICL 1900, which applies the principle of making a double-precision float out of two single-precision floats, usually used with hardware Group formats, to a base floating-point format which belongs to Group; this appears to be the result of either successive implementations of the architecture evolving from hardware multiply to full hardware floating-point or the availability of hardware floating-point as an option.

Another case where the same machine had floating point formats belonging to different groups is the Harris 800, which added a Group quad-precision floating-point format to an existing architecture whose single and double precision floating-point formats belonged to Group: here, the hardware level seems to have remained constant, and what happened was that the larger size of the quad-precision format made it reasonable to use a full word instead of a partial word for the exponent, and once that was done, a Group format appeared more reasonable than a Group format. The Univac 418 single-precision floating-point format belongs to Group, and its double-precision format to Group . Hardware floating-point was only introduced to this architecture with the Univac 418-, and so this combination is not too surprising.

Group Floating-Point Formats

The floating-point formats of many 24-bit computers followed the model shown in the third line of the diagram at the top of the page, but they varied in minor ways from it, and are illustrated below.

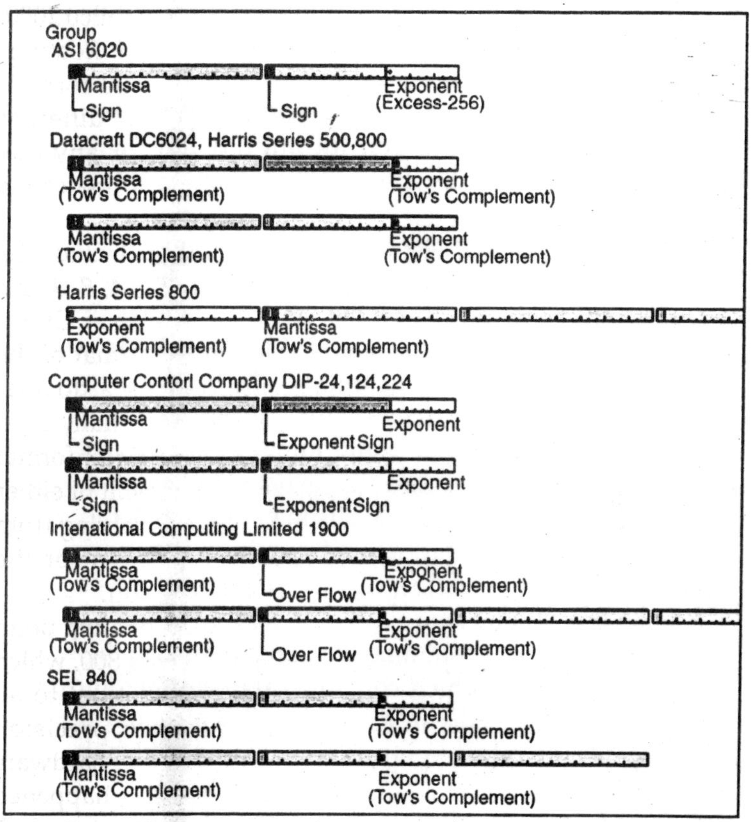

The ASI 6020 computer used a 39-bit mantissa in sign-magnitude format, followed by a nine-bit exponent in excess-256 notation, a rare instance of excess-n format being used in a Group representation of floating-point numbers. The Datacraft 6024 computer, and its successors from Harris, used two's complement form to represent integers. The exponent field, including sign, was eight bits long. The basic format shown above was used for double-precision floating-point; in single-precision floating point, numbers still occupied two 24-bit words in memory, but the portion of the mantissa in the second word was not used.

The Harris 800 computer added a quad-precision floating-point format that used a full 24-bit word for the exponent. In this format, the exponent came first instead of last, so it belongs to Group . The sign bits of the second and third words of the mantissa were unused, but this is even found in some of the double-precision formats in Group .

The DDP-24 computer, from 3C and then Honeywell, used sign-magnitude representation for integers, and a multiply instruction ensured both words of the product contained the same sign.

It also left the mantissa portion of the second word unused for single-precision numbers. The eight least significant bits of the second word contained the value of the exponent; the sign of the exponent was contained in the sign bit of the second word, instead of that bit being unused. The ICL 1900 computer used two's complement notation for integers.

In double-length fixed-point numbers, the first bit of the second word was always zero. The exponent field of a floating-point number consisted of nine bits in excess-256 notation; the first bit of the second word was a flag which, if one, indicated that a floating-point overflow had taken place. Single-precision numbers were 48 bits long.

A double-precision number was 96 bits long; in the second half of the number, which contained the least significant 35 bits of the mantissa, the first bit of each word, and the area corresponding to the exponent field in the first half, were ignored.

The SEL 820 computer, which I believe to be the last of the major members of the"classic"group of 24-bit computers to be described on these pages has its floating-point format illustrated here as well. Despite the fact that the exponent is at the end of the number and not the beginning, the double-precision format simply appends a word of mantissa to an unaltered single-precision floating-point number.

DETECTION AND CORRECTION CODES

ERROR-CORRECTING CODES

Introduction

The theory of error detecting and correcting codes is that branch of engineering and mathematics which deals with the reliable transmission and storage of data. Information media are not 100% reliable in practice, in the sense that noise (any form of interference) frequently causes data to be distorted. To deal with this undesirable but inevitable situation, some form of redundancy is incorporated in the original data.

With this redundancy, even if errors are introduced (up to some tolerance level), the original information can be recovered, or at least the presence of errors can be detected. We saw in class how adding to the original message the parity bit or the arithmetic sum allows the detection of a (certain type of) error.

However, that kind of redundancy doesn't allow for the correction of the error. Error-correcting codes do exactly this: they add redundancy to the original message in such a way that it is possible for the receiver to detect the error and correct it, recovering the original message.

This is crucial for certain applications where the re-sending of the message is not possible (for example, for interplanetary communications and storage of data). The crucial problem to be resolved then is how to add this redundancy in order to detect and correct as many errors as possible in the most efficient way.

This document starts with an overview of the applications of the error-correcting codes, followed by a session describing the fundamental concepts. It then addresses some of the issues involved in the design of the codes. The last session is a brief introduction of the very last discovery in the theory of error-correcting codes: the turbo codes.

Applications of Error Correcting Codes

The increasing reliance on digital communication and the emergence of the digital computer as an essential tool in a technological society have placed error-correcting codes in a most prominent position. We cite here a few specific applications, in an attempt to indicate their practicality and importance.

Many computers now have error-correcting capabilities built into their random access memories; it is less expensive to compensate for errors through the use of error-correcting codes than to build integrated circuits that are 100% reliable. The single error-correcting Hamming codes, and linear codes in general, are of use here. Disk storage is another area of computing where error-coding is employed. Storage capacity has been greatly increased through the use of disks of higher and higher density. With this increase in density, error probability also increases, and therefore information is now stored on many disks using error-correcting codes.

In 1972, the *Mariner* space probe flew past Mars and transmitted pictures back to earth. The channel for such transmissions is space and the earth's atmosphere. Solar activity and atmospheric conditions can introduce errors into weak signals coming from the spacecraft. In order that most of the pictures sent could be correctly recovered here on earth, the following coding scheme was used. The source alphabet consisted of 64 shades of gray. The source encoder encoded each of these into binary 6-tuples and the channel encoder produced binary 32-tuples. The source decoder could correct up to 7 errors in any 32-tuple. This was done with the Reed-Muller codes.

In 1979, the *Voyager* probes began transmitting colour pictures of Jupiter. For colour pictures the source alphabet needed to be much larger and was chosen to have 4096 colour shades. The source encoder produced binary 12-tuples for each colour shade and the channel encoder produced 24-tuples (i.e.

24 dimensional vectors). This code would correct up to 3 errors in any 24-tuple, and is the Golay code. The increasing popularity of digital audio is due in part to the powerful error-correcting codes that the digitization process facilitates. Information is typically stored on a small aluminized disk as a series of microscopic pits and smooth areas, the pattern representing a sequence of 0's and 1's. A laser beam is used as the playback mechanism to retrieve stored data.

Because the data is digital, error correction schemes can be easily incorporated into such a system. Given an error-coded digital recording, a digital audio system can on playback, correct errors introduced by fingerprints, scratches, or even imperfections originally present in the storage medium. The compact disc system pioneered by Philips Corporation of the Netherlands in cooperation with Sony Corporation of Japan, allowing playback of pre-recorded digital audio disks, is an excellent example of the application of error-correcting codes to digital communication; *cross interleaved Reed-Solomon* codes are used for error correction in this system. Digital audio tape (DAT) systems have also been developed, allowing digital recording as well as playback.

Error-correcting codes are particularly suited when the transmission channel is noisy. This is the case of wireless communication. Nowadays, all digital wireless communications use error-correcting codes.

Fundamental Concepts

We begin with a few definitions, in order to develop a working vocabulary.

Let A be an alphabet of q symbols. For example, A = {a,b,c...,z) is the standard lower case alphabet for the English language, and A = (0,1) is the binary alphabet.

Definition: A block code of length n containing M codewords over the alphabet A is a set of M n-tuples where each n-tuple takes its components from A. We refer to such a block code as an [n,M]-code over A.

In practice, we most frequently take A to be the binary alphabet. Given a code C of block length n over an alphabet

A, those specific n-tuples over A which are in C are referred to as codewords.

Note that while the channel encoder transmits codewords, the n-tuples received by the channel decoder may or may not be codewords, due to the possible occurrence of errors during transmission.

Example 1: Suppose the information we are to transmit comes from the set of symbols {A, B, C, D}. For practical considerations we associate sequences of 0's and l's with each of these symbols.

$$A \rightarrow 00$$
$$B \rightarrow 01$$
$$C \rightarrow 10$$
$$D \rightarrow 11$$

This is the source encoding. Now we want to add some redundancy (channel encoding).

$$A \rightarrow 00 \rightarrow 00000$$
$$B \rightarrow 01 \rightarrow 10110$$
$$C \rightarrow 10 \rightarrow 01011$$
$$D \rightarrow 11 \rightarrow 11101$$

We have just constructed a [5,4]-code over a binary alphabet. That is, we constructed a code with 4 codewords, each being a 5-tuple (block length 5), with each component of the 5-tuple being O or 1. The code is the set of n-tuples produced by the channel encoder (as opposed to the source encoder). The source encoder transforms messages into k-tuples (k=2 in the example above) over the code alphabet A, and the channel encoder assigns to each of these information k-tuples a codeword of length n (n=5 in the example).

Since the channel encoder is adding redundancy, we have $n > k$ and hence we have message expansion. While the added redundancy is desirable from the point of view of error control, it decreases the efficiency of the communication channel by reducing its effective capacity. The ratio k to n is a measure of the fraction of information in the channel which is non-redundant.

Definition: The rate of an [n,M]-code which encodes information k-tuples is

$$R = K/n$$

The rate of the simple code given in example 1 is 2/5.

The quantity r = n-k is sometimes called the redundancy of the code.

A fundamental parametre associated with an [n,M]-code C is the Hamming distance for C. Before we can define the Hamming distance for a code, we must define the Hamming distance between two codeword's.

*Definition:*The Hamming distance d(x,y) between two codewords x and y is the number of coordinate positions in which they differ.

Example 2: Over the alphabet A = (0,1}, the codewords x and y x=(10110) y=(11O11) have Hamming distance d(x,y) =3.

Example 3: The codeword's u and v over the alphabet A = (0,1,2), given by u= (21002) v=(12001) have Hamming distance d(u,v) =3.

Definition: Let C be an [n,M]-code.

The Hamming distance d of the code C is d= min {d(x,y): x,y belong to C, x != y}.

In other words, the Hamming distance of a code is the minimum distance between two distinct codeword's, over all pairs of codeword's.

Example 4: Consider C = (c0,c1,c2,c3} where c0=(00000) c1 =(10110) c2= (01011) c3= (11101) This code has distance d = 3. It is the [5,4] code constructed earlier.

Suppose we have an [n,M]-code C with distance d. We need to adopt a strategy for the channel decoder (or just decoder). When the decoder receives an n-tuple r it must make some decision.

This decision may be one of:

- No errors have occurred; accept r as a codeword.
- Errors have occurred; correct r to a codeword c.
- Errors have occurred; no correction is possible.

In general, the decoder will not always make the correct decision; for example, consider the possibility of an error pattern occurring which changes a transmitted codeword into another codeword. The goal is that the decoder takes the course of action which has the greatest probability of being correct.

One usually makes the assumption that errors are introduced by the channel at random, and that the probability of an error in one coordinate is independent of errors in adjacent coordinates.

The decoding strategy we shall adopt, called nearest neighbour decoding, can then be specified as follows.

Nearest Neighbour Decoding: If an n-tuple r is received, and there is a unique codeword c that belongs to C such that d(r,c) is a minimun, then correct r to the c. If no such c exists, report that errors have been detected, but no correction is possible. By nearest neighbour decoding, a received vector is decoded to the codewords"closest"to it, with respect to Hamming distance.

The figure below illustrates the concept. The red dots are the codeword's, the green ones are the received words that can be corrected to the closest codeword's and the blue dot is a received word that is equidistant from 2 codeword's and therefore cannot be corrected.

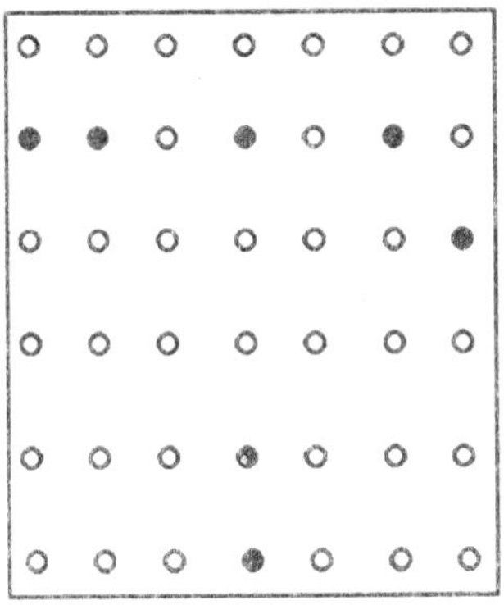

A code is said to correct e errors if a decoder using the above scheme is capable of correcting any pattern of e or fewer errors introduced by the channel. In this case, the decoder can correct any transmitted codeword which has been altered in e or fewer coordinate positions.

Theorem: Let C be an [n,M]-code having distance d = 2e+1. Then C can correct e errors. If used for error detection only, C can detect 2e errors. Let c be one codeword of C and S be the set of all n-tuples over the alphabet of C and define,

$$S(c) = \{x \text{ belongs to } S: d(x,c) \Leftarrow e).$$

S(c) is called the sphere of radius e about the codeword c. It consists of all n-tuples within distance e of the codeword c, which we think of as being at the centre of the sphere.

In the figure below, the"spheres"arount the codewords of the previous figure. The radius is in this case is 1.

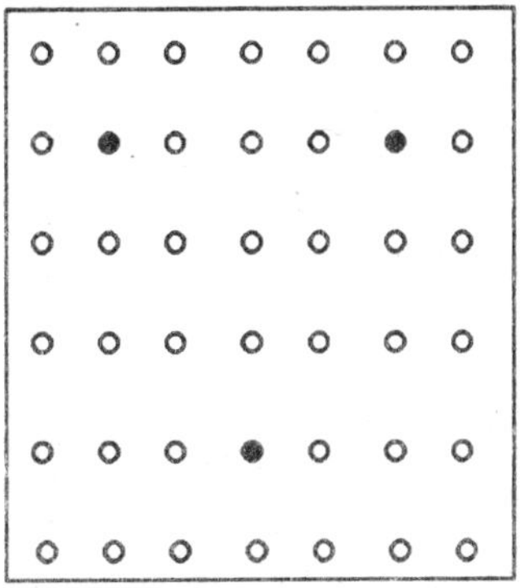

Given 2 code words, their spheres don't intersect, hence if codeword c is transmitted and t<= e errors are introduced, the received word r is an n-tuple in the sphere S(c) and thus c is the unique codeword closest to r. The decoder can always correct any error pattern of this type. If we use the code only for error detection, then at least 2e+1 errors must occur in a codeword to carry it into another codeword. If at least 1 and at most 2e errors are introduced, the received word will never be a codeword and error detection is always possible.

The spheres have to be disjoint in order to be able to correct errors. But if a received word happens to be in the space between the spheres, correction is not possible: that space doesn't belong to any sphere, i.e. to any codeword: the error is detected but not corrected.

Therefore, we want to find codes such that the the spheres around the codewords are disjoint (to correctly correct the errors) but as close as possible to each other, to correct ALL the errors. If all the space is taken by the sphere, all the words received will fall into the sphere of a codeword and therefore can be corrected to that codeword. These are the perfect codes. Lets give the formal definition of perfect codes.

Definition: A perfect code is an e-error-correcting [n, M]-code over an alphabet A such that every n-tuple over A is in the sphere of radius e about some codework.

In a perfect code of block length n, the sphere of radius e about code works are not only disjoint (since the code is e-error-correcting) but exhaust the entire space of n-tuples.

Issues

Designing a good code is a very hard problem. Also, lots of factors need to be taken in account. For instance, in practice the code should be designed appropriately depending on the expected rate of errors for the particular channel being employed. If it is known that the probability that the channel will introduce 2 errors into any transmitted codeword is extremely small, then it is likely not necessary to construct a code that will correct all 2-bit error patterns. A single error correcting code will likely suffice. Conversely, if double errors are frequent and a single error correcting code is being used, then decoding errors will be frequent.

From this brief introduction, a number of questions arise:

- Given n, M and d, can we determine if an [n Al] code with distance d exists?
- Assuming such a code does exist, how would one be constructed in practice?
- How should information k-tuples be associated with codeword n-tuples to facilitate efficient channel encoding?
- How should channel decoding be performed?

Lets examine the issue of channel decoding in greater detail. When a word is received and it's not a codeword, finding the closest codeword involves computing the distance from the received word to each codeword, requiring M comparisons. While this might be acceptable for small M, in practice we usually find M quite large. Suppose a code C is used with M = 2^50 codewords, which is not unrealistic. If we could carry out 1 million distance computations per second, it would take around 20 years to make a single correction. Clearly, this is not tolerable and more efficient techniques are required. Wishing to retain the nearest neighbour decoding strategy, we seek more efficient techniques for its implementation. The theory of error-correcting code is concerned with constructing codes for various values of n, M and d, and the consideration of appropriate encoding and decoding techniques.

Most of the best known codes are algebraic in nature like the linear codes. Linear codes are an important and general class of error-correcting codes. For example, theBCH codes used for CDs are linear codes. They are heavily mathematical and an appropriate description here is not possible. The next session describes instead the last"discovery"in the theory of error correcting codes, the Turbo codes.

Turbo Codes

In session 3, when we introduced the Nearest Neighbour Decoding, we didn't mention the fact that what the decoding actually does is maximizing the probability P(r|c) that r is received, given that c is sent. i.e. choosing the nearest codeword is equivalent to choosing the most likely input message c given the received tuple r. This decoding strategy is known as maximum likelihood decoding

We can then state the decoding problem in the following manner. Let U be the original message, X the encoded message and Y the message received after the noisy channel. This is schematized in the following figure.

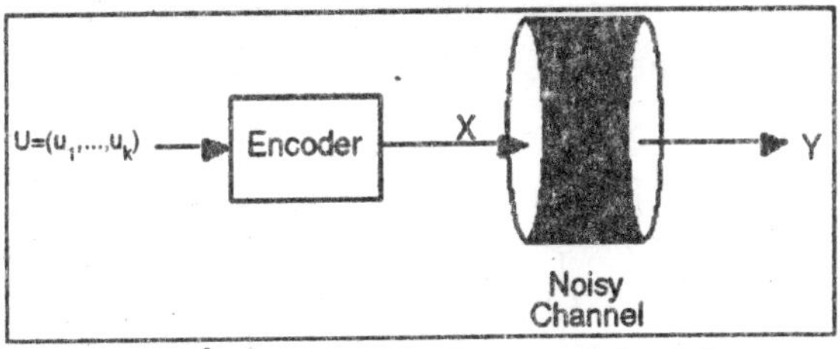

The receiver knows Y and the model of the encoder, i.e. is has a knowledge of how the original message was originally encoded. The problem now is finding the U that maximizes the probability that U was sent given that Y was received, i.e. the probability P(U|Y).

Having stated the decoding problem in probabilistic terms, we can take advantage of various methods that deal with probability estimations. A class of such methods is the class of graphical models.

The simplest graphical model:

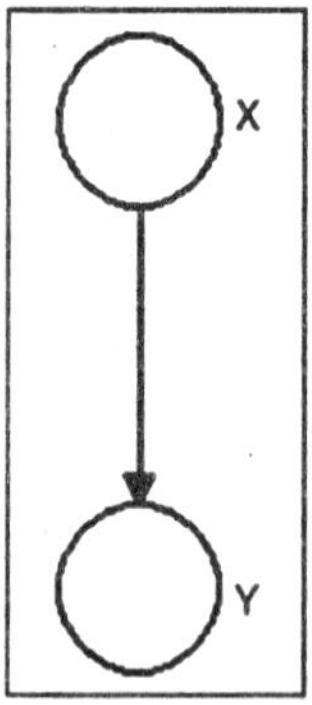

A classical problem of probability estimation is finding the probability distribution P(X | Y) where X and Y are 2 random variables. The graphical model framework allows for such probability estimations to be calculated in an efficient way. Note that the calculation of P(X | Y) from P(Y | X) and P(X) is just Bayes rule - P(X | Y) = P(Y | X)P(X)/P(Y) - and that graphical model inference algorithms can be viewed as generalizations of Bayes rule to arbitrary graphs.

Lets now see how we can view error correcting codes as graphical models. In the figure below, a convolution code as a graphical model.Let U be the original message, X the encoded message and Y the message received after the noisy channel.

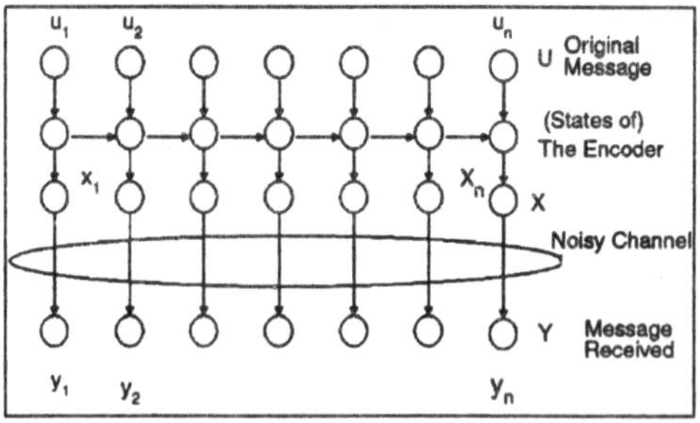

Now, the decoding problem of finding U that maximizes p(U | Y) can be tackled within the framework of graphical models. 345We have introduced the convolution codes mainly because the Turbo codes are two convolution codes put together. The following figure illustrate the graphical representation of a turbo code.

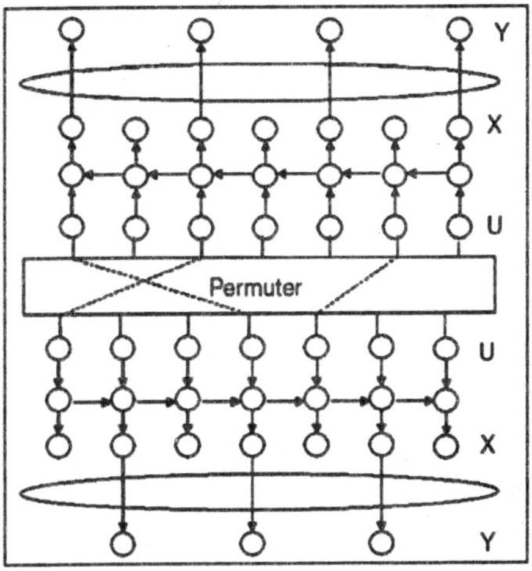

It should be mentioned that general inference in graphical models is NP-hard, and, in particular, exact inference, calculating P(U | Y), for turbo codes is infeasible and therefore an approximate inference algorithm is used.

Turbo codes were discovered very recently. There is much excitement about them. They outperform all other kinds of error-correcting codes in the case of long block lengths, although the reason why they do so is not yet clear.

ERROR DETECTING

R. W. Hamming wrote the paper that both opened and closed this field in 1950. His interest was in providing a means of self-checking in computers, which were just being developed at the time he wrote this. the paper appeared in the Bell System Technical Journal, April, 1950. Definitely worth tracking down in the library and reading.

Bit Strings

The best starting point for understanding ECC codes is to consider bit strings as addresses in a binary hypercube. A hypercube is a generalization of a cube to various dimensions; we're probably most familiar with the notion of a four-dimensional hypercube.

Here's a picture of binary hypercubes for several different dimensionalities:

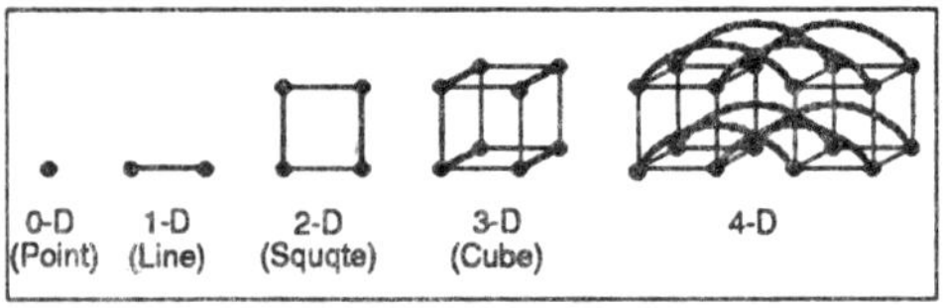

Each of them was created by copying the one to the left twice, and connecting corresponding vertices. We can assign each vertex in a hypercube a location in a coordinate space determined by the dimensionality of the hypercube.

- A zero-dimensional hypercube requires no coordinates to know where you are
- A one-dimensional hypercube can use one bit to tell whether you're at the bottom or the top of the line segment.
- A two-dimensional hypercube can use two bits: first bit is left vs. right, second is inherited from the line.
- A three-dimensional hypercube can use a bit to tell front square from back, and inherit two bits from the square.
- A four-dimensional hypercube can use a bit to tell left cube from right, and inherits three bits from cube.

The Hamming distance between two bit strings is the number of bits you have to change to convert one to the other: this is the same as the number of edges you have to traverse in a binary hypercube to get from one of the vertices to the other. The basic idea of an error correcting code is to use extra bits to increase the dimensionality of the hypercube, and make sure the Hamming distance between any two valid points is greater than one.

- If the Hamming distance between valid strings is only one, a single-bit error results in another valid string. This means we can't detect an error.
- If it's two, then changing one bit results in an invalid

string, and can be detected as an error. Unfortunately, changing just one more bit can result in another valid string, which means we can't know which bit was wrong: so we can detect an error but not correct it.

- If the Hamming distance between valid strings is three, then changing one bit leaves us only one bit away from the original error, but two bits away from any other valid string. This means if we have a one-bit error, we can figure out which bit is the error; but if we have a two-bit error, it looks like one bit from the other direction. So we can have single bit correction, but that's all.
- Finally, if the Hamming distance is four, then we can correct a single-bit error and detect a double-bit error. This is frequently referred to as a SECDED.

Parity

The simplest case is by adding a parity bit. Suppose we have a three-bit word (so the bit strings define points in a cube). If we add a fourth bit, we can decree that any time we want to switch a bit in the original three-bit string, we also have to switch the parity bit. If we start with 000 in the left cube, so the full string is 0000, changing any one of the original three bits requires us to change to the other cube: 1001, 1010, and 1100. Now if we change a second bit, we have to move back to the left cube: 0011, 0101, 0110.

And if we change the third bit, we move back to the right cube: 0111. So, there is a Hamming distance of two between any two valid strings. If we get a one-bit error, we know it is an error because it's on one of the invalid vertices. This can be computed by counting the number of 1's, and making sure it's always even (so this is called even parity). We could have selected exactly the opposite set of vertices as the valid ones, which would have given us odd parity.

HAMMING CODE

Several Teletext packets contain information protected by hamming. This is a method for encoding data such that errors in reception can be detected, and if the error is sufficiently small, corrected. Teletext uses two hamming codes.

The simpler and more robust version encodes 4 bits of data in one 8-bit byte. This code is used extensively to protect the fields that have meaning to the Teletext system itself. The more efficient code encodes 18 bits of data in three 8-bit bytes. It is used for to protect some of the data fields inside Teletext packets.

Both codes are designed such that any one-bit error can be corrected, and any 2-bit error can be detected.

8/4 HAMMING

The 8/4 code is quite simple; if the input nibble is the 4-bit value:

```
b3, b2, b1, b0
```

with b3 being the most significant bit, then the output hammed byte is the 8-bit value:

```
b3, b3^b2^b1, b2, !b2^b1^b0, b1, !b3^b1^b0, b0,
!b3^b2^b0
```

where ^ represents bitwise exclusive-or and ! is bitwise not.

This code has the property that every value is four bits different from all other such values. A one-bit error is therefore unambiguously correctable, being only one bit away from a valid code.

A two-bit error is detectable but not correctable, being equidistant between two valid codes.

Here is the table of all 16 encoded nibbles:

```
Data nibble Hammed byte
0 = 0 0 0 0 15 = 0 0 0 1 0 1 0 1
1 = 0 0 0 1 02 = 0 0 0 0 0 0 1 0
2 = 0 0 1 0 49 = 0 1 0 0 1 0 0 1
3 = 0 0 1 1 5E = 0 1 0 1 1 1 1 0
4 = 0 1 0 0 64 = 0 1 1 0 0 1 0 0
5 = 0 1 0 1 73 = 0 1 1 1 0 0 1 1
6 = 0 1 1 0 38 = 0 0 1 1 1 0 0 0
7 = 0 1 1 1 2F = 0 0 1 0 1 1 1 1
8 = 1 0 0 0 D0 = 1 1 0 1 0 0 0 0
9 = 1 0 0 1 C7 = 1 1 0 0 0 1 1 1
A = 1 0 1 0 8C = 1 0 0 0 1 1 0 0
```

```
B = 1 0 1 1 9B = 1 0 0 1 1 0 1 1
C = 1 1 0 0 A1 = 1 0 1 0 0 0 0 1
D = 1 1 0 1 B6 = 1 0 1 1 0 1 1 0
E = 1 1 1 0 FD = 1 1 1 1 1 1 0 1
F = 1 1 1 1 EA = 1 1 1 0 1 0 1 0
          | | | |             | | | | | | | |
b3b2b1b0             b3 |b2 |b1 |b0 |
                                |    | | |
                             321 !210 !310 !320
```

Decoding a hammed byte back in to a 4-bit nibble can be done using the table below, or by a bit-twiddling algorithm. In the table, the hammed byte value is used to index the row (most significant 4 bits) and column (least significant four bits), and the decoded nibble is read out of the table. Assuming the hammed byte is

`h7, h6, h5, h4, h3, h2, h1, h0`

with h7 being the most significant bit, we compute

```
     p = h7 ^ h6 ^ h5 ^ h4 ^ h3 ^ h2 ^ h1 ^ h0
c0 = h7 ^ h5 ^ h1 ^ h0
c1 = h7 ^ h3 ^ h2 ^ h1
c2 = h5 ^ h4 ^ h3 ^ h1
```

If the parity, p, is correct (equal to 1) then either 0 or 2 errors occurred. If all the check bits, c0, c1, c2 are correct (equal to 1) then the byte was received intact, (no errors) otherwise it was damaged beyond repair (two errors).

If p is 0, then there was a single bit error which can be recovered:

```
c0 c1c2 meaning
1 1 1 error in bit h6
1 1 0 error in bit h4
1 0 1 error in bit h2
0 1 1 error in bit h0
0 0 1 error in bit h7
0 1 0 error in bit h5
1 0 0 error in bit h3
0 0 0 error in bit h1
```

The erroneous bit should be flipped. Note that there is actually no need to fix errors in bits h6, h4, h2 and h0 since they are not used in the decoded byte.

After flipping bits if necessary, the decoded byte is then:

`h7, h5, h3, h1`

24/18 HAMMING

The more efficient 24/18 code is based on the same principle of interleaved check bits and an overall parity bit as the simpler 8/4 code.

Assuming the input bits are:

```
b17, b16, b15, b14, b13, b12, b11, b10, b9,b8,
                    b7, b6, b5, b4, b3, b2, b1, b0
```

with b17 being the most significant bit, the six hamming check bits are:

```
c0 = ! b17 ^ b15 ^ b13 ^ b11 ^ b10 ^ b8 ^ b6
  ^ b4 ^ b3 ^ b1 ^ b0
c1 = ! b17 ^ b16 ^ b13 ^ b12 ^ b10 ^ b9 ^ b6
  ^ b5 ^ b3 ^ b2 ^ b0
c2 = ! b17 ^ b16 ^ b15 ^ b14 ^ b10 ^ b9 ^ b8
  ^ b7 ^ b3 ^ b2 ^ b1
c3 = ! b10 ^ b9 ^ b8 ^ b7 ^ b6 ^ b5 ^ b4
c4 = ! b17 ^ b16 ^ b15 ^ b14 ^ b13 ^ b12 ^
  b11
c5 = b17 ^ b14 ^ b12 ^ b11 ^ b10 ^ b7 ^ b5
  ^ b4 ^ b2 ^ b1 ^ b0
```

where ^ represents bitwise exclusive-or and ! is bitwise not.C5 can alternatively and equivalently be computed as the odd parity of all the other data and check bits.

The output bytes are then:

```
c3, b3, b2, b1, c2, b0, c1, c0
c4, b10, b9, b8, b7, b6, b5, b4
c5, b17, b16, b15, b14, b13, b12, b11
```

in byte transmission order, with the most significant bit of each byte on the left.

To decode a hammed byte triplet:

```
h7, h6, h5, h4, h3, h2, h1, h0
h15, h14, h13, h12, h11, h10, h9, h8
h23, h22, h21, h20, h19, h18, h17, h16
```

with h0 being the least significant bit of the first byte and h23 being the most significant bit of the third byte, we compute

```
p = h23 ^ h22 ^ h21 ^ h20 ^ ... ^ h1 ^ h0
c0 = h0 ^ h2 ^ h4 ^ h6 ^ h8 ^ h10 ^ h12 ^ h14
   ^ h16 ^ h18 ^ h20 ^ h22
c1 = h1 ^ h2 ^ h5 ^ h6 ^ h9 ^ h10 ^ h13 ^ h14
   ^ h17 ^ h18 ^ h21 ^ h22
c2 = h3 ^ h4 ^ h5 ^ h6 ^ h11 ^ h12 ^ h13 ^ h14
   ^ h19 ^ h20 ^ h21 ^ h22
c3 = h7 ^ h8 ^ h9 ^ h10 ^ h11 ^ h12 ^ h13 ^ h14
c4 = h15 ^ h16 ^ h17 ^ h18 ^ h19 ^ h20 ^ h21
   ^ h22
```

If the parity, p, is correct (equal to 1) then either 0 or 2 errors occurred. If all the check bits, c0, c1, c2, c3, c4, c5 are correct (equal to 1), then the byte was received intact, (no errors) otherwise it was damaged beyond repair (two errors).

If p is 0, then there was a single bit error which can be recovered.

For the check bits which are incorrect (equal to 0), add the following powers of two together:

```
if c0 = 0 add 1
if c1 = 0 add 2
if c2 = 0 add 4
if c3 = 0 add 8
if c4 = 0 add 16
```

The sum gives the bit position 1--24 corresponding to h0--h23 which is in error. The erroneous bit should be flipped. Note that there is actually no need to fix errors in bits h23, h15, h7, h3, h1 and h0 since they are not used in the decoded byte.

The output data bits, d17--d0 are:

```
h22, h21, h20, h19, h18, h17, h16, h14, h13,h12,
h11, h10, h9, h8, h6, h5, h4, h2
```

Chapter 2

Digital Computer Generation

Digital computers perform arithmetic and logic functions on separate discrete data, like numbers, or combinations of discrete data, such as name, rate, and division. This makes them different from analog computers that operate on continuous data, like measuring temperature changes. We generally use digital computers for business and scientific data processing.

ACCOUNTING

Computers are ideal for keeping payroll records, printing paychecks, billing customers, preparing tax returns, and taking care of many of the other accounting tasks in an organization.

RECORDKEEPING

Computers can record information like inventories and personnel files. They can also keep track of books checked out of a library. Airline ticket counters are much more efficient than they used to be, thanks to centralized reservation computers that can be reached over the telephone lines.

INDUSTRIAL USES

Industrial computers save considerable time and reduce waste by efficiently performing hundreds of industrial tasks, ranging from filling sales orders and routing parts to various locations on an assembly line, to designing earthquake-resistant structures, and controlling an entire oil refinery.

SCIENCE

The research and development applications are the most

numerous. Digital computers are being used to do lengthy and complicated mathematical calculations millions of times faster than human beings. They are also used to collect, store, and evaluate data from experiments, analyse weather patterns, forecast crop statistics, and, believe it or not, design other computers.

WORD PROCESSING

Remember, these words were typed into a desktop computer! Word processing is among the most common applications for personal computers. If you have not discovered the advantages of computer writing, it's time to visit a computer dealer for a personalized demonstration.

None of this work could be performed by a computer without first instructing the computer how to do it by means of a list of instructions called a programme. The instructions in the programme must be written in one of the languages the computer understands.

The most popular generic term for computer programmes is software Hardware of course, refers to the computer and related equipment. It is easy to say that both computer hardware and software are interdependent because neither can perform useful work without the other. Digital computers may be either special or general purpose.

ACCURACY OF COMPUTERS

The fundamental difference between analog and digital computers is that digital computers deal with discrete quantities such as beads on an abacus, notches on a toothed wheel, or electrical pulses, while analog computers deal with continuous physical variables such as electrical voltages or mechanical shaft rotations.

Computation with analog computers depends on the relation of information to a measurement of some physical quantity. For example, you can determine the number of boards in a picket fence by either a digital or an analog system as follows. In the digital method (fig. 1-5, view A), you use an adding machine and count the boards one by one. In the analog method (fig. 1-5, view B), you draw a string (marked off in inches for the width of each board including the gap) over the length of the fence, then measure the length of the string.

The number of boards may then be determined by dividing the length of string by the number of inches per board.

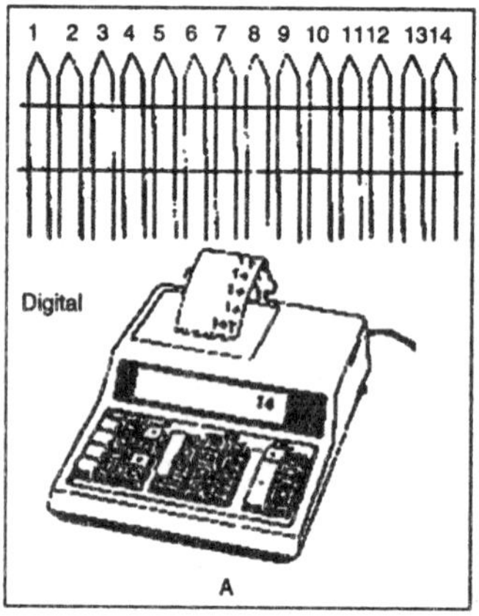

Fig. Digital Computation.

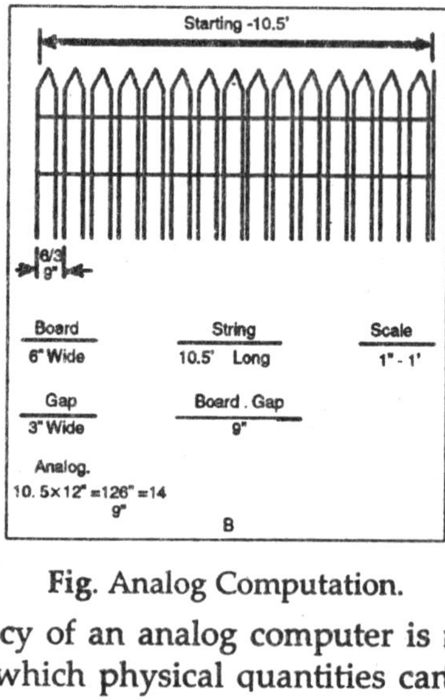

Fig. Analog Computation.

The accuracy of an analog computer is restricted to the accuracy with which physical quantities can be sensed and displayed. This, in turn, is related to the quality of the components used in constructing the computer; for example, the tolerance of electrical resistors or mechanical shafts and the quality of the output equipment.

In an analog computer, for example, if the constant is represented by a voltage, it probably could be read only to the third decimal place. On the other hand, the accuracy of a digital computer is governed by the number of significant figures carried in the computations. This, in turn, is determined by the computer's design.

In a digital computer, the number of decimal places in the constant could be many, depending on the design of the computer processing unit.

The digital computer is, therefore, capable of higher precision and accuracy. However, a computer, regardless of its accuracy, would do you no good if the wrong one were chosen for a given task.

GENERATIONS

FIRST GENERATION

The computers of the first generation (1951-1958) were physically very large machines characterized by the vacuum tube. Because they used vacuum tubes, they were very unreliable, required a lot of power to run, and produced so much heat that adequate air conditioning was critical to protect the computer parts.

Compared to today's computers, they had slow input and output devices, were slow in processing, and had small storage capacities. Many of the internal processing functions were measured in thousandths of a second (millisecond).

The software (computer programme) used on first generation computers was unsophisticated and machine oriented. This meant that the programmers had to code all computer instructions and data in actual machine language.

They also had to keep track of where instructions and data were stored in memory. Using such a machine language was efficient for the computer but difficult for the programmer.

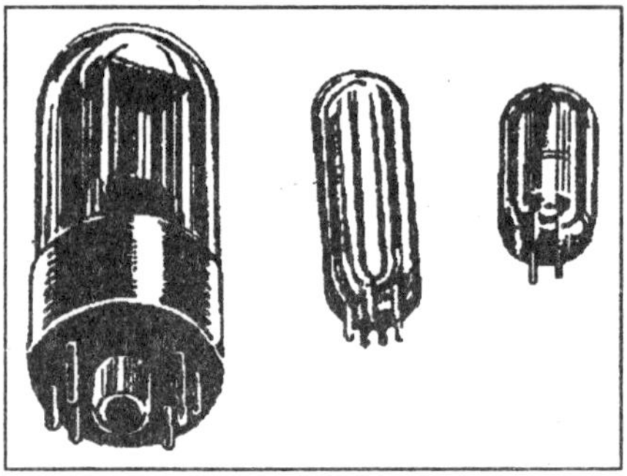

Fig. First generation Computers used Vacuum Tubes.

First Generation (1939-1954) - Vacuum Tube

- *1937*: John V. Atanasoff designed the first digital electronic computer
- *1939*: Atanasoff and Clifford Berry demonstrate in Nov. the ABC prototype
- *1941*: Konrad Zuse in Germany developed in secret the Z3
- *1943*: In Britain, the Colossus was designed in secret at Bletchley Park to decode German messages
- *1944*: Howard Aiken developed the Harvard Mark I mechanical computer for the Navy
- *1945*: John W. Mauchly and J. Presper Eckert built ENIAC at U of PA for the U.S. Army
- *1946*: Mauchly and Eckert start Electronic Control Co., received grant from National Bureau of Standards to build a ENIAC-type computer with magnetic tape input/output, renamed UNIVAC in 1947 but run out of money, formed in Dec. 1947 the new company Eckert-Mauchly Computer Corporation (EMCC).
- *1948*: Howard Aiken developed the Harvard Mark III electronic computer with 5000 tubes
- *1948*: U of Manchester in Britain developed the SSEM Baby electronic computer with CRT memory

- *1949*: Mauchly and Eckert in March successfully tested the BINAC stored-programme computer for Northrop Aircraft, with mercury delay line memory and a primitive magentic tape drive; Remington Rand bought EMCC Feb. 1950 and provided funds to finish UNIVAC
- *1950*: Commander William C. Norris led Engineering Research Associates to develop the Atlas, based on the secret code-breaking computers used by the Navy in WWII; the Atlas was 38 feet long, 20 feet wide, and used 2700 vacuum tubes
- *1951*: S. A. Lebedev developed the MESM computer in Russia
- *1951*: Remington Rand successfully tested UNIVAC March 30, 1951, and announced to the public its sale to the Census Bureau June 14, 1951, the first commercial computer to feature a magnetic tape storage system, the eight UNISERVO tape drives that stood separate from the CPU and control console on the other side of a garage-size room. Each tape drive was six feet high and three feet wide, used 1/2-inch metal tape of nickel-plated bronze 1200 feet long, recorded data on eight channels at 100 inches per second with a transfer rate of 7,200 characters per second. The complete UNIVAC system weighed 29,000 pounds, included 5200 vacuum tubes, and an offline typewriter-printer UNIPRINTER with an attached metal tape drive. Later, a punched card-to-tape machine was added to read IBM 80-column and Remington Rand 90-column cards.
- *1952*: Remington Rand bought the ERA in Dec. 1951 and combined the UNIVAC product line in 1952: the ERA 1101 computer became the UNIVAC 1101. The UNIVAC I was used in November to calculate the presidential election returns and successfully predict the winner, although it was not trusted by the TV networks who refused to use the prediction.
- *1954*: The aircraft-warning system was the largest

vacuum tube computer system ever built. It began in 1954 at MIT's Lincoln Lab with funding from the Air Force. The first of 23 Direction Centres went online in Nov. 1956, and the last in 1962. Each Centre had two 55,000-tube computers built by IBM, MIT, AND Bell Labs. The 275-ton computers known as"Clyde"were based on Jay Forrester's Whirlwind I and had magnetic core memory, magentic drum and magnetic tape storage. The Centres were connected by an early network, and pioneered development of the modem and graphics display.

SECOND GENERATION

The computers of the second generation (1959-1963), were characterized by transistors instead of vacuum tubes. Transistors were smaller, less expensive, generated almost no heat, and required very little power. Thus second generation computers were smaller, required less power, and produced a lot less heat.

The use of small, long lasting transistors also increased processing speeds and reliability. Cost performance also improved. The storage capacity was greatly increased with the introduction of magnetic disk storage and the use of magnetic cores for main storage.

High speed card readers, printers, and magnetic tape units were also introduced. Internal processing speeds increased. Functions were measured in millionths of a second (microseconds).

Like the first generation, a particular computer of the second generation was designed to process either scientific or business oriented problems but not both. The software was also improved.

Symbolic machine languages or assembly languages were used instead of actual machine languages. This allowed the programmer to use mnemonic operation codes for instruction operations and symbolic names for storage locations or stored variables. Compiler languages were also developed for the second generation computers.

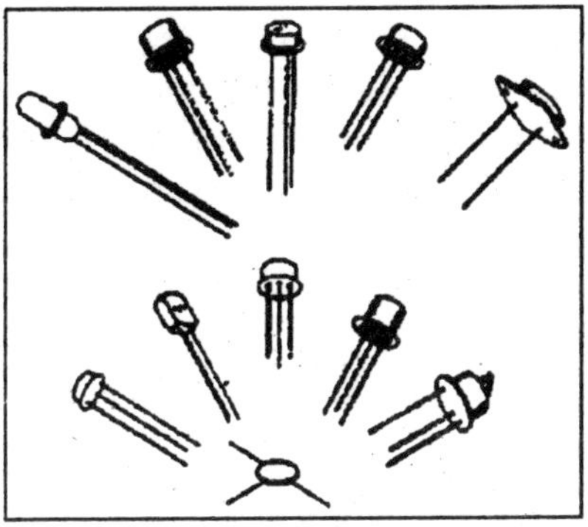

Fig. Second Generation Computers used Transistors.

Second Generation Computers (1954 -1959) - Transistor

- *1950*: National Bureau of Standards (NBS) introduced its Standards Eastern Automatic Computer (SEAC) with 10,000 newly developed germanium diodes in its logic circuits, and the first magnetic disk drive designed by Jacob Rabinow
- *1953*: Tom Watson, Jr., led IBM to introduce the model 604 computer, its first with transistors, that became the basis of the model 608 of 1957, the first solid-state computer for the commercial market. Transistors were expensive at first, cost $8 vs. $.75 for a vacuum tube. But Watson was impressed with the new transistor radios and gave them to his engineers to study. IBM also developed the 650 Magnetic Drum Calculator, the first by IBM to use magnetic drum memory rather punched cards, and began shipment of the 701 scientific"Defence Calculator"that was the first of the Model 700 line that dominated main frame computers for the next decade
- *1955*: IBM introduced the 702 business computer; Watson on the cover of Time magazine March 28
- *1956*: Bendix G-15A small business computer sold for only $45,000, designed by Harry Huskey of NBS

- *1959*: General Electric Corporation delivered its Electronic Recording Machine Accounting (ERMA) computing system to the Bank of America in California; based on a design by SRI, the ERMA system employed Magnetic Ink Character Recognition (MICR) as the means to capture data from the checks and introduced automation in banking that continued with ATM machines in 1974

THIRD GENERATION

The computers of this generation, many of which are still in use, are characterized by miniaturized circuits. This reduces the physical size of computers even more and increases their durability and internal processing speeds.

One design employs solid-state logic microcircuits for which conductors, resistors, diodes, and transistors have been miniaturized and combined on half-inch ceramic squares. Another smaller design uses silicon wafers on which the circuit and its components are etched.

The smaller circuits allow for faster internal processing speeds resulting in faster execution of instructions. Internal processing speeds are measured in billionths of a second (nanoseconds).

The faster computers make it possible to run jobs that were considered impractical or impossible on first or second generation equipment. Because the miniature components are more reliable, maintenance is reduced.

New mass storage, such as the data cell, was introduced during this generation, giving a storage capacity of over 100 million characters.

Drum and disk capacities and speed have been increased, the portable disk pack has been developed, and faster, higher density magnetic tapes have come into use.

Considerable improvements were made to card readers and printers, while the overall cost has been greatly reduced. Applications using online processing, real-time processing, time sharing, multiprogramming, multiprocessing, and teleprocessing have become widely accepted.

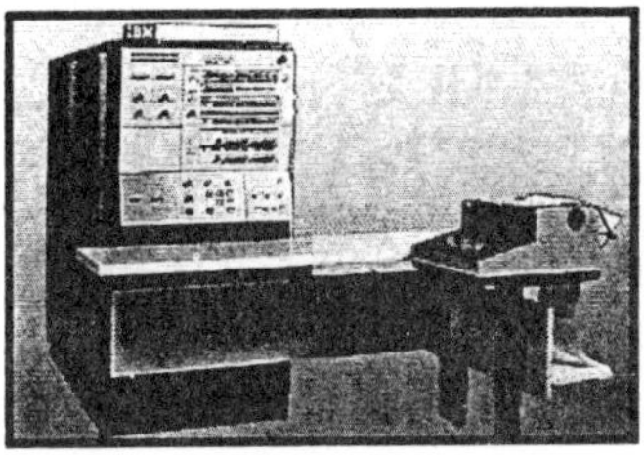

Fig. Third Generation Computers used MicroCircuits.

Manufacturers of third generation computers are producing a series of similar and compatible computers. This allows programmes written for one computer model to run on larger models of the same series. Most third generation systems are designed to handle both scientific and business data processing applications.

Improved programme and operating software has been designed to provide better control, resulting in faster processing. These enhancements are of significant importance to the computer operator. They simplify system initialization (booting) and minimize the need for inputs to the programme from a keyboard (console intervention) by the operator.

Third Generation Computers (1959 -1971) - IC

- *1959*: Jack Kilby of Texas Instruments patented the first integrated circuit; Kilby had made his first germanium IC in Oct. 1958; Robert Noyce at Fairchild used planar process to make connections of components within a silicon IC in early 1959; the first commercial product using IC was the hearing aid in Dec. 1963; General Instrument made LSI chip (100+ components) for Hammond organs 1968
- *1964*: IBM produced SABRE, the first airline reservation tracking system for American Airlines; IBM announced the System/360 all-purpose computer, using 8-bit character word length (a"byte") that was pioneered in the 7030 of April 1961 that grew out of the AF contract of Oct. 1958 following Sputnik to develop transistor computers for BMEWS

- *1968*: DEC introduced the first"mini-computer", the PDP-8, named after the mini-skirt; DEC was founded in 1957 by Kenneth H. Olsen who came for the SAGE project at MIT and began sales of the PDP-1 in 1960
- *1969*: Development began on ARPAnet, funded by the DOD
- *1971*: Intel produced large scale integrated (LSI) circuits that were used in the digital delay line, the first digital audio device

FOURTH GENERATION AND BEYOND

The computers of the fourth generation are not easily distinguished from earlier generations, yet there are some striking and important differences. The manufacturing of integrated circuits has advanced to the point where thousands of circuits (active components) can be placed on a silicon wafer only a fraction of an inch in size (the computer on a chip).

This has led to what is called large scale integration (LSI) and very large scale integration (VLSI). As a result of this technology, computers are significantly smaller in physical size and lower in cost. Yet they have retained large memory capacities and are ultra fast.

Large mainframe computers are increasingly complex. Medium sized computers can perform the same tasks as large third generation computers. An entirely new breed of computers called microcomputers and minicomputers are small and inexpensive, and yet they provide a large amount of computing power.

What is in store for the future? The computer industry still has a long way to go in the field of miniaturization. You can expect to see the power of large mainframe computers on a single super chip.

Massive data bases, such as the Navy's supply system, may be written into read-only memory (ROM) on a piece of equipment no bigger than a desktop calculator. The future challenge will not be in increasing the storage or increasing the computer's power, but rather in properly and effectively using the computing power available.

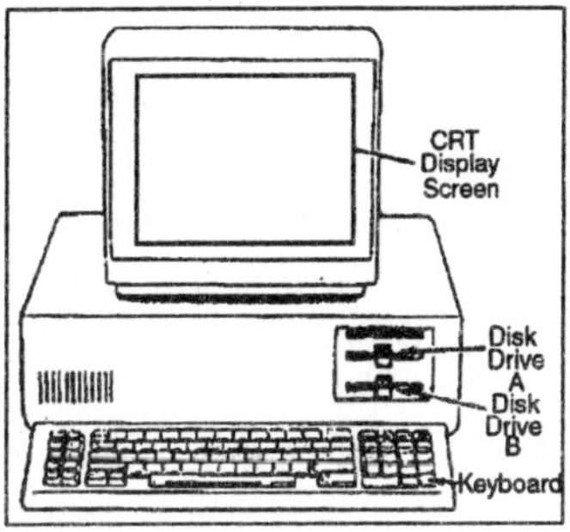

Fig. Fourth Generation Desktop (Personal) Computer.

This is where software (programmes such as assemblers, report generators, subroutine libraries, compilers, operating systems, and applications programmes) will come into play. Some believe developments in software and in learning how to use these extraordinary, powerful machines we already possess will be far more important than further developments in hardware over the next 10 to 20 years.

As a result, the next 20 years (during your career) may be even more interesting and surprising than the last 20 years.

Fourth Generation (1971-1991) - Microprocessor

- *1971*: Gilbert Hyatt at Micro Computer Co. patented the microprocessor; Ted Hoff at Intel in February introduced the 4-bit 4004, a VSLI of 2300 components, for the Japanese company Busicom to create a single chip for a calculator; IBM introduced the first 8-inch"memory disk", as it was called then, or the"floppy disk"later; Hoffmann-La Roche patented the passive LCD display for calculators and watches; in November Intel announced the first microcomputer, the MCS-4; Nolan Bushnell designed the first commercial arcade video game"Computer Space"
- *1972*: Intel made the 8-bit 8008 and 8080 microprocessors; Gary Kildall wrote his Control Programme/Microprocessor (CP/M) disk operating

system to provide instructions for floppy disk drives to work with the 8080 processor. He offered it to Intel, but was turned down, so he sold it on his own, and soon CP/M was the standard operating system for 8-bit microcomputers; Bushnell created Atari and introduced the successful"Pong"game

- *1973*: IBM developed the first true sealed hard disk drive, called the"Winchester"after the rifle company, using two 30 Mb platters; Robert Metcalfe at Xerox PARC created Ethernet as the basis for a local area network, and later founded 3COM
- *1974*: Xerox developed the Alto workstation at PARC, with a monitor, a graphical user interface, a mouse, and an ethernet card for networking
- *1975*: the Altair personal computer is sold in kit form, and influenced Steve Jobs and Steve Wozniak
- *1976*: Jobs and Wozniak developed the Apple personal computer; Alan Shugart introduced the 5.25-inch floppy disk
- *1977*: Nintendo in Japan began to make computer games that stored the data on chips inside a game cartridge that sold for around $40 but only cost a few dollars to manufacture. It introduced its most popular game"Donkey Kong"in 1981, Super Mario Bros in 1985
- *1978*: Visicalc spreadsheet software was written by Daniel Bricklin and Bob Frankston
- *1979*: Micropro released Wordstar that set the standard for word processing software
- *1980*: IBM signed a contract with the Microsoft Co. of Bill Gates and Paul Allen and Steve Ballmer to supply an operating system for IBM's new PC model. Microsoft paid $25,000 to Seattle Computer for the rights to QDOS that became Microsoft DOS, and Microsoft began its climb to become the dominant computer company in the world.
- *1984*: Apple Computer introduced the Macintosh personal computer January 24.

- *1987*: Bill Atkinson of Apple Computers created a software programme called HyperCard that was bundled free with all Macintosh computers. This programme for the first time made hypertext popular and useable to a wide number of people. Ted Nelson coined the terms"hypertext"and"hypermedia"in 1965 based on the pre-computer ideas of Vannevar Bush published in his"As We May Think"article in the July 1945 issue of The Atlantic Monthly.

FIFTH GENERATION (1991 AND BEYOND)

- *1991*: World-Wide Web was developed by Tim Berners-Lee and released by CERN.
- *1993*: The first Web browser called Mosaic was created by student Marc Andreesen and programmer Eric Bina at NCSA in the first 3 months of 1993. The beta version 0.5 of X Mosaic for UNIX was released Jan. 23 1993 and was instant success. The PC and Mac versions of Mosaic followed quickly in 1993. Mosaic was the first software to interpret a new IMG tag, and to display graphics along with text. Berners-Lee objected to the IMG tag, considered it frivolous, but image display became one of the most used features of the Web. The Web grew fast because the infrastructure was already in place: the Internet, desktop PC, home modems connected to online services such as AOL and CompuServe
- *1994*: Netscape Navigator 1.0 was released Dec. 1994, and was given away free, soon gaining 75% of world browser market.
- *1996*: Microsoft failed to recognize the importance of the Web, but finally released the much improved browser Explorer 3.0 in the summer.

COMPUTER TYPES AND CLASSIFICATION

CLASSIFICATION OF COMPUTERS

Computers are available in different shapes, sizes and

weights, due to these different shapes and sizes they perform different sorts of jobs from one another. They can also be classified in different ways. All the computers are designed by the qualified computer architectures that design these machines as their requirements.

A computer that is used in a home differs in size and shape from the computer being used in a hospital. Computers act as a server in large buildings, while the computer also differs in size and shape performing its job as a weather forecaster.

A student carrying a laptop with him to his college is different in shape and size from all the computers mentioned above. Here we are going to introduce different classifications of computers one by one. We will discuss what are in classifications and what job they perform.

Super Computer

The biggest in size, the most expensive in price than any other is classified and known as super computer. It can process trillions of instructions in seconds. This computer is not used as a PC in a home neither by a student in a college.

Governments specially use this type of computer for their different calculations and heavy jobs. Different industries also use this huge computer for designing their products. In most of the Hollywood's movies it is used for animation purposes. This kind of computer is also helpful for forecasting weather reports worldwide.

Mainframes

Another giant in computers after the super computer is Mainframe, which can also process millions of instruction per second and capable of accessing billions of data.

This computer is commonly used in big hospitals, air line reservations companies, and many other huge companies prefer mainframe because of its capability of retrieving data on a huge basis. This is normally to expensive and out of reach from a salary-based person who wants a computer for his home. This kind of computer can cost up to thousands of dollars.

Minicomputer

This computer is next in he line but less offers less than mainframe in work and performance. These are the computers, which are mostly preferred by the small type of business personals, colleges, etc.

Personal Computers

Almost all the computer users are familiar with the personal computers. They normally know what the personal computer is and what its functions are. This is the computer mostly preferred by the home users.

These computers are lesser in cost than the computers given above and also, small in size; they are also called PCs in short for Personal computers. This computer is small in size and you can easily arrange it to fit in your single bedroom with its all accommodation. Today this is thought to be the most popular computer in all.

Notebook Computers

Having a small size and low weight the notebook is easy to carry to anywhere. A student can take it with him/her to his/her school in his/her bag with his/her book.

This is easy to carry around and preferred by students and business people to meet their assignments and other necessary tasks. The approach of this computer is also the same as the Personal computer. It can store the same amount of data and having a memory of the same size as that of a personal computer. One can say that it is the replacement of personal desktop computer.

TYPES OF COMPUTERS

Different types of computer systems are nowadays available for different purposes according the user needs. When you'll have to order yours or even to build it, you should first define the expected use of your computer.

In general terms, computers can be classified into three categories: mainframe computers minicomputers, and microcomputers. A computer's power is determined by the technology it uses, NOT its physical size. Greater speed, greater capability and capacity to store information, and greater facility to accommodate additional peripheral (external)equipment will make one computer more powerful than another regardless of their overall physical sizes.

We do not go into detail on each of the different types of computers. Rather, we identify examples of each and point out their physical and internal differences. This will prove valuable when you are maintaining them.

Colossus Computer

The Colossus was a giant computer build by British Secret Service during World War II. It was build by an engineer called Tommy Flowers, and used vacuum tubes to perform the calculations.

Colossus computers were used by the British to break the German codes. They were the world's first programmable, digital, electronic, computing devices.

Z3 Computers

The Z3 computer was build by Konrad Zuse, between 1936 and 1941, in Germany. It was first reliable, freely programmable, working computer in the world, and was completely constructed from 2000 relays.

The Z3 contained almost all of the features of modern computer. The success of Zuse's Z3is often attributed to its use of the simple binary system - that is, all the data is stored in the form of just 2 numbers, 0 and 1.

Harvard Mark-I

Many consider that the modern computer era commenced with the first large - scale automatic digital computer, which was developed between 1939 and 1944. This device, the brain child of Harvard graduate Howard.

H. Aiken, was commonly referred to as the Harvard Mark - I was constructed out of switches, relays, rotating shafts, and clutches, and was described as sounding like a'roomful of ladies knitting.'The machine contained more than 750,000 components, was 15 metre long, 2.4 metre tall, and weighed approximately 5 tons.

Atanasoff-Berry Computers

The Atanasoff - Berry Computer was the world's first electronic digital computer. It was build by John Vincent Atanasoff and Clifford Berry at lova state university during 1937 - 42.

It incorporated several major innovations in computing. The machine was capable of solving up to 29 simultaneous linear equations.

The machine was, however, the implement three critical ideas that are still part of every modern computer. It used binary digits, it performed all calculations using electronics rather than wheels or mechanical switches, and it organized

Micro Computers

Micro computers have a micro processor as their central processing unit, and are therefore relatively small in size. When they have a key board and monitor, they are used as personal computers, which is type of computer that you have in your home.

Microcomputers, personal computers (PCs), are small, lightweight, and portable. Some of them aremore powerful than some of the older, larger mainframes and minicomputers.

Microcomputers are unique in that the heart of the computer (the CPU) is contained on a single integrated chip (IC) and the entire computer system is contained on a handful of printed circuit boards located inside a small compact frame or cabinet.

In some cases a complete microcomputer is located on a single chip; the CPU, co-processor, and memory. Some micros/ PCs are high-speed, multi-user,multi-tasking units. Traditionally micros are used forward processing, database management, spreadsheets, graphics, desktop publishing, and other general office applications.

Currently, micros and PCs are being used for tactical support systems, such as Naval Intelligence Processing

Systems (NIPS) and Joint Operational Tactical System (JOTS). Micros and PC scan also be used as a SNAP system for shore based operational commands, such as ASWOC.

The operational programmes for PCs used for a tactical support system are supported externally by technical teams. These operational programmes are also updated as systems are added or replaced.

Programmes that are used for word processing, graphics, and soon are abundant and can be obtained through civilian vendors and software support teams such as Commander Naval Computer and Telecommunications Command.

Training for micro-computers is obtained through formal A schools, civilian contractor schools, and OJT. Training for micros is not NEC producing.

The physical features of microcomputers are very different from mainframes and minis. The following isa brief description of a typical PC/desktop system. PCs are unique in that the frame or cabinet contains the majority ofthe components for a complete system.

A typical PC frame or cabinet contains the following components: Backplane or motherboard for printed circuit boards. A central processor unit (CPU) and memory printed circuit board(s) (pcb) (NOTE: In some cases the CPU and memory are located on the same pcb.)Input/output pcb Disk controller pcb Video controller pcb Data storage devices: Hard disk drive units, floppy disk drive units, and/or tape cassette units I/O connector: Parallel or serial communications.

A small fan: No special cooling requirements; the unit relies on ambient temperature of the room or space Power supply: No special requirements Display monitors are output devices for visual displays of data, and may have monochrome or colour displays.

Lap Top Computers

A lap top computer or note book computer is a small lightweight computer that you can carry around easily. It can perform all the functions of a regular computer, and has build in key board, pointing devise and a lightweight, non - bulky screen. Lap top computers can run both on batteries and from an external adaptor that charges the battery while supping power. If you have a lap top computer, you can work on it while traveling or even you are outdoors.

Desktóp Computers

A desktop computer is a small computer that you can use from a fixed power source. It gets its name from a fact that it is small enough to fit on a table or desk. Desktop computers have separate key boards and screens, and come in a variety of styles and models.

Pocket PC

A pocket PC is a scaled down version of a full sized computer that you use in home or office. Although they are the size of a small diary, pocket PCs are proper computers. They have many of capabilities of full size computers, and can run sophisticated software applications. They are compact enough to fit in your shirt pocket... hence the clever name.

Tablet PC

A tablet PC is cross between a note book PC, and a handheld computer. It is a flat - panel portable PC in a form of a slate. You can enter information by typing the screen with a stylus, or electronic pen. You can use the pen directly on the screen just as you would a mouse to do things like select, drag, and open files.

You can also use it a place of a key board to hand write notes and communications. Unlike a touch screen, the tablet PC screen only receives information from this special pen.

Handheld Computer

A handheld computer is a portable computer that is small enough to be held one hand. They are about the size of spectacle case, and a capable of storing thousands of address, appointment and memos.

So, they are also called Personal Digital Assistants or PDAs. Handheld computers have extremely small screens and key boards. Today, the key board has been replaced with an electronic pen in some handheld computers. You can connect a handheld computer to a desk top computer to exchange information between the two. A portable computer that is small enough to be held in one's hand.

Although extremely convenient to carry, handheld computers have not replaced notebook computers because of their small keyboards and screens. The most popular hand-held computers are those that are specifically designed to provide PIM (personal information manager) functions, such as a calendar and address book.

Some manufacturers are trying to solve the small keyboard problem by replacing the keyboard with an electronic pen. However, these pen-based devices rely on handwriting recognition technologies, which are still in their infancy. Hand-held computers are also called PDAs, palmtops and pocket computers.

Ultra Mobile PC

The ultra - mobile PC or UMPC is a small, mobile computer that runs on the Windows Vista operating system. The UMPC goes anywhere, and can be used any time, just like a mobile PC.

The UMPC has many advantages. It is smaller and lighter than traditional lap top computers and has multiple input methods like tough screen, tablet pen, the USB key board and others. It can also operate on different systems.

Super Computers

The fastest and most powerful computers available at a particular time are called super computers. Super computers are very expensive and employed for specialized tasks that required immense amount of mathematical calculations. The New York World, referring to tabulators manufactured by IBM, coined the term super computer in 1929.

To modern computer users, these tabulators would probably appear awkward and slow. In the constantly changing the world of computing, it should come as no surprise to learn that most super computers are considered to be'super'only few years, in fact, today's super computer will become tomorrow's ordinary computer. Supercomputer is a broad term for one of the fastest computers currently available. Supercomputers are very expensive and are employed for specialized applications that require immense amounts of mathematical calculations (number crunching). For example, weather forecasting requires a supercomputer.

Other uses of supercomputers scientific simulations, graphics, fluid dynamic calculations, nuclear energy research, electronic design, and analysis of geological data (e.g. in petrochemical prospecting). Perhaps the best known supercomputer manufacturer is Cray Research.

Minisuper and Supermini Computers

A minisuper computer is super computer that is about a quarter to a half as fast as the most powerful super computers, but cost much less. A minisuper computer a mini computer with high performance compared to ordinary mini computers.

Biological Computer

Biological computers are special types of micro computers that are specifically designed to be used for medical applications.

The biological computer is planted inside the body and is mainly used for tasks like monitoring the body's activities, or diagnosing and treating diseases. Biological computers are important because they enable a doctor to focus on, find a treat only damaged or diseased cells.

Quantum Computers

We already know that a bit is a fundamental unit of information which is represented as a 0 or 1 in digital computer. Ordinary computers interrupt information according to the well understood laws of classical physics.

In quantum computer, fundamental unit of information is called quantum bit or qubit. A quantum computer obeys the laws of quantum mechanics which are very different from classical physics. Scientists have already built basic quantum computers that can perform certain calculations, but a practical quantum computer is still years away.

DNA Computers

DNA or deoxyribonucleic acid molecules, material our genes are made of, have the potential to perform calculations many times faster than the world's most powerful human built computers.

A computer that uses DNA to store information and perform complex calculations is called a DNA computer. It was in 1994 that University of Southern California computer scientist Leonard Adelman suggested that DNA could be used to solve complex mathematical problems.

While still in their infancy, DNA computers will be capable of storing billons of times more data than your personal computer.

Optical Computer

An optical computer is a computer that uses light instead of electricity. An optical computer uses photons to manipulate, store and transmit data. You also know the modern electric computer use transistors. In optical computers electronic components are replaced with optical ones and'optical transistors'must be used. Optical computer technology is still in early stages.

Wetware Computers

A wetware computer is an organic computer. Organic refers any thing that is derived from living organisms. A wetware computer is from living neurons, which are cells found in brain, spinal column and nerves. A wetware computer is some times called an artificial organic brain or a neurocomputer. A wetware computer has already been constructed from leech neurons.

Shoe Computers

A shoe computer is a type of computer that uses law level

electrical impulses emitted by our bodies, when we walk we generate the energy, and this energy powers the processors of the computer.

Chamical Computers

A chemical computer is an unconventional computer based on a semi - solid chemical'soup,'where data is represented by varying concentration of chemicals. The computations are performed by naturally occurring chemical reactions. So far, it still in very early experimental stage, but may have great potential for the computer industry.

Nano Computer

A nano computer is a computer that is microscopic size. It is smaller than micro computer, which is smaller than mini computer. We can also say it is a computer whose fundamental parts are no bigger than a few nanometers. It is commonly used nano technology which is the building of extremely small machines.

PDA

Short for personal digital assistant, a handheld device that combines computing, telephone/fax, and networking features. A typical PDA can function as a cellular phone, fax sender, and personal organizer. Unlike portable computers, most PDAs are pen-based, using a stylus rather than a keyboard for input.

This means that they also incorporate handwriting recognition features. Some PDAs can also react to voice input by using voice recognition technologies.

The field of PDA was pioneered by Apple Computer, which introduced the Newton Message Pad in 1993. Shortly thereafter, several other manufacturers offered similar products.

To date, PDAs have had only modest success in the marketplace, due to their high price tags and limited applications. However, many experts believe that PDAs will eventually become common gadgets.

FUNCTIONAL UNITS AND THEIR INTERCONNECTIONS

Digital computer systems consist of three distinct units. These units are as follows:

- Input unit
- Central Processing unit
- Output unit

These units are interconnected by electrical cables to permit communication between them. This allows the computer to function as a system.

INPUT UNIT

A computer must receive both data and programme statements to function properly and be able to solve problems. The method of feeding data and programmes to a computer is accomplished by an input device. Computer input devices read data from a source, such as magnetic disks, and translate that data into electronic impulses for transfer into the CPU. Some typical input devices are a keyboard, a mouse, or a scanner.

CENTRAL PROCESSING UNIT

The brain of a computer system is the central processing unit (CPU). The CPU processes data transferred to it from one of the various input devices. It then transfers either an intermediate or final result of the CPU to one or more output devices. A central control section and work areas are required to perform calculations or manipulate data. The CPU is the computing centre of the system.

It consists of a control section, an arithmetic-logic section and an internal storage section (main memory). Each section within the CPU serves a specific function and has a particular relationship with the other sections within the CPU.

Control Section

The control section directs the flow of traffic (operations) and data. It also maintains order within the computer. The flow of control is indicated by dotted arrows in figure.

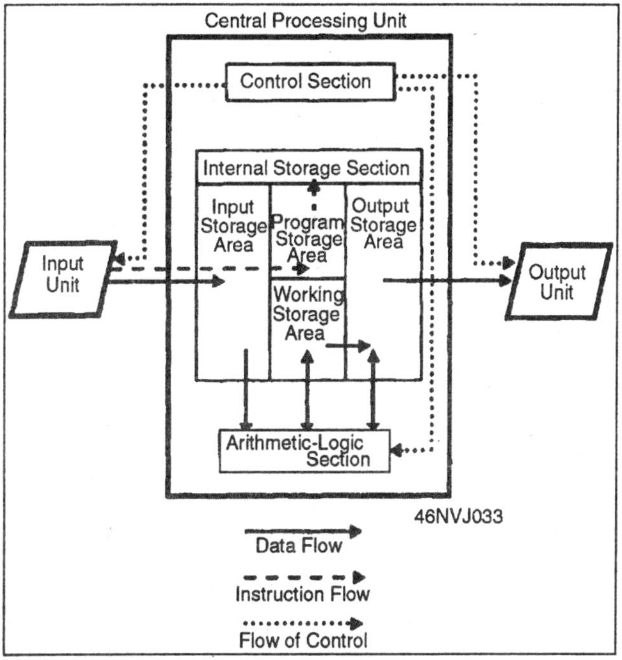

The control section selects one programme statement at a time from the programme storage area, interprets the statement, and sends the appropriate electronic impulses to the arithmetic-logic and storage sections so they can carryout the instructions. The control section does not perform actual processing operations on the data. The control section instructs the input device on when to start and stop transferring data to the input storage area. It also tells the output device when to start and stop receiving data from the output storage area.

Arithmetic-logic Section

The arithmetic-logic section performs arithmetic operations, such as addition, subtraction, multiplication and division. Through internal logic capability, it tests various conditions encountered during processing and takes action based on the result. As indicated by the solid arrows in figure 3-1, data flows between the arithmetic-logic section and the internal storage section during processing. Specifically, data is transferred as needed from the storage section to the arithmetic-logic section, processed, and returned to internal storage. At no time does processing take place in the storage section.

Data maybe transferred back and forth between these two sections several times before processing is completed. The results are then transferred from internal storage to an output device, as indicated by the solid arrow.

Internal Storage Section

The internal storage section is sometimes called primary storage, main storage, or main memory, because this section functions similar to our own human memory. The storage section serves four purposes; three relate to retention (holding) of data during processing. First, as indicated by the solid arrow (fig.), data is transferred from an input device to the Input Storage Area where it remains until the computers ready to process it.

Second, a Workings Storage Area ("scratch pad"memory) within the storage section holds both the data being processed and the intermediate results of the arithmetic-logic operations. Third, the storage section retains the processing results in the Output Storage Area. From there the processing results can be transferred to an output device.

The fourth storage section, the Programme Storage Area, contains the programme statements transferred from an input device to process the data. Please note that the four areas (input, working storage, output, and programme storage) are NOT fumed or location but are determined by individual programme requirements.

OUTPUT UNIT

As programme statements and data are received by the CPU from an input device, the results of the processed data are sent from the CPU to an Output Device. These results are transferred from the output storage area onto an output medium, such as a floppy disk, hard drive, video display, printer, and so on By now, you should have an idea of the functions performed by a CPU. It is the CPU that executes stored programmes and does all of the processing and manipulating of data. The input and output (I/O) devices simply aid the computer by sending and receiving data and programmes

BUSES

A bus, in computing, is a set of physical connections (cables, printed circuits, etc.) which can be shared by multiple hardware components in order to communicate with one another.

The purpose of buses is to reduce the number of"pathways"needed for communication between the components, by carrying out all communications over a single data channel. This is why the metaphor of a"data highway"is sometimes used.

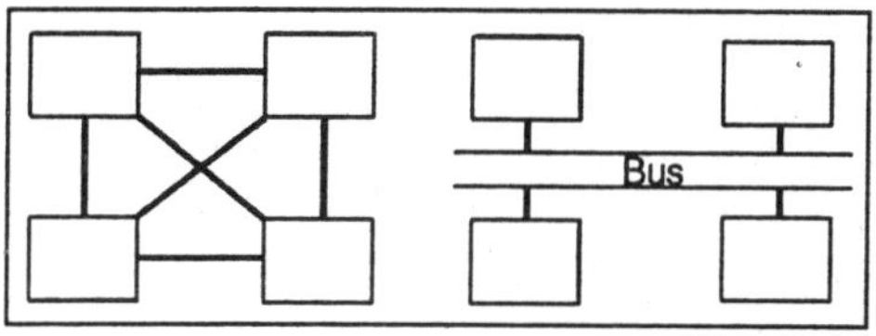

If only two hardware components communicate over the line, it is called a hardware port (such as a serial port or parallel port).

CHARACTERISTICS OF A BUS

A bus is characterized by the amount of information that can be transmitted at once. This amount, expressed in bits, corresponds to the number of physical lines over which data is sent simultaneously. A 32-wire ribbon cable can transmit 32 bits in parallel. The term"width"is used to refer to the number of bits that a bus can transmit at once.

Additionally, the bus speed is also defined by its frequency (expressed in Hertz), the number of data packets sent or received per second. Each time that data is sent or received is called a cycle. This way, it is possible to find the maximum transfer speed of the bus, the amount of data which it can transport per unit of time, by multiplying its width by its frequency. A bus with a width of 16 bits and a frequency of 133 MHz, therefore, has a transfer speed equal to:

```
16 * 133.106 = 2128*106 bit/s,
or 2128*106/8 = 266*106 bytes/s
or 266*106/1000 = 266*103 KB/s
or 259.7*103/1000 = 266 MB/s
```

BUS SUBASSEMBLY

In reality, each bus is generally constituted of 50 to 100 distinct physical lines, divided into three subassemblies:

- The address bus (sometimes called the memory bus) transports memory addresses which the processor wants to access in order to read or write data. It is a unidirectional bus.
- The data bus transfers instructions coming from or going to the processor. It is a bidirectional bus.
- The control bus (or command bus) transports orders and synchonisation signals coming from the control unit and travelling to all other hardware components. It is a bidirectional bus, as it also transmits response signals from the hardware.

THE PRIMARY BUSES

There are generally two buses within a computer:

- The internal bus (sometimes called the front-side bus, or FSB for short). The internal bus allows the processor to communicate with the system's central memory (the RAM).
- The expansion bus (sometimes called the input/output bus) allows various motherboard components (USB, serial, and parallel ports, cards inserted in PCI connectors, hard drives, CD-ROM and CD-RW drives, etc.) to communicate with one another. However, it is mainly used to add new devices using what are called expansion slots connected to the input/outpour bus.

THE CHIPSET

A chipset is the component which routes data between the computer's buses, so that all the components which make up the computer can communicate with each other. The chipset originally was made up of a large number of electronic chips, hence the name.

It generally has two components:

- The Northbridge (also called the memory controller) is in charge of controlling transfers between the processor and the RAM, which is way it is located physically near the processor. It is sometimes called the GMCH, forr Graphic and Memory Controller Hub.
- The Southbridge (also called the input/output controller or expansion controller) handles communications between peripheral devices. It is also called the ICH (I/O Controller Hub). The tembridge is generally used to designate a component which connects two buses.

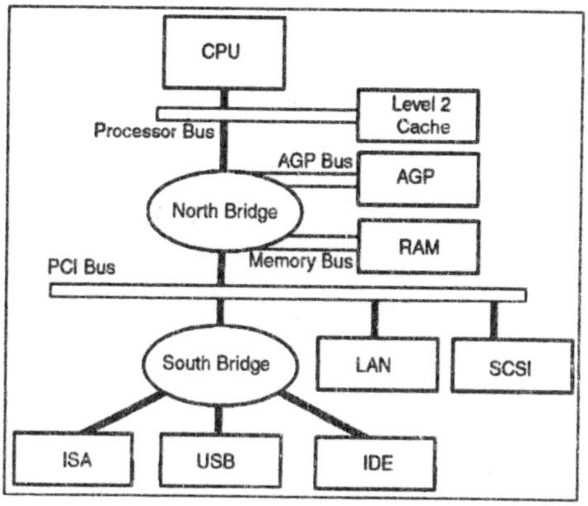

It is interesting to note that, in order to communicate, two buses must have the same width.

The explains why RAM modules sometimes have to be installed in pairs (for example, early Pentium chips, whose processor buses were 64-bit, required two memory modules each 32 bits wide).

Here is a table which gives the specifications for the most commonly used buses:

Standard	Bus width(bits)	Bus speed (MHz)	Bandwidth (MB/sec)
ISA 8-bit	8	8.3	7.9
ISA 16-bit	16	8.3	15.9
EISA	32	8.3	31.8
VLB	32	33	127.2
PCI 32-bit	32	33	127.2
PCI 64-bit 2.1	64	66	508.6
AGP	32	66	254.3
AGP (x2 Mode)	32	66x2	528
AGP (x4 Mode)	32	66x4	1056
AGP (x8 Mode)	32	66x8	2112
ATA33	16	33	33
ATA100	16	50	100
ATA133	16	66	133
Serial ATA (S-ATA)	1		180
Serial ATA II (S-ATA2)	2		380
USB	1		1.5
USB 2.0	1		60
FireWire	1		100
FireWire 2	1		200
SCSI-1	8	4.77	5
SCSI-2 - Fast	8	10	10
SCSI-2 - Wide	16	10	20
SCSI-2 - Fast Wide 32 bits	32	10	40
SCSI-3 - Ultra	8	20	20
SCSI-3 - Ultra Wide	16	20	40
SCSI-3 - Ultra 2	8	40	40
SCSI-3 - Ultra 2 Wide	16	40	80
SCSI-3 - Ultra 160 (Ultra 3)	16	80	160

SCSI-3 - Ultra 320 (Ultra 4)	16	80 DDR	320
SCSI-3 - Ultra 640 (Ultra 5)	16	80 QDR	640

REGISTERS

DEFINITION

A small, high-speed computer circuit that holds values of internal operations, such as the address of the instruction being executed and the data being processed. When a programme is debugged, register contents may be analysed to determine the computer's status at the time of failure. In microcomputer assembly language programming, programmers look at the contents of registers routinely. Assembly languages in larger computers are often at a higher level.

In a computer, a register is one of a small set of data holding places that are part of a computer processor . A register may hold a computer instruction, a storage address, or any kind of data (such as a bit sequence or individual characters). Some instructions specify registers as part of the instruction. For example, an instruction may specify that the contents of two defined registers be added together and then placed in a specified register.

A register must be large enough to hold an instruction - for example, in a 32-bit instruction computer, a register must be 32 bits in length. In some computer designs, there are smaller registers - for example, half-registers - for shorter instructions. Depending on the processor design and language rules, registers may be numbered or have arbitrary names.

MEMORY TRANSFER

MEMORY UNIT INSTALLATION

- Make sure the memory units you wish to use are properly installed. On the front of the console are two ports labeled"Memory Unit A"and"Memory Unit

B"that can be used when you need to transfer data between two memory units. You can also use the hard drive to install files, and it attaches to the top of the console.

ACCESSING THE SYSTEM MEMORY

- Turn on the Xbox 360 system and while in the dashboard go to"My Xbox."Scroll through the blades to the right and find"System,"then"Memory."From this screen, pick the memory unit you wish to access.

TYPES OF FILES

- After you have selected the proper memory unit, you can scroll through the various file types. The list includes games, gamer profiles, demos, videos, themes, gamer pictures, system items and music. The Xbox 360 also lists how much memory each type of content is taking up on the hard drive or memory unit. Music, videos and game demos often take up a lot of memory, so be sure to delete the ones you don't need or move them to a storage device with extra memory available.

MOVING AND COPYING

- Select one of the file categories and find the file you want to move or copy. You can choose"Move"to transfer the file from one memory unit to another or"Copy"to make a duplicate file on a second memory unit. Follow the on-screen prompts to complete the task of your choosing.

REMOVING THE MEMORY UNIT

- Do not remove the memory unit while you are transferring files because you could cause damage to the unit or prevent the entire file from being transferred. Wait until the console alerts you that the process is done before removing the memory unit from the memory unit slot.

Chapter 3

Central Processing Unit

ADDITION AND SUBTRACTION OF SIGNED NUMBER

ADDITION AND SUBTRACTION

For purposes of addition and subtraction, one can think of negative numbers as debts.

Adding a negative number is the same as subtracting the corresponding positive number:

5 + (–3) = 5 – 3 = 2 (if you have $5 and acquire a debt of $3, then you have a net worth of $2)

$$-2 + (-5) = -2 - 5 = -7$$

Subtracting a positive number from a smaller positive number yields a negative result:

4 – 6 = –2 (if you have $4 and spend $6 then you have a debt of $2).

Subtracting a positive number from any negative number yields a negative result:

–3 – 6 = –9 (if you have a debt of $3 and spend another $6, you have a debt of $9).

Subtracting a negative is equivalent to adding the corresponding positive:

5 – (–2) = 5 + 2 = 7 (if you have a net worth of $5 and you get rid of a debt of $2, then your new net worth is $7).

Also: (–8) – (–3) = –5 (if you have a debt of $8 and get rid of a debt of $3, then you still have a debt of $5).

SIGNED NUMBER

A negative number is a number that is less than zero, such

as –3. A positive number is a number that is greater than zero, such as 3. Zero itself is neither negative nor positive. The non-negative numbers are the positive numbers together with zero. Note that some numbers are neither negative nor non-negative, for example the imaginary unit i.

Negative Numbers

These include negative integers, negative rational numbers, negative real numbers, negative hyperreal numbers, and negative surreal numbers.

Negative integers can be regarded as an extension of the natural numbers, such that the equation x – y= z has a meaningful solution for all values of x and y. The other sets of numbers are then derived as progressively more elaborate extensions and generalizations from the integers.

Negative numbers are useful to describe values on a scale that goes below zero, such as temperature, and also in bookkeeping where they can be used to represent debts. In bookkeeping, debts are often represented by red numbers, or a number in parentheses.

Positive Numbers

In the context of complex numbers positive implies real, but for clarity one may say"positive real number". Zero is not a positive number, though in computing zero is sometimes treated as though it were a positive number (due to the way that numbers are typically represented).

Non-negative Numbers

A number is nonnegative if and only if it is greater than or equal to zero, i.e. positive or zero. Thus thenonnegative integers are all the integers from zero on upwards, and the nonnegative reals are all the real numbers from zero on upwards. A real matrix A is called nonnegative if every entry of A is nonnegative.A real matrix A is called totally nonnegative by matrix theorists or totally positive by computer scientists if the determinant of every square submatrix of A is nonnegative.

Arithmetic Involving Signed Numbers

Addition and Subtraction

For purposes of addition and subtraction, one can think of negative numbers as debts.

Adding a negative number is the same as subtracting the corresponding positive number:

$5 + (-3) = 5 - 3 = 2$ (if you have \$5 and acquire a debt of \$3, then you have a net worth of \$2)

$-2 + (-5) = -2 - 5 = -7$

Subtracting a positive number from a smaller positive number yields a negative result:

$4 - 6 = -2$ (if you have \$4 and spend \$6 then you have a debt of \$2).

Subtracting a positive number from any negative number yields a negative result:

$-3 - 6 = -9$ (if you have a debt of \$3 and spend another \$6, you have a debt of \$9).

Subtracting a negative is equivalent to adding the corresponding positive:

$5 - (-2) = 5 + 2 = 7$ (if you have a net worth of \$5 and you get rid of a debt of \$2, then your new net worth is \$7).

Also:

$(-8) - (-3) = -5$ (if you have a debt of \$8 and get rid of a debt of \$3, then you still have a debt of \$5).

Multiplication

Multiplication of a negative number by a positive number yields a negative result: $(-2) \cdot 3 = -6$. The reason is that this multiplication can be understood as repeated addition: $(-2) \cdot 3 = (-2) + (-2) + (-2) = -6$. Alternatively: if you have a debt of \$2, and then your debt is tripled, you end up with a debt of \$6. Multiplication of two negative numbers yields a positive result: $(-3) \cdot (-4) = 12$.

This situation cannot be understood as repeated addition, and the analogy to debts doesn't help either. The ultimate reason for this rule is that we want the distributive law to work:

$$(3 + (-3)) \cdot (-4) = 3 \cdot (-4) + (-3) \cdot (-4).$$

The left hand side of this equation equals 0 · (–4) = 0. The right hand side is a sum of –12 + (–3) · (–4); for the two to be equal, we need (–3) · (–4) = 12.

Computing

On a computer, the sign of a number (whether it is positive or negative) is usually expressed using the left-most bit. If the bit is 1, the whole number is negative, otherwise the number is not negative (zero or positive). Such an integer or variable is called signed.

There are many different ways to represent numbers;. The most common system for representing negative integers in a fixed set of bits is termed"two's complement", in which negative numbers are represented by complementing the absolute value and then adding one to the value as if it were unsigned. For example, if an integer is expressed by 8 bits,

```
digits   binary     actual value
0        00000000   0
1        00000001   1
....
126      01111110   126
127      01111111   127
128      10000000   -128
129      10000001   -127
130      10000010   -126
....
254      11111110   -2
255      11111111   -1
```

Usually, the computer's central processing unit (CPU) can use both signed and unsigned variables. In typical computer architectures there is no way to determine if a given digit is signed or unsigned at runtime because 255 and -1, for instance, appear the same in memory, and both addition, subtraction and multiplication are identical between signed and unsigned values, assuming overflow is ignored, by simply cutting off higher bits than can be stored. The data type of the value dictates which operation should be applied. There is a duplicate material at Computer numbering formats.

Complement

Complementing a binary number means changing all the 0s to 1s and all the 1s to 0s; a Boolean NOT on each bit. A byte, holding 8 bits, can represent the values 00000000 (0) to 11111111 (25510), if all bits are used to represent the magnitude of the number.

This is called an unsigned integer. To represent both positive and negative (signed) integers, the convention is that the most significant bit of the binary representation of the number will be used to indicate the sign of the number, rather than contributing to its magnitude; three formats have been used for representing the magnitude: sign-and-magnitude, one's complement, and two's complement, the latter being by far the most common nowadays.

Sign-and-Magnitude

Sign-and-magnitude is the simplest and most like human writing forms. The MSB is set to 0 for a positive number or zero, and set to 1 for a negative number. The remaining bits in the number indicate the (positive) magnitude. Hence in a byte with only seven bits (apart from the sign bit), the magnitude can range from 0000000 (0) to 1111111 (127). Thus you can represent numbers from -127_{10} to $+127_{10}$. –43 encoded in a byte this way is 10101011.

Ones'Complement

The ones'-complement representation of a negative number is created by taking the complement of its positive counterpart. For example, negated 00101011 (43) becomes 11010100 (–43) (Notice how this is different from the sign-and-magnitude convention where the same bit pattern would be -84). The PDP-1and UNIVAC 1100/2200 series use ones'-complement arithmetic. The range of signed numbers using one's complement in a byte is -127_{10} to $+127_{10}$.

Two's Complement

Both ones'-complement and sign-and-magnitude have two ways to represent zero: 00000000 (+0) and 11111111 (–0) in one's-complement and 10000000 in sign-and-magnitude. This is sometimes problematic (since hardware for adding and subtracting becomes more complicated, as does testing for 0). To avoid this, and to also make integer addition simpler, the two's-complement representation is the one generally used. The two's-complement representation is created by first complementing the positive number, then adding 1 to it. Thus 00101011 (43) becomes 11010101 (–43).

In two's-complement, there is only one zero (00000000). Negating a negative number involves the same operation: complementing, then adding 1. The pattern 11111111 now represents -1_{10} and 10000000 represents -128_{10}; that is, the range of two's-complement integers is -128_{10} to $+127_{10}$. To add two two's-complement integers, treat them as unsigned numbers, add them, and ignore any potential carry over (this is essentially the great advantage that two's-complement has over the other conventions). The result will be the correct two's-complement number, unless both summands were positive and the result is negative or both summands were negative and the result is non-negative. The latter cases are referred to as"overflow"or"wrap around"; the addition cannot be carried out in 8 bit two's-complement in these cases.

For example:

00101011 (+43) 11010101 (–43) 00101011 (+43) 10011010 (–101) + 11010101 (–43) + 11100011 (–29) + 11100011 (–29) + 10110001 (– 79) ----------------------------------
00000000 (0) 10111000 (–72) 00001110 (+14) 01001011 (overflow)

LOOK AHEAD CARRY ADDERS

TYPES OF ADDERS

A half adder can add two bits. It has two inputs, generally labeled A and B, and two outputs, the sum S and carry C. S is the two-bit XOR of A and B, and C is the AND of A and B. Essentially the output of a half adder is the sum of two one-bit numbers, with C being the most significant of these two outputs. A full adder is capable of adding three bits: two bits and one carry bit. It has three inputs - A, B, and carry C, such that multiple full adders can be used to add larger numbers. To remove ambiguity between the input and output carry lines, the carry in is labelled C_i or C_{in} while the carry out is labelled C_o or Cout.

Half Adder

Schematic Symbol of Half Adder

```
____________
A ------| |
| Half |-----
| Adder |
| |-----
B ------|___________|
```

A half adder is a logical circuit that performs an addition operation on two one-bit binary numbers. The half adder outputs a sum of the two inputs and a carry value. The drawback of this circuit is that in case of a multibit addition, it cannot include a carry.

Following is the logic table for a half adder:

0	0	0	0
0	1	0	1
1	0	0	1
1	1	1	0

Full Adder

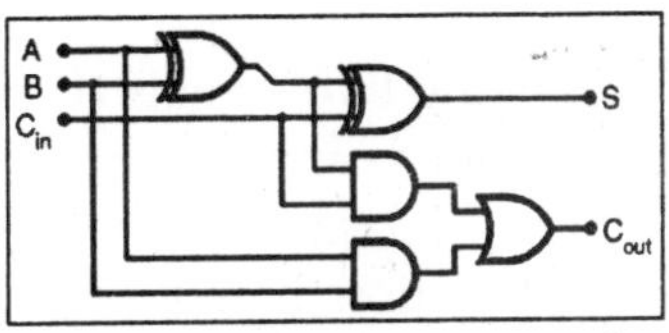

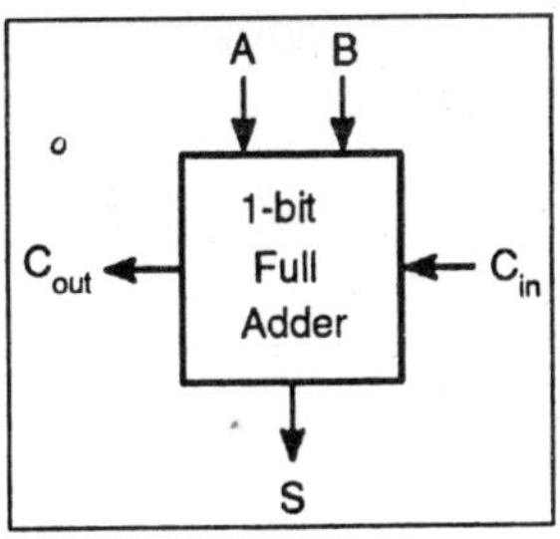

A full adder is a logical circuit that performs an addition operation on three one-bit binary numbers. The full adder produces a sum of the two inputs and carry value. It can be combined with other full adders or work on its own.

RIPPLE CARRY ADDER

It is possible to create a logical circuit using multiple full adders to add N-bit numbers. Each full adder inputs a C_{in}, which is the C_{out} of the previous adder. This kind of adder is a ripple carry adder, since each carry bit"ripples"to the next full adder.

Note that the first (and only the first) full adder may be replaced by a half adder. The layout of ripple carry adder is simple, which allows for fast design time; however, the ripple carry adder is relatively slow, since each full adder must wait for the carry bit to be calculated from the previous full adder. The gate delay can easily be calculated by inspection of the full adder circuit.

Following the path from C_{in} to C_{out} shows two gates that must be passed through. Therefore, a 32-bit adder requires 31 carry computations and the final sum calculation for a total of gate delays.

CARRY LOOK-AHEAD ADDERS

To reduce the computation time, engineers devised faster ways to add two binary numbers by using carry look ahead adders.

They work by creating two signals (P and G) for each bit position, based on whether a carry is propagated through from a less significant bit position (at least one input is a'1'), a carry is generated in that bit position (both inputs are'1'), or if a carry is killed in that bit position (both inputs are'0'). In most cases, P is simply the sum output of a half-adder and G is the carry output of the same adder.

After P and G are generated the carries for every bit position are created. Some advanced carry look ahead architectures are the Manchester carry chain, Brent-Kung adder, and the Kogge-Stone adder.

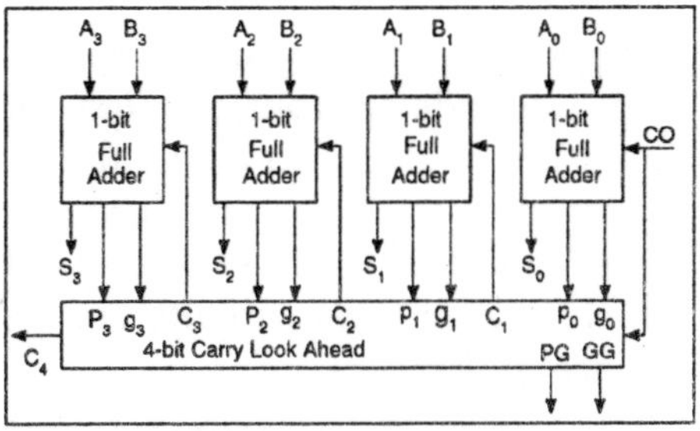

Some other multi-bit adder architectures break the adder into blocks. It is possible to vary the length of these blocks based on the propagation delay of the circuits to optimize computation time.

These block based adders include the carry bypass adder which will determine P andG values for each block rather than each bit, and the carry select adder which pre-generates sum and carry values for either possible carry input to the block.

Other adder designs include the conditional sum adder, carry skip adder, and carry complete adder.

LOOKAHEAD CARRY UNIT

By combining multiple carry look-ahead adders even larger adders can be created. This can be used at multiple levels to make even larger adders.

For example, the following adder is a 64-bit adder that uses 4 16-bit CLAs with two levels of LCUs.

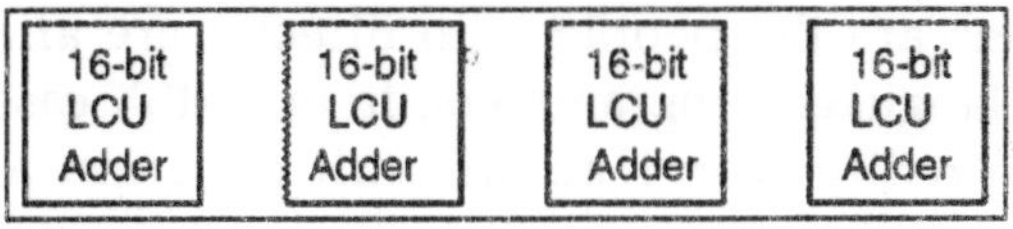

COMPRESSORS

We can view a full adder as a 3:2 compressor: it sums three one-bit inputs, and returns the result as a single two-bit number. Thus, for example, an input of 101 results in an output of 1+0+1=10 (2). The carry-out represents bit one of the result, while the sum represents bit zero. Likewise, a half adder can be used as a 2:2 compressor. 3:2 compressors can be used to speed up the summation of three or more addends. If the addends are exactly three, the layout is known as the carry-save adder. If the addends are four or more, more than one layer of compressors is necessary and there are various possible design for the circuit: the most common are Dadda and Wallace trees. This kind of circuit is most notably used in multipliers, which is why these circuits are also known as Dadda and Wallace multipliers.

MULTIPLICATION

DEFINITION

Multiplication is one of those'difficult'operations for a processor, one that eats up a lot of transistors and therefore uses a lot of CPU power and takes up much space on the silicium. So it doesn't surprise us that in the early days technicians didn't directly integrate multiplication instructions into the processor. So it wasn't build in in the - at that time - advanced Z80 8-bit CPU. Multiplication was left to be implemented by the programmers which needed it.

Most programmers won't care about the fact that multiplication wasn't built into the processor. If you use a higher level programming language it will most certainly provide the necessary commands or code libraries which will solve multiplication arithmetic's for us.

The only people who will worry about the missing CPU instructions are the people who directly are affected: the assembly language programmers. In our MSX case the only ones who really worry about multiplication are demo-programmers; they need a really fast solution for performance reasons. More normal applications can still use a relatively slow multiplication, since once assembled, ML is still the most perform and for the occasional multiplication one won't see the difference between 40 or 140 microseconds.

If you need however thousands of multiplications like in real time 3D algorithms or a real time spectrum analyser this 1000 times 100 microseconds will be a difference of 100 milliseconds between possible screen updates. With the fast code you get at maximum 1/40 ms = 25 Hz, so 25 frames per second. With the slow code you will obtain 7 frames per second. This means that your frame rate can vary 357 per cent depending on the code!

The Solutions

Let's have a look at some of the possible solutions for multiplication on a Z80. Remember, just like in real life there is no best solution, it all depends upon the priorities needed for the programming project at hand.

Solution

Let's start off easy. Most novice assembly writers will solve multiplication with something that resembles the following code:

```
        ML-listing: SOLUT1.ASC
; INPUT: THE VALUES IN REGISTER B EN C
; OUTPUT: HL = B * C
; CHANGES: AF,DE,HL,B
;
              LD HL,0
              LD A,B
              OR A
              RET Z
              LD D,0
              LD E,C
LOOP:         ADD HL,DE
              DJNZ LOOP
              RET
```

This is almost literally the definition of multiplication like most of us have learned in elementary school. 5 times 3 equals 3+3+3+3+3, 8 times 2 equals 2+2+2+2+2+2+2+2 etc. It is clear that this approach can be optimized quite a bit, like making sure that register B contains the smallest value. Extra functionality can be easily implemented like adapting the routine so that it can multiply if there are one or two bytes in two's complement format and accordingly outputting a two's complements value in HL.

Advantages

It's simple, it's short. No more memory used than needed

to store the code. And it is very easy to understand for outsiders. If you write code it is always nice if somebody else can read and maintain it later.

Disadvantages

Time needed by this routine can vary a lot. When B is zero it will be very fast. 11+4+4+7 is 26 T-states, on a regular 3.5 MHz Z80 this corresponds to ± 7.5 microseconds.

In the worst case however this routine will need 11+4+4+7+7+4+254*(11+12)+11+7+7=5904 T-states, meaning milliseconds! Well all right, not really multiple milliseconds, one multiplication can take about 1.45 millisecond considering this worst case scenario. And don't forget on an MSX there is for every instruction an extra T-state wasted to make it even worse. This means that our Z80's 1.455 milliseconds will become 1.834 milliseconds when run on our beloved MSX.

Solution

Like in most assembly written applications you will need to make a choice between space and speed. The previous solution is probably the best choice if you were going for a very short solution, that needs the least amount of memory. If you however have some amperages free you can percale all the information in advance in one huge matrix and then do lookups.

Let's say you need multiplications where number one can be from zero up until 255 and number two is in the range of zero up until 63. Now we can use 32 kB to percale all this. Let us say we are going to use the memory from #4000 to #BFFF to store this data.

We will calculate the data with the following pseudo-code:

```
     Pseudo-listing: PRECALC
for a=0 to 63
for b=0 to 255
solution=a*b
poke #4000+a*256+b,low-byte(solution)
poke #8000+a*256+b,high-byte(solution)
next b,a
```

If we have the data stored in this format we can use the following code to multiply:

```
    ML-listing: SOLUT2.ASC
  ; IN: L NUMBER ONE (0-255)
  ;       A NUMBER TWO (0-63)
  ; OUT: BC IS RESULT
  ; CHANGES: AF,BC,HL
  ;
              OR A,#40
              LD H,A
              LD C,(HL)
              ADD A,#40
              LD H,A
              LD B,(HL)
              RET
```

Advantages

Fast, this solution will always, no matter what the input is, use 7+4+7+7+4+7+7=43 T–States. If you want to use two's complement numbers the code doesn't change, just make the needed matrix.

Or you could alter your routine to take into account the signs of the numbers. Just introduce a litle overhead to transform both numbers to positive numbers and afterwards change HL to its two's complement when the final result had to be negative.

This approach would let you multiply numbers from -63 up until 63 with any other number from -255 up until 255 using the same matrix.

Disadvantages

You need a lot of memory! At least you will have to store the result matrix. If you are going to store a 128×256 matrix your entire view range of 64 kB will be filled and you will have to introduce an extra overhead to use the memory mapper.

Making a matrix for 256×256 possibilities is going to use up 128 kB of memory. So for a regular European MSX2 this is not even possible, because there would be no mapperpage left for the programme, stack and system variables!

THE PERFECT COMPROMISE

Let's introduce a method of which the speed is constant and which doesn't fill the entire memory range. We still need a lookup table of 512 bytes to do our lookups. How are we going to go about it? Let me show you the code. First, the lookup table. This one must start at #xx00. Most demo programmers will already have the habit of aligning lookup tables this way. It speeds up the indexing since there is no offset to take into account and all lookups can be calculated using boolean operations on addresses. We did this in the previous example also, it was not by coincidence that the lookup table started at #4000.

ML-listing: MULTAB.ASC

```
MULTAB DB  0, 0, 1, 2, 4, 6, 9, 12, 16, 20
       DB  25, 30, 36, 42, 49, 56, 64, 72, 81, 90
       DB  100, 110, 121, 132, 144, 156, 169,
           182, 196, 210
       DB  225, 240, 0, 16, 33, 50, 68, 86, 105,
           124
       DB  144, 164, 185, 206, 228, 250, 17, 40,
           64, 88
       DB  113, 138, 164, 190, 217, 244, 16, 44,
           73, 102
       DB  132, 162, 193, 224, 0, 32, 65, 98,
           132, 166
       DB  201, 236, 16, 52, 89, 126, 164, 202,
           241, 24
       DB  64, 104, 145, 186, 228, 14, 57, 100,
           144, 188
       DB  233, 22, 68, 114, 161, 208, 0, 48,
           97, 146
       DB  196, 246, 41, 92, 144, 196, 249, 46,
           100, 154
       DB  209, 8, 64, 120, 177, 234, 36, 94,
           153, 212
```

```
    DB  16, 76, 137, 198, 4, 66, 129, 192
    DB  0, 192, 129, 66, 4, 198, 137, 76, 16,
        212
    DB  153, 94, 36, 234, 177, 120, 64, 8,
        209, 154
    DB  100, 46, 249, 196, 144, 92, 41, 246,
        196, 146
    DB  97, 48, 0, 208, 161, 114, 68, 22, 233,
        188
    DB  144, 100, 57, 14, 228, 186, 145, 104,
        64, 24
    DB  241, 202, 164, 126, 89, 52, 16, 236,
        201, 166
    DB  132, 98, 65, 32, 0, 224, 193, 162,
      132, 102
DB  73, 44, 16, 244, 217, 190, 164, 138,
    113, 88
DB  64, 40, 17, 250, 228, 206, 185, 164,
    144, 124
DB  105, 86, 68, 50, 33, 16, 0, 240, 225,
    210
DB  196, 182, 169, 156, 144, 132, 121, 110,
    100, 90
DB  81, 72, 64, 56, 49, 42, 36, 30, 25, 20
DB  16, 12, 9, 6, 4, 2, 1, 0
DB  0, 0, 0, 0, 0, 0, 0, 0, 0, 0
DB  0, 0, 0, 0, 0, 0, 0, 0, 0, 0
DB  0, 0, 0, 0, 0, 0, 0, 0, 0, 0
DB  0, 0, 1, 1, 1, 1, 1, 1, 1, 1
DB  1, 1, 1, 1, 1, 1, 2, 2, 2, 2
DB  2, 2, 2, 2, 2, 2, 3, 3, 3, 3
DB  3, 3, 3, 3, 4, 4, 4, 4, 4, 4
DB  4, 4, 5, 5, 5, 5, 5, 5, 5, 6
DB  6, 6, 6, 6, 6, 7, 7, 7, 7, 7
DB  7, 8, 8, 8, 8, 8, 9, 9, 9, 9
DB  9, 9, 10, 10, 10, 10, 10, 11, 11, 11
DB  11, 12, 12, 12, 12, 12, 13, 13, 13, 13
DB  14, 14, 14, 14, 15, 15, 15, 15
```

```
DB  16, 15, 15, 15, 15, 14, 14, 14, 14, 13
DB  13, 13, 13, 12, 12, 12, 12, 12, 11, 11
DB  11, 11, 10, 10, 10, 10, 10, 9, 9, 9
DB  9, 9, 9, 8, 8, 8, 8, 8, 7, 7
DB  7, 7, 7, 7, 6, 6, 6, 6, 6, 6
DB  5, 5, 5, 5, 5, 5, 5, 4, 4, 4
DB  4, 4, 4, 4, 4, 3, 3, 3, 3, 3
DB  3, 3, 3, 2, 2, 2, 2, 2, 2, 2
DB  2, 2, 2, 1, 1, 1, 1, 1, 1, 1
DB  1, 1, 1, 1, 1, 1, 1, 0, 0, 0
DB  0, 0, 0, 0, 0, 0, 0, 0, 0, 0
DB  0, 0, 0, 0, 0, 0, 0, 0, 0, 0
DB  0, 0, 0, 0, 0, 0, 0, 0
```

He precalced table may seem long and boring - which it is actually - but the code itself is much shorter and cleaner:

```
    ML-listing: MULTROUT.ASC
; IN: A and D are to be multiplied
; OUT: HL is result
; CHANGES: AF,BC,E,HL
;
        LD      E,A
        SUB     D
        LD      H,MULTAB/256
        LD      L,A
        LD      C,(HL)
        INC     H
        LD      B,(HL)
        LD      A,E
        ADD     A,D
        LD      L,A
        LD      E,(HL)
        DEC     H
        LD      L,(HL)
        LD      H,E
        OR      A
        SBC     HL,BC
```

ome people would by now feel the urge to take paper and pencil and they would try to figure out how this works. If you are one of those people I'll give you a hint and afterwards you will find it much easier to figure out how it works. Ok, here is the hint.

MULTAB is made using the following pseudo-code:

```
Pseudo-listing: PRECALC
for i=0 to 255
if i<128 then a=i else a=i-256
solution=int((a*a)/4)
poke i,low-byte(solution)
poke 256+i,high-byte(solution)
next
```

Those who feel they can tackle the programme alone can start working now. For those who didn't find a piece of paper or whose pencils are blunt I will explain the code. Nobody would read this far and then appear too lazy to figure it out himself, right? Everybody has once during his scolar career heard about the'special products'. And we learned that$(a+b)(a-b)=a^2-b^2$ and that $(a+b)^2=a^2+2ab+b^2$. First of all, we make a lookup table for the function $(x)=(x^2)/4$. The trick is that now we can say that $a*b=f(a+b)-f(a-b)$. Let's prove that this is true. We are going to work out this function.

$a*b = f(a+b) - f(a-b)$	this is our original function
$a*b = ((a+b)^2)/4 - ((a-b)^2)/4$	we replaced the funtion by it's definition
$a*b = ((a+b)^2 - (a-b)^2)/4$	here we say $a/b - c/b = (a-c)/b$
$a*b = ((a^2+2ab+b^2) - (a^2-2ab+b^2))/4$	we worked out the special products
$a*b = (a^2-2ab+b^2 - a^2+2ab-b^2)/4$	just dropped the brackets that weren't needed Pay attention to alter the signs if needed, -(-X) becomes +X
$a*b = (a^2-a^2 +b^2-b^2 +2ab+2ab)/4$	rearranged the components between the brackets
$a*b = (4ab)/4$	Since *x-x* can be dropped this simplifies a lot
$a*b = ab$	Voilà, it seems that our initial (complex) function can be reduced to the result of a simple multiplication

It's use a simple example to make it clearer:

5*8	=	f(5+8)-f(5-8)
5*8	=	f(13)-f(-3)
5*8	=	13*13/4 - (-3)(-3)/4

5*8 = 169/4 - 9/4
5*8 = 42.25 - 2.25
5*8 = 40

---

ur pre-built list contains the values for $x^2/4$ for all x's in the range of –128 up until +127. So the constraints for the registers A and D in our programme are –128 <= A+D <=127 and –128 <= A-D <=127. If we are sure that A and D are always between -64 and +63 these conditions will always be true. Little remark however for those who saw the light. Our lookup table doesn't contain $x^2/4$ but int($x^2/4$)! So for the case of 3 we don't get 2.25 but 2 as result of the lookup. Rest assured however that this doesn't affect the final result.

hope that this article has made it clear that, even on a slow CPU, fast solutions exist to what seem to be long and tedious problems. Just as in real life, there are multiple solutions to one and the same problem, every solution having its good and bad sides. For those who were looking for a fast multiplying routine, feel free to use the given solution. I'm waiting to see the results of your imagination.

SIGNED OPERAND MULTIPLICATION

Code	Mnemonic	Description
F6 /5	IMUL r/m8	AX AL * r/m byte
F7 /5	IMUL r/m16	DX:AX AX * r/m word
F7 /5	IMUL r/m32	EDX:EAX EAX * r/m doubleword
0F AF / r	IMUL r16, r/m16	word register word register * r/m word
0F AF / r	IMUL r32, r/m32	doubleword register doubleword register * r/m doubleword
6B / r ib	IMUL r16, r/m16, imm8	word register r/m16 * sign-extended immediate byte
6B / r ib	IMUL r32, r/m32, imm8	doubleword register r/m32 * sign-extended immediate byte
6B / r ib	IMUL r16, imm8	word register word register *sign-extended immediate byte
6B / r ib	IMUL r32, imm8	doubleword register doubleword register *sign-extended immediate byte
69 / r iw	IMUL r16, r/m16, imm16	word register r/m16 * immediate word
69 / r id	IMUL r32,r /m32, imm32	doubleword register r/m32 * immediate doubleword
69 / r iw	IMUL r16, imm16	word register r/m16 * immediate word
69 / r id	IMUL r32, imm32	doubleword register r/m32 * immediate doubleword

DESCRIPTION

Performs a signed multiplication of two operands. This

instruction has three forms, depending on the number of operands. This form is identical to that used by the MUL instruction. Here, the source operand (in a general-purpose register or memory location) is multiplied by the value in the AL, AX, or EAX register (depending on the operand size) and the product is stored in the AX, DX:AX, or EDX:EAX registers, respectively.

Two-operand Form

With this form the destination operand (the first operand) is multiplied by the source operand (second operand). The destination operand is a general-purpose register and the source operand is an immediate value, a general-purpose register, or a memory location. The product is then stored in the destination operand location.

Three-operand Form

This form requires a destination operand (the first operand) and two source operands (the second and the third operands). Here, the first source operand (which can be a general-purpose register or a memory location) is multiplied by the second source operand (an immediate value). The product is then stored in the destination operand (a general-purpose register).

When an immediate value is used as an operand, it is sign-extended to the length of the destination operand format. The CF and OF flags are set when significant bits are carried into the upper half of the result. The CF and OF flags are cleared when the result fits exactly in the lower half of the result. The three forms of the IMUL instruction are similar in that the length of the product is calculated to twice the length of the operands. With the one-operand form, the product is stored exactly in the destination.

With the two- and three- operand forms, however, result is truncated to the length of the destination before it is stored in the destination register. Because of this truncation, the CF or OF flag should be tested to ensure that no significant bits are lost. The two- and three-operand forms may also be used with unsigned operands because the lower half of the product is the same regardless if the operands are signed or unsigned. The CF and OF flags, however, cannot be used to determine if the upper half of the result is non-zero.

Accumulator Operands	Multiplies Bytes	Clocks	
• r8	2	11	NP
r16	2	11	NP
r32	2	10	NP
mem8	2 + d(0 - 2)	11	NP
mem16	2 + d(0 - 2)	11	NP
mem32	2 + d(0 - 2)	10	NP

Implied Multiplicand	Operand (Multiplier)		Result
AL	*	byte	= AX
AX	*	word	= DX:AX
EAX	*	dword	= EDX:EAX

2 AND 3 OPERAND MULTIPLIES

Operands	Bytes	Clocks	
r16, imm	2 + i(1, 2)	10	NP
r32, imm	2 + i(1, 2)	10	NP
r16, r16, imm	2 + i(1, 2)	10	NP
r32, r32, imm	2 + i(1, 2)	10	NP
r16, m16, imm	2 + d(0 - 2) + i(1, 2)	10	NP
r32, m32, imm	2 + d(0 - 2) + i(1, 2)	10	NP
r16, r16	2 + i(1, 2)	10	NP
r32, r32	2 + i(1, 2)	10	NP
r16, m16	2 + d(0 - 2) + i(1, 2)	10	NP
r32, m32	2 + d(0 - 2) + i(1, 2)	10	NP

FLAGS

ID	unaffected	DF	unaffected
VIP	unaffected	IF	unaffected
VIF	unaffected	TF	unaffected
AC	unaffected	SF	undefined

VM	unaffected	ZF	undefined
RF	unaffected	AF	undefined
NT	unaffected	PF	undefined
IOPL	unaffected	CF	For the one operand form of the instruction, sets when significant bits are carried into the upper half of the result and cleared when the result fits exactly in the lower half of the result. For the two- and three-operand forms of the instruction, sets when the result must be truncated to fit in the destination operand size and cleared when the result fit exactly in the destination operand size.
OF	For the one operand form of the instruction, sets when significant bits are carried into the upper half of the result and cleared when the result fits exactly in the lower half of the result. For the two- and three-operand forms of the instruction, sets when the result must be truncated to fit in the destination operand		

size and cleared when the result fits exactly in the destination operand size

BOOTHS ALGORITHM AND ARRAY MULTIPLIER

PROCEDURE

Booth's algorithm involves repeatedly adding one of two predetermined values A and S to a product P, then performing a rightward arithmetic shift on P. Let m and r be the multiplicand and multiplier, respectively; and let x and y represent jhghugyg the number of bits in m and r.

- Determine the values of A and S, and the initial value of P. All of these numbers should have a length equal to (x + y + 1).
  - *A*: Fill the most significant (leftmost) bits with the value of m. Fill the remaining (y + 1) bits with zeros.
  - *S*: Fill the most significant bits with the value of (?m) in two's complement notation. Fill the remaining (y + 1) bits with zeros.
  - *P*: Fill the most significant x bits with zeros. To the right of this, append the value of r. Fill the least significant (rightmost) bit with a zero.
- Determine the two least significant (rightmost) bits of P.
  - If they are 01, find the value of P + A. Ignore any overflow.
  - If they are 10, find the value of P + S. Ignore any overflow.
  - If they are 00, do nothing. Use P directly in the next step.
  - If they are 11, do nothing. Use P directly in the next step.
- Arithmetically shift the value obtained in the 2nd

step by a single place to the right. Let P now equal this new value.

- Repeat steps 2 and 3 until they have been done y times.
- Drop the least significant (rightmost) bit from P. This is the product of m and r.

Example

Find 3 × (–4), with m = 3 and r = –4, and x = 4 and y = 4:

- A = 0011 0000 0
- S = 1101 0000 0
- P = 0000 1100 0
- *Perform the loop four times:*
  - – P = 0000 1100 0. The last two bits are 00.
  - a. P = 0000 0110 0. Arithmetic right shift.
  - – P = 0000 0110 0. The last two bits are 00.
  - a. P = 0000 0011 0. Arithmetic right shift.
  - – P = 0000 0011 0. The last two bits are 10.
  - a. P = 1101 0011 0. P = P + S.
  - b. P = 1110 1001 1. Arithmetic right shift.
  - – P = 1110 1001 1. The last two bits are 11.
  - a. P = 1111 0100 1. Arithmetic right shift.
  - b. The product is 1111 0100, which is –12.

The above mentioned technique is inadequate when the multiplicand is the largest negative number that can be represented (i.e. if the multiplicand has 8 bits then this value is –128). One possible correction to this problem is to add one more bit to the left of A, S and P.

Below, we demonstrate the improved technique by multiplying –8 by 2 using 4 bits for the multiplicand and the multiplier:

- A = 1 1000 0000 0
- S = 0 1000 0000 0
- P = 0 0000 0010 0
- *Perform the loop four times:*
  - – P = 0 0000 0010 0. The last two bits are 00.
  - a. P = 0 0000 0001 0. Right shift.
  - – P = 0 0000 0001 0. The last two bits are 10.

a) P = 0 1000 0001 0. P = P + S.
b) P = 0 0100 0000 1. Right shift.
– P = 0 0100 0000 1. The last two bits are 01.
a) P = 1 1100 0000 1. P = P + A.
b) P = 1 1110 0000 0. Right shift.
– P = 1 1110 0000 0. The last two bits are 00.
a) P = 0 1111 0000 0. Right shift.
b) The product is 11110000 (after discarding the first and the last bit) which is –16.

WORKING

Consider a positive multiplier consisting of a block of 1s surrounded by 0s.

For example, 00111110. The product is given by:

$$M \times "00111110" = M \times (2^5 + 2^4 + 2^3 + 2^2 + 2^1) = M \times 62$$

where M is the multiplicand. The number of operations can be reduced to two by rewriting the same as

$$M \times "010000 - 10" = M \times (2^6 - 2^1) = M \times 62.$$

In fact, it can be shown that any sequence of 1's in a binary number can be broken into the difference of two binary numbers:

$$(\cdots\overbrace{01\cdots10}^{n}\cdots)_2 \equiv (\cdots\overbrace{10\cdots00}^{n}\cdots)_2 - (\cdots\overbrace{00\cdots10}^{n}\cdots)_2.$$

Hence, we can actually replace the multiplication by the string of ones in the original number by simpler operations, adding the multiplier, shifting the partial product thus formed by appropriate places, and then finally subtracting the multiplier. It is making use of the fact that we do not have to do anything but shift while we are dealing with 0s in a binary multiplier, and is similar to using the mathematical property that 99 = 100 – 1 while multiplying by 99. This scheme can be extended to any number of blocks of 1s in a multiplier (including the case of single 1 in a block). Thus,

$$M \times "00111010" = M \times (2^5 + 2^4 + 2^3 + 2^1) = M \times 58$$

$$M \times "0100 - 1010" = M(2^6 - 2^3 + 2^1) = M \times 58.$$

Booth's algorithm follows this scheme by performing an addition when it encounters the first digit of a block of ones

(0 1) and a subtraction when it encounters the end of the block (1 0). This works for a negative multiplier as well. When the ones in a multiplier are grouped into long blocks, Booth's algorithm performs fewer additions and subtractions than the normal multiplication algorithm.

DIVISION AND LOGIC OPERATION

In computer's programming we also have another kind of operators, called logical operators, they are used in logical expressions and just return true or false, take a look at the following tables with the most used arithmetical and logical operators in computer programming.

ARITHMETICAL

```
** Exponentiation
+x, -x Positive, Negative
*,/,% Multiplication, Division, Remainder
+, - Addition, Subtraction
```

You should at least know the majority of the operators above, the only one that a few people may know is the Remainder (%), it returns the remainder of a division, for example: 3% 2 would return 1 because 3 divided by 1 is 1 and 1 remains, the operator% returns the reminder of a division.

The operators above are processed from top to bottom, so the expression:

```
1 + 3 * 2
```

Is processed in the following order: first 3 * 2 that will result in 6, then 6 + 1 that will result in 7, test it, open up a Python shell and type? 1 + 3 * 2. And as I'm a nice guy, I'll not make you remember the order of the operators (like some teachers that never did real code in their life do), there is a way for you to organize the expression so it executes in the order that you want, using parenthesis, like in mathematics, the most internal parenthesis are processed first, so if we want the sum to be processed before the multiplication we need to write our expression like this:

```
(1 + 3) * 2
```

Type the above code in Python and see what happens

LOGICAL

```
or Boolean operator OR
and Boolean Operator AND
not Boolean Operator NOT
<, <=, >, >=, !=, == Comparisons
```

Like we have learned in our previous lesson a Boolean variable have just 2 possible values (true or false), logical operators are used in logical expressions and they always return true or false, take a look at the expression:

```
5 > 3
```

The above expression is a logical expression and returns true, because its true that 5 is bigger than 3, now a little more complex expression:

```
5 > 3 ou 3 > 4
```

The expression above would return false too, because the operator OR returns true if one of the two expressions is true.

The following expressions return false:

```
10 != 10 → is 10 different from 10? false!
10 > 10 → is 10 bigger 10? false!
10 == 11 → is 10 equals 11? false!
```

Like we have learned before, true or false to the computer means 1 (true) or 0 (false), on and off, so to process this expressions, the computer multiplies or sum, depending on the operator, it looks complicated at first sight:

OPERATOR AND

```
1 0 | 1 * 0 = 0 → false
0 * 1 = 0 → false
1 * 1 = 1 → true
0 * 0 = 0 → false
```

So for the operator AND return true, both variables need to be true.

OPERATOR OR

```
1 + 0 = 1 → true
0 + 1 = 1 → true
1 + 1 = 1 → true
0 + 0 = 0 → false
```

It the OR operator's case, its necessary just one of the variables to be true, the expression will be false just when both variables are false, what is exactly the contrary of the AND operator.

OPERATOR NOT

The operator not just returns the inverse value of the Boolean variable, so not true is false, and not false is true,

```
not 1 → 0
not 0 → 1
```

LOGICAL OPERATORS (!, &&, | |)

The Operator ! is the C++ operator to perform the Boolean operation NOT, it has only one operand, located at its right, and the only thing that it does is to inverse the value of it, producing false if its operand is true and true if its operand is false. Basically, it returns the opposite Boolean value of evaluating its operand.

For example:

```
1!(5 == 5)// evaluates to false because the
expression at its right (5 == 5) is true.
2!(6 <= 4)// evaluates to true because (6 <=
4) would be false.
3!true// evaluates to false
4 !false// evaluates to true.
```

The logical operators && and | | are used when evaluating two expressions to obtain a single relational result. The operator &&corresponds with Boolean logical operation AND. This operation results true if both its two operands are true, and false otherwise. The following panel shows the result of operator && evaluating the expression a && b:

&& OPERATOR

a	b	a && b
true	true	true
true	false	false
false	true	false
false	false	false

The operator || corresponds with Boolean logical operation OR. This operation results true if either one of its two operands is true, thus being false only when both operands are false themselves. Here are the possible results of a || b:

|| OPERATOR

a	b	a || b
true	true	true
true	false	true
false	true	true
false	false	false

For example:

```
((5 == 5) && (3 > 6))// evaluates to false
(true && false).
((5 == 5) || (3 > 6))// evaluates to true
(true || false).
```

CONDITIONAL OPERATOR (?)

The conditional operator evaluates an expression returning a value if that expression is true and a different one if the expression is evaluated as false. Its format is:

```
condition ? result1: result2
```

If condition is true the expression will return result1, if it is not it will return result2.

```
7==5 ? 4: 3// returns 3, since 7 is not
equal to 5.
7==5+2 ? 4: 3// returns 4, since 7 is
equal    to 5+2.
5>3 ? a: b// returns the value of a,
since 5 is greater than 3.
a>b ? a: b// returns whichever is greater,
a or b.
```

```
// conditional operator          7

  #include <iostream>
```

```
using namespace std;
int main ()
{
 int a,b,c;
a=2;
 b=7;
c = (a>b) ? a: b;
cout << c;
 return 0;
  }
```

In this example a was 2 and b was 7, so the expression being evaluated (a>b) was not true, thus the first value specified after the question mark was discarded in favour of the second value (the one after the colon) which was b, with a value of 7.

COMMA OPERATOR (,)

The comma operator (,) is used to separate two or more expressions that are included where only one expression is expected. When the set of expressions has to be evaluated for a value, only the rightmost expression is considered.

For example, the following code:

```
a = (b=3, b+2);
```

Would first assign the value 3 to b, and then assign b+2 to variable a. So, at the end, variable a would contain the value 5 while variable b would contain value 3.

BITWISE OPERATORS (&, |, ^, ~, <<, >>)

Bitwise operators modify variables considering the bit patterns that represent the values they store.

Operator	Asm Equivalent	Description
&	AND	Bitwise AND
|	OR	Bitwise Inclusive OR
^	XOR	Bitwise Exclusive OR
~	NOT	Unary complement (bit inversion)
<<	SHL	Shift Left
>>	SHR	Shift Right

EXPLICIT TYPE CASTING OPERATOR

Type casting operators allow you to convert a datum of a given type to another. There are several ways to do this in C++. The simplest one, which has been inherited from the C language, is to precede the expression to be converted by the new type enclosed between parentheses (()):

```
int i;
float f = 3.14;
i = (int) f;
```

The previous code converts the float number 3.14 to an integer value (3), the remainder is lost. Here, the typecasting operator was (int). Another way to do the same thing in C++ is using the functional notation: preceding the expression to be converted by the type and enclosing the expression between parentheses:

```
i = int (f);
```

Both ways of type casting are valid in C++.

Sizeof()

This operator accepts one parametre, which can be either a type or a variable itself and returns the size in bytes of that type or object:

```
a = sizeof (char);
```

This will assign the value 1 to a because char is a one-byte long type. The value returned by sizeof is a constant, so it is always determined before programme execution.

OTHER OPERATORS

Later in these tutorials, we will see a few more operators,

like the ones referring to pointers or the specifics for object-oriented programming. Each one is treated in its respective section.

PRECEDENCE OF OPERATORS

When writing complex expressions with several operands, we may have some doubts about which operand is evaluated first and which later.

For example, in this expression:

```
a = 5 + 7% 2
```

we may doubt if it really means:

```
1 a = 5 + (7% 2)// with a result of 6, or
2 a = (5 + 7)% 2// with a result of 0
```

The correct answer is the first of the two expressions, with a result of 6. There is an established order with the priority of each operator, and not only the arithmetic ones (those whose preference come from mathematics) but for all the operators which can appear in C++.

From greatest to lowest priority, the priority order is as follows:

Level	Operator	Description	Grouping
1	::	scope	Left-to-right
2	() [] . → ++ -- dynamic_cast static_cast reinterpret_cast const_cast typeid	postfix	Left-to-right
3	++ -- ~ ! sizeof new delete	unary (prefix)	Right-to-left
	* &	indirection and reference (pointers)	
	+ -	unary sign operator	
4	(type)	type casting	Right-to-left
5	.* →*	pointer-to-member	Left-to-right
6	*/%	multiplicative	Left-to-right
7	+ -	additive	Left-to-right
8	<< >>	shift	Left-to-right

9	< > <= >=	relational	Left-to-right
10	== !=	equality	Left-to-right
11	&	bitwise AND	Left-to-right
12	^	bitwise XOR	Left-to-right
13	|	bitwise OR	Left-to-right
14	&&	logical AND	Left-to-right
15	||	logical OR	Left-to-right
16	?:	conditional	Right-to-left
17	= *=/=%= += -= >>= <<= &= ^= |=	assignment	Right-to-left
18	,	comma	Left-to-right

Grouping defines the precedence order in which operators are evaluated in the case that there are several operators of the same level in an expression.

All these precedence levels for operators can be manipulated or become more legible by removing possible ambiguities using parentheses signs (and), as in this example:

```
a = 5 + 7% 2;
```

Might be written either as:

```
a = 5 + (7% 2);
```

or

```
a = (5 + 7)% 2;
```

depending on the operation that we want to perform.

So if you want to write complicated expressions and you are not completely sure of the precedence levels, always include parentheses. It will also become a code easier to read.

DIVISION

You cannot synthesize a general n-bit/m-bit division operation using the div and idiv instructions. Such an operation must be performed using a sequence of shift and subtract instructions.

Such an operation is extremely messy. A less general operation, dividing an n bit quantity by a 32 bit (on the 80386 or later) or 16 bit quantity is easily synthesized using the div instruction. The following code demonstrates how to divide a 64 bit quantity by a 16 bit divisor, producing a 64 bit quotient and a 16 bit remainder:

```
dseg        segment para public'DATA'
dividend    dword 0FFFFFFFFh, 12345678h
divisor     word 16
Quotient    dword 0,0
Modulo      word 0
dseg ends
cseg      segment para public'CODE'
          assume cs:cseg, ds:dseg
; Divide a 64 bit quantity by a 16 bit quantity:
Divide64    proc near
            mov ax, word ptr dividend+6
            sub dx, dx
            div divisor
            mov word ptr Quotient+6, ax
            mov ax, word ptr dividend+4
            div divisor
            mov word ptr Quotient+4, ax
            mov ax, word ptr dividend+2
            div divisor
            mov word ptr Quotient+2, ax
            mov ax, word ptr dividend
            div divisor
            mov word ptr Quotient, ax
            mov Modulo, dx
            ret
Divide64    endp
cseg        ends
```

This code can be extended to any number of bits by simply adding additional mov/ div/ mov instructions at the beginning of the sequence. Of course, on the 80386 and later processors you can divide by a 32 bit value by using edx and eax in the above sequence (with a few other appropriate adjustments). If you need to use a divisor larger than 16 bits (32 bits on an 80386 or later), you're going to have to implement the division using a shift and subtract strategy.

Unfortunately, such algorithms are very slow. In this section we'll develop two division algorithms that operate on an arbitrary number of bits. The first is slow but easier to understand, the second is quite a bit faster (in general). As for multiplication, the best way to understand how the computer performs division is to study how you were taught to perform long division by hand.

Consider the operation 3456/12 and the steps you would take to manually perform this operation:

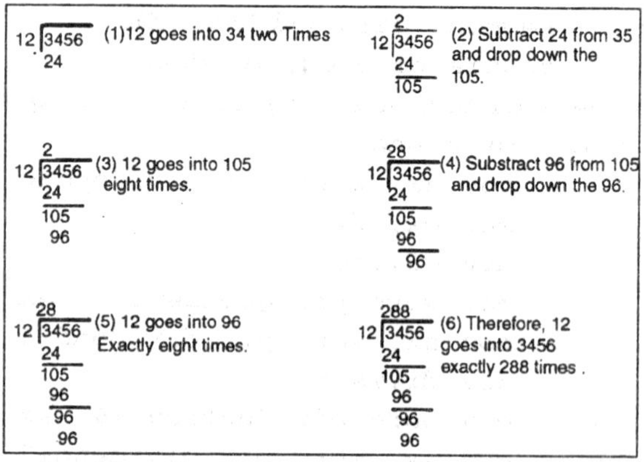

This algorithm is actually easier in binary since at each step you do not have to guess how many times 12 goes into the remainder nor do you have to multiply 12 by your guess to obtain the amount to subtract. At each step in the binary algorithm the divisor goes into the remainder exactly zero or one times.

As an example, consider the division of 27 (11011) by three (11):

```
11)11011        11 goes into 11 one time.
   11

   1
11)11011        Subtract out the 11 and bring down the zero
   11
   --
   00

   1
11)11011        11 goes into zero times.
   11
   --
   00
   00
```

```
     10
  11)11011        subtract out the zero and bring the one.
     11
     --
     00
     00
     --
      01
```

```
     10
  11)11011        11 goes int o 01 zero times.
     11
     --
     00
     00
     --
      01
      00
```

```
     100
  11)11011 Subtract out the zero and bring down the one.
     11
     --
     00
     00
     --
      01
      00
      --
       11
```

```
     100
  11)11011        11 goes into 11 one time.
     11
     --
     00
     00
     --
      01
      00
      --
       11
       11
```

```
     1001
  11)11011        This produces the final result of 1001.
     11
     --
     00
     00
     --
      01
      00
      --
       11
       11
       --
       00
```

There is a novel way to implement this binary division algorithm that computes the quotient and the remainder at the same time.

The algorithm is the following:

```
Quotient:= Dividend;
Remainder:= 0;
for i:= 1 to NumberBits do

  Remainder:Quotient:= Remainder:Quotient SHL
  1;
  if Remainder >= Divisor then

    Remainder:= Remainder - Divisor;
    Quotient:= Quotient + 1;

  endif
endfor
```

NumberBits is the number of bits in the Remainder, Quotient, Divisor, and Dividend variables. Note that the Quotient:= Quotient + 1 statement sets the L.O. bit of Quotientto one since this algorithm previously shifts Quotient one bit to the left. The 80x86 code to implement this algorithm is

```
; Assume Dividend (and Quotient) is DX:AX,
Divisor is in CX:BX,
; and Remainder is in SI:DI.
        mov bp, 32;Count off 32 bits in
                    BP
        sub si, si;Set remainder to zero
        sub di, di
BitLoop:    shl ax, 1;See the section on
                            shifts
            rcl dx, 1       ; that describes
                                how this
rcl di, 1           ; 64 bit SHL
                      operation works
rcl si, 1
cmp si, cx          ;Compare H.O. words
                    of Rem,
ja GoesInto; Divisor.
jb TryNext
```

```
cmp di, bx;Compare L.O. words.
jb TryNext
GoesInto:  sub di, bx;Remainder:=
                      Remainder -
           sbb si, cx; Divisor
           inc ax;Set L.O. bit of AX
TryNext: dec bp;Repeat 32 times.
           jne BitLoop
```

This code looks short and simple, but there are a few problems with it. First, it does not check for division by zero (it will produce the value 0FFFFFFFFh if you attempt to divide by zero), it only handles unsigned values, and it is very slow. Handling division by zero is very simple, just check the divisor against zero prior to running this code and return an appropriate error code if the divisor is zero.

Dealing with signed values is equally simple, you'll see how to do that in a little bit. The performance of this algorithm, however, leaves a lot to be desired. Assuming one pass through the loop takes about 30 clock cycles[2], this algorithm would require almost 1,000 clock cycles to complete! That's an order of magnitude worse than the DIV/IDIV instructions on the 80x86 that are among the slowest instructions on the 80x86.

There is a technique you can use to boost the performance of this division by a fair amount: check to see if the divisor variable really uses 32 bits. Often, even though the divisor is a 32 bit variable, the value itself fits just fine into 16 bits (i.e., the H.O. word of Divisor is zero). In this special case, that occurs frequently, you can use the DIV instruction which is much faster.

Chapter 4

Floating Point Arithmetic Operations

INTRODUCTION

Builders of computer systems often need information about floating-point arithmetic. There are, however, remarkably few sources of detailed information about it. One of the few books on the subject, Floating-Point Computation by Pat Sterbenz, is long out of print. This paper is a tutorial on those aspects of floating-point arithmetic (floating-point hereafter) that have a direct connection to systems building. It consists of three loosely connected parts. The first section, Rounding Error, discusses the implications of using different rounding strategies for the basic operations of addition, subtraction, multiplication and division.

It also contains background information on the two methods of measuring rounding error, ulps and relative error. The second part discusses the IEEE floating-point standard, which is becoming rapidly accepted by commercial hardware manufacturers. Included in the IEEE standard is the rounding method for basic operations.

The discussion of the standard draws on the material in the section Rounding Error. The third part discusses the connections between floating-point and the design of various aspects of computer systems. Topics include instruction set design, optimizing compilers and exception handling. I have tried to avoid making statements about floating-point without also giving reasons why the statements are true, especially since the justifications involve nothing more complicated than elementary calculus. Those explanations that are not central to the main argument have been grouped into a section called"The Details,"so that they can be skipped if desired. In particular, the proofs of many of the theorems appear in this section. The end of each proof is marked with the z symbol. When a proof is not included, the z appears immediately following the statement of the theorem.

ROUNDING ERROR

Squeezing infinitely many real numbers into a finite number of bits requires an approximate representation. Although there are infinitely many integers, in most programmes the result of integer computations can be stored in 32 bits. In contrast, given any fixed number of bits, most calculations with real numbers will produce quantities that cannot be exactly represented using that many bits.

Therefore the result of a floating-point calculation must often be rounded in order to fit back into its finite representation. This rounding error is the characteristic feature of floating-point computation. The section Relative Error and Ulpsdescribes how it is measured. Since most floating-point calculations have rounding error anyway, does it matter if the basic arithmetic operations introduce a little bit more rounding error than necessary? That question is a main theme throughout this section.

The section Guard Digits discusses guard digits, a means of reducing the error when subtracting two nearby numbers. Guard digits were considered sufficiently important by IBM that in 1968 it added a guard digit to the double precision format in the System/360 architecture (single precision already had a guard digit), and retrofitted all existing machines in the field. Two examples are given to illustrate the utility of guard digits.

The IEEE standard goes further than just requiring the use of a guard digit. It gives an algorithm for addition, subtraction, multiplication, division and square root, and requires that implementations produce the same result as that algorithm.

Thus, when a programme is moved from one machine to another, the results of the basic operations will be the same in every bit if both machines support the IEEE standard. This greatly simplifies the porting of programmes. Other uses of this precise specification are given in Exactly Rounded Operations.

FLOATING-POINT FORMATS

Several different representations of real numbers have been proposed, but by far the most widely used is the floating-point representation. Floating-point representations have a base β (which is always assumed to be even) and a precision p. If β = 10 and p = 3, then the number 0.1 is represented as 1.00 × 10-1. If β = 2 andp = 24, then the decimal number 0.1 cannot be represented exactly, but is approximately 1.10011001100110011001101 × 2-4.

In general, a floating-point number will be represented as ± d.dd... d × β^e, where d.dd... d is called the significand and has p digits. More precisely ± d0 . d1 d2 ... dp-1 × β^e represents the number

$$(1) \pm(d_0 + d_1\beta^{-1} + \cdots + d_{p-1}\beta^{-(p-1)})\beta^c, (o \le d_i < \beta).$$

The term floating-point number will be used to mean a real number that can be exactly represented in the format under discussion. Two other parametres associated with floating-point representations are the largest and smallest allowable exponents, e_{max} and e_{min}. Since there are βp possible significands, and emax - emin + 1 possible exponents, a floating-point number can be encoded in

$$[\log_2(e_{max} - e_{min} + 1)] + [\log_2(\beta^p)] + 1$$

bits, where the final +1 is for the sign bit. The precise encoding is not important for now.

There are two reasons why a real number might not be exactly representable as a floating-point number. The most common situation is illustrated by the decimal number 0.1. Although it has a finite decimal representation, in binary it has an infinite repeating representation. Thus when β = 2, the number 0.1 lies strictly between two floating-point numbers and is exactly representable by neither of them. A less common situation is that a real number is out of range, that is, its absolute value is larger than $\beta \times \beta^{e_{max}}$ or smaller than $1.0\times \beta^{e_{min}}$. Most of this paper discusses issues due to the first reason. However, numbers that are out of range will be discussed in the sections Infinity and Denormalized Numbers.

Floating-point representations are not necessarily unique. For example, both 0.01 × 101 and 1.00 × 10-1represent 0.1. If the leading digit is nonzero (d0 ≠ 0 in equation above), then the representation is said to be normalized. The floating-point number 1.00 × 10-1 is normalized, while 0.01 × 101 is not. When $\beta = 2$,p = 3, emin = -1 and emax = 2 there are 16 normalized floating-point numbers. The bold hash marks correspond to numbers whose significand is 1.00. Requiring that a floating-point representation be normalized makes the representation unique. Unfortunately, this restriction makes it impossible to represent zero! A natural way to represent 0 is with 1.0 $\times \beta^{c_{min}-1}$, since this preserves the fact that the numerical ordering of nonnegative real numbers corresponds to the lexicographic ordering of their floating-point representations. When the exponent is stored in a k bit field, that means that only 2k - 1 values are available for use as exponents, since one must be reserved to represent 0.

Note that the × in a floating-point number is part of the notation, and different from a floating-point multiply operation. The meaning of the × symbol should be clear from the context. For example, the expression (2.5 ×10-3) × (4.0 × 102) involves only a single floating-point multiplication.

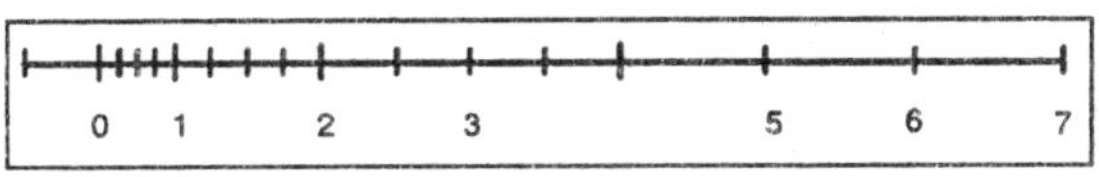

Normalized numbers when $\beta = 2$, p = 3, $e^{min} = -1$, $e^{max} = 2$

RELATIVE ERROR

Since rounding error is inherent in floating-point computation, it is important to have a way to measure this error. Consider the floating-point format with $\beta = 10$ and p =

3, which will be used throughout this section. If the result of a floating-point computation is 3.12×10^{-2}, and the answer when computed to infinite precision is .0314, it is clear that this is in error by 2 units in the last place. Similarly, if the real number .0314159 is represented as 3.14 × 10-2, then it is in error by .159 units in the last place. In general, if the floating-point number d.d...d × β^e is used to represent z, then it is in error by $|d.d...d - (z/\beta^e)| \beta^{p-1}$ units in the last place.

The term ulps will be used as shorthand for"units in the last place."If the result of a calculation is the floating-point number nearest to the correct result, it still might be in error by as much as .5 ulp. Another way to measure the difference between a floating-point number and the real number it is approximating isrelative error, which is simply the difference between the two numbers divided by the real number. For example the relative error committed when approximating 3.14159 by 3.14 × 100 is .00159/3.14159 ≈ .0005.

To compute the relative error that corresponds to .5 ulp, observe that when a real number is approximated by the closest possible floating-point number d.dd...dd × β^e, the error can be as large as 0.00...00β^I × β^e, whereβ^I is the digit β/2, there are p units in the significand of the floating-point number, and p units of 0 in the significand of the error. This error is ((β/2)β-p) × β^e. Since numbers of the form d.dd...dd × β^e all have the same absolute error, but have values that range between βe and β ×βe, the relative error ranges between $((\beta/2)\beta^{-p}) \times \beta^e/\beta^e$ and $((\beta/2)\beta^{-p}) \times \beta^e/\beta^{e+1}$. That is,

$$(2)\ \frac{1}{2}\beta{-}p \le \frac{1}{2}\text{ulp} \le \frac{\beta}{2}\beta^{-p}$$

In particular, the relative error corresponding to .5 ulp can vary by a factor of β. This factor is called the wobble. Setting ε = $(\beta/2)\beta^{-p}$ to the largest of the bounds in above, we can say that when a real number is rounded to the closest floating-point number, the relative error is always bounded by e, which is referred to as machine epsilon.

In the example above, the relative error was .00159/3.14159 ≈ .0005. In order to avoid such small numbers, the relative error is normally written as a factor times ε, which in this case is ε =

$(\beta/2)\beta^{-p}$ = 5(10)-3 = .005. Thus the relative error would be expressed as (.00159/3.14159)/.005) ε ≈ 0.1ε. To illustrate the difference between ulps and relative error, consider the real number x = 12.35.

It is approximated by $\bar{x}$ = 1.24 × 10^1. The error is 0.5 ulps, the relative error is 0.8ε. Next consider the computation 8$\bar{x}$. The exact value is 8x = 98.8, while the computed value is 8$\bar{x}$ = 9.92 × 101. The error is now 4.0 ulps, but the relative error is still 0.8ε. The error measured in ulps is 8 times larger, even though the relative error is the same. In general, when the base is β, a fixed relative error expressed in ulps can wobble by a factor of up to β. And conversely, as equation above shows, a fixed error of .5 ulps results in a relative error that can wobble by β.

The most natural way to measure rounding error is in ulps. For example rounding to the nearest floating-point number corresponds to an error of less than or equal to .5 ulp. However, when analyzing the rounding error caused by various formulas, relative error is a better measure.

A good illustration of this is the analysis in the section Theorem 9. Since ε can overestimate the effect of rounding to the nearest floating-point number by the wobble factor of β, error estimates of formulas will be tighter on machines with a small β.

When only the order of magnitude of rounding error is of interest, ulps and ε may be used interchangeably, since they differ by at most a factor of β. For example, when a floating-point number is in error by n ulps, that means that the number of contaminated digits is logβ n. If the relative error in a computation is n ε, then

(3) Contaminated digits ≈ log β n.

GUARD DIGITS

One method of computing the difference between two floating-point numbers is to compute the difference exactly and then round it to the nearest floating-point number. This is very expensive if the operands differ greatly in size. Assuming p = 3, 2.15 × 10^{12} - 1.25 × 10-5 would be calculated as

$x = 2.15 \times 10^{12}$
$y = .0000000000000000125 \times 10^{12}$
$x - y = 2.1499999999999999875 \times 10^{12}$

which rounds to 2.15×10^{12}. Rather than using all these digits, floating-point hardware normally operates on a fixed number of digits. Suppose that the number of digits kept is p, and that when the smaller operand is shifted right, digits are simply discarded (as opposed to rounding). Then 2.15×10^{12} - 1.25×10-5 becomes

$x = 2.15 \times 10^{12}$
$y = 0.00 \times 10^{12}$
$x - y = 2.15 \times 10^{12}$

The answer is exactly the same as if the difference had been computed exactly and then rounded. Take another example: 10.1 - 9.93. This becomes

$x = 1.01 \times 10^1$
$y = 0.99 \times 10^1$
$x - y = .02 \times 10^1$

The correct answer is .17, so the computed difference is off by 30 ulps and is wrong in every digit! How bad can the error be?

THEOREM 1

Using a floating-point format with parametres β and p, and computing differences using p digits, the relative error of the result can be as large as β - 1.

Proof

A relative error of β - 1 in the expression x - y occurs when x = 1.00...0 and y = .ρρ...ρ, where ρ = β - 1. Here y has p digits (all equal to ρ). The exact difference is $x - y = \beta/^{-p}$. However, when computing the answer using only p digits, the rightmost digit of y gets shifted off, and so the computed difference is β^{-p+1}. Thus the error is $\beta^{-p} - \beta^{-p+1} = \beta^{-p}(\beta - 1)$, and the relative error is $\beta^{-p}(\beta - 1)/\beta^{-p} = \beta - 1$. z

When β = 2, the relative error can be as large as the result, and when β = 10, it can be 9 times larger. Or to put it another way, when β=2, equation shows that the number of contaminated digits is $\log_2(1/\varepsilon) = \log_2(2^p) = p$. That is, all of the p digits in the result are wrong! Suppose that one extra digit is added to guard against this situation (a guard digit). That is, the smaller number is truncated to p + 1 digits, and then the result of the subtraction is rounded to p digits. With a guard digit, the previous example becomes

$x = 1.010 \times 10^1$

$y = 0.993 \times 10^1$

$x - y = .017 \times 10^1$

and the answer is exact. With a single guard digit, the relative error of the result may be greater than ε, as in 110 - 8.59.

$x = 1.10 \times 10^2$

$y = .085 \times 10^2$

$x - y = 1.015 \times 10^2$

This rounds to 10^2, compared with the correct answer of 101.41, for a relative error of .006, which is greater than ε = .005. In general, the relative error of the result can be only slightly larger than ε . More precisely,

THEOREM 2

If x and y are floating-point numbers in a format with parametres β and p, and if subtraction is done with p + 1 digits (i.e. one guard digit), then the relative rounding error in the result is less than 2ε.

This theorem will be proven in Rounding Error. Addition is included in the above theorem since x and y can be positive or negative.

Cancellation

The last section can be summarized by saying that without a guard digit, the relative error committed when subtracting two nearby quantities can be very large. In other words, the evaluation of any expression containing a subtraction (or an addition of quantities with opposite signs) could result in a relative error so large that all the digits are meaningless (Theorem 1). When subtracting nearby quantities, the most significant digits in the operands match and cancel each other.

There are two kinds of cancellation: catastrophic and benign. Catastrophic cancellation occurs when the operands are subject to rounding errors. For example in the quadratic formula, the expression $b^2 - 4ac$ occurs. The quantities b^2 and $4ac$ are subject to rounding errors since they are the results of floating-point multiplications.

Suppose that they are rounded to the nearest floating-point number, and so are accurate to within .5 ulp. When they are subtracted, cancellation can cause many of the accurate digits to disappear, leaving behind mainly digits contaminated by rounding error. Hence the difference might have an error of many ulps. For example, consider $b = 3.34$, $a = 1.22$, and $c = 2.28$. The exact value of $b^2 - 4ac$ is .0292.

But b^2 rounds to 11.2 and 4ac rounds to 11.1, hence the final answer is .1 which is an error by 70 ulps, even though 11.2 - 11.1 is exactly equal to .1[6]. The subtraction did not introduce any error, but rather exposed the error introduced in the earlier multiplications. Benign cancellation occurs when subtracting exactly known quantities. If x and y have no rounding error, then by Theorem 2 if the subtraction is done with a guard digit, the difference x-y has a very small relative error (less than 2 ε). A formula that exhibits catastrophic cancellation can sometimes be rearranged to eliminate the problem. Again consider the quadratic formula

$$(4)\ r_1 = \frac{-b+\sqrt{b^2-4ac}}{2a}, r_2 = \frac{-b-\sqrt{b^2-4ac}}{2a}$$

When $b^2 \gg \alpha c$, then $b^2 - 4\alpha c$ does not involve a cancellation and

To avoid this, multiply the numerator and denominator of r1 by $-b-\sqrt{b^2-4\alpha c}$

(and similarly for r2) to obtain

$$(5)\ r_1 = \frac{2c}{-b-\sqrt{b^2-4\alpha c}}, r_2 = \frac{2c}{-b+\sqrt{b^2-4\alpha c}}$$

If $b^2 \gg ac$ and $b > 0$, then computing r_1 using formula will involve a cancellation. Therefore, use formula for computing

r_1 and for r_2. On the other hand, if b < 0, use for computing r_1 and for r_2. The expression $x^2 - y^2$ is another formula that exhibits catastrophic cancellation. It is more accurate to evaluate it as $(x - y)(x + y)$.

Unlike the quadratic formula, this improved form still has a subtraction, but it is a benign cancellation of quantities without rounding error, not a catastrophic one. By Theorem 2, the relative error in x – y is at most 2ε. The same is true of x + y. Multiplying two quantities with a small relative error results in a product with a small relative error (see the section Rounding Error).

In order to avoid confusion between exact and computed values, the following notation is used. Whereas x -y denotes the exact difference of x and y, x $ y denotes the computed difference (i.e., with rounding error). Similarly Å, Ä, and% denote computed addition, multiplication, and division, respectively. All caps indicate the computed value of a function, as in LN(x) or SQRT(x). Lowercase functions and traditional mathematical notation denote their exact values as in ln(x) and $\sqrt{x}$.

Although (x $ y) Ä(x Å y) is an excellent approximation to $x^2 - y^2$, the floating-point numbers x and y might themselves be approximations to some true quantities $\hat{x}$ and $\hat{y}$. For example, $\hat{x}$ and $\hat{y}$ might be exactly known decimal numbers that cannot be expressed exactly in binary. In this case, even though x $ y is a good approximation to x - y, it can have a huge relative error compared to the true expression $\hat{x} - \hat{y}$, and so the advantage of (x + y)(x - y) over $x^2 - y^2$ is not as dramatic. Since computing (x + y)(x – y) is about the same amount of work as computing $x^2 - y^2$, it is clearly the preferred form in this case.

In general, however, replacing a catastrophic cancellation by a benign one is not worthwhile if the expense is large, because the input is often (but not always) an approximation. But eliminating a cancellation entirely (as in the quadratic formula) is worthwhile even if the data are not exact. Throughout this paper, it will be assumed that the floating-point inputs to an algorithm are exact and that the results are computed as accurately as possible. The expression $x^2 - y^2$ is more accurate when rewritten as $(x - y)(x + y)$ because a catastrophic cancellation is replaced with a benign one. We next present more interesting examples of formulas exhibiting catastrophic cancellation that can be rewritten to exhibit only benign cancellation.

The area of a triangle can be expressed directly in terms of the lengths of its sides a, b, and c as

$$(6)\ A = \sqrt{s(s-a)(s-b)(s-c)},\ \text{Where } s = (a+b+c)/2$$

(Suppose the triangle is very flat; that is, $a \approx b + c$. Then $s \approx a$, and the term $(s - a)$ in formula (6) subtracts two nearby numbers, one of which may have rounding error. For example, if a = 9.0, b = c = 4.53, the correct value of s is 9.03 and A is 2.342.... Even though the computed value of s (9.05) is in error by only 2 ulps, the computed value of A is 3.04, an error of 70 ulps.

There is a way to rewrite formula (6) so that it will return accurate results even for flat triangles. It is

$$(7)\ A = \frac{\sqrt{(a+(b+c))(a-b))(c+(a-b))(a+(b-c))}}{4},\ a \geq b \geq c$$

If a, b, and c do not satisfy $a \geq b \geq c$, rename them before applying. It is straightforward to check that the right-hand sides are algebraically identical. Using the values of a, b, and c above gives a computed area of 2.35, which is 1 ulp in error and much more accurate than the first formula.

Although formula (7) is much more accurate than (6) for this example, it would be nice to know how well (7)performs in general.

THEOREM 3

The rounding error incurred when using (7) to compute the area of a triangle is at most 11e, provided that subtraction is performed with a guard digit, $e \leq .005$, and that square roots are computed to within 1/2 ulp.

The condition that $e < .005$ is met in virtually every actual floating-point system. For example when $\beta = 2$, $p \geq 8$ ensures that $e < .005$, and when $\beta = 10$, $p \geq 3$ is enough.

In statements like Theorem 3 that discuss the relative error of an expression, it is understood that the expression is computed using floating-point arithmetic. Because of the cumbersome nature of (8), in the statement of theorems we will usually say the computed value of E rather than writing out E with circle notation.

Error bounds are usually too pessimistic. In the numerical example given above, the computed value of (7) is 2.35, compared with a true value of 2.34216 for a relative error of 0.7ε, which is much less than 11ε. The main reason for computing error bounds is not to get precise bounds but rather to verify that the formula does not contain numerical problems. A final example of an expression that can be rewritten to use benign cancellation is $(1 + x)^n$, where $x \ll 1$.

This expression arises in financial calculations. Consider depositing $100 every day into a bank account that earns an annual interest rate of 6%, compounded daily. If n = 365 and i = .06, the amount of money accumulated at the end of one year is

$$100\frac{(1+i/\mu)^{\mu}-1}{1-\mu}$$

dollars. If this is computed using $\beta = 2$ and $p = 24$, the result is $37615.45 compared to the exact answer of $37614.05, a discrepancy of $1.40. The reason for the problem is easy to see. The expression 1 + i/n involves adding 1 to .0001643836, so the low order bits of i/n are lost. This rounding error is amplified when 1 + i/n is raised to the nth power.

The troublesome expression $(1 + i/n)^n$ can be rewritten as $e^{n\ln(1 + i/n)}$, where now the problem is to compute ln(1 + x) for small x. One approach is to use the approximation $\ln(1 + x) \approx x$, in which case the payment becomes $37617.26, which is off by $3.21 and even less accurate than the obvious formula. But there is a way to compute ln(1 + x) very accurately, as Theorem 4 shows [Hewlett-Packard 1982]. This formula yields $37614.07, accurate to within two cents!

Theorem 4 assumes that $^{LN(x)}$ approximates ln(x) to within 1/2 ulp. The problem it solves is that when x is small, $_{LN}(1 \oplus x)$ is not close to ln(1 + x) because $1 \oplus x$ has lost the information in the low order bits of x. That is, the computed value of ln(1 + x) is not close to its actual value when $x \ll 1$.

THEOREM 4

If ln(1 + x) is computed using the formula

$$(8)\quad \ln(1+x) = \begin{cases} x & \text{for } 1 \oplus x = 1 \\ \dfrac{x\ln(1+x)}{(1+x)-1} & \text{for } 1 \oplus x \neq 1 \end{cases}$$

the relative error is at most 5ε when $0 \leq x < 3/4$, provided subtraction is performed with a guard digit, e < 0.1, and ln is computed to within 1/2 ulp.

This formula will work for any value of x but is only interesting for $x \ll 1$, which is where catastrophic cancellation occurs in the naive formula ln(1 + x). Although the formula may seem mysterious, there is a simple explanation for why it works. Write ln(1 + x) as $x\left(\dfrac{\ln(1+x)}{x}\right) = x\mu(x)$

The left hand factor can be computed exactly, but the right hand factor μ(x) = ln(1 + x)/x will suffer a large rounding error when adding 1 to x. However, μ is almost constant, since ln(1 + x) » x. So changing x slightly will not introduce much error. In other words, if $\tilde{x} \ll x$, computing $x\mu(\tilde{x})$ will be a good approximation to $x\mu(x)$ = ln(1 + x).

Is there a value for $\tilde{x}$ for which $\tilde{x}$ and $\tilde{x}+1$ can be computed accurately? There is; namely $\tilde{x} = (1 \oplus x) \ominus 1$, because then $1 + \tilde{x}$ is exactly equal to $1 \oplus x$. The results of this section can be summarized by saying that a guard digit guarantees accuracy when nearby precisely known quantities are subtracted (benign cancellation). Sometimes a formula that gives inaccurate results can be rewritten to have much higher numerical accuracy by using benign cancellation; however, the procedure only works if subtraction is performed using a guard digit.

The price of a guard digit is not high, because it merely requires making the adder one bit wider. For a 54 bit double precision adder, the additional cost is less than 2%. For this price, you gain the ability to run many algorithms such as formula (6) for computing the area of a triangle and the expression ln(1 + x). Although most modern computers have a guard digit, there are a few that do not.

EXACTLY ROUNDED OPERATIONS

When floating-point operations are done with a guard digit, they are not as accurate as if they were computed exactly then rounded to the nearest floating-point number. Operations performed in this manner will be called exactly rounded.8 The example immediately preceding Theorem 2 shows that a single guard digit will not always give exactly rounded results. The previous section gave several examples of algorithms that require a guard digit in order to work properly. This section gives examples of algorithms that require exact rounding.

So far, the definition of rounding has not been given. Rounding is straightforward, with the exception of how to round halfway cases; for example, should 12.5 round to 12 or 13? One school of thought divides the 10 digits in half, letting {0, 1, 2, 3, 4} round down, and {5, 6, 7, 8, 9} round up; thus 12.5 would round to 13. This is how rounding works on Digital Equipment Corporation's VAX computers.

Another school of thought says that since numbers ending in 5 are halfway between two possible rounding's, they should round down half the time and round up the other half. One way of obtaining this 50% behaviour to require that the rounded result have its least significant digit be even. Thus 12.5 rounds to 12 rather than 13 because 2 is even. Which of these methods is best, round up or round to even? Reiser and Knuth offer the following reason for preferring round to even.

THEOREM 5

Let x and y be floating-point numbers, and define $x_0 = x$, $x_1 = (x_0 \ominus y) \oplus y, \ldots, x_n = (x_{n-1} \ominus y) \oplus y$. If $\oplus$ and $\ominus$ are exactly rounded using round to even, then either xn = x for all n or $x_n = x_1$ for all $n \geq 1$. z

To clarify this result, consider $\beta = 10$, $p = 3$ and let $x = 1.00$, $y = -.555$. When rounding up, the sequence becomes1.57, and each successive value of xn increases by .01, until xn =

9.45 ($n \leq 845$)9. Under round to even, x_n is always 1.00. This example suggests that when using the round up rule, computations can gradually drift upward, whereas when using round to even the theorem says this cannot happen. Throughout the rest of this paper, round to even will be used. One application of exact rounding occurs in multiple precision arithmetic. There are two basic approaches to higher precision.

One approach represents floating-point numbers using a very large significand, which is stored in an array of words, and codes the routines for manipulating these numbers in assembly language. The second approach represents higher precision floating-point numbers as an array of ordinary floating-point numbers, where adding the elements of the array in infinite precision recovers the high precision floating-point number. It is this second approach that will be discussed here. The advantage of using an array of floating-point numbers is that it can be coded portably in a high level language, but it requires exactly rounded arithmetic.

The key to multiplication in this system is representing a product xy as a sum, where each summand has the same precision as x and y. This can be done by splitting x and y. Writing $x = x_h + x_l$ and $y = y_h + y_l$, the exact product is

$$xy = xh\ yh + xh\ yl + xl\ yh + xl\ yl.$$

If x and y have p bit significands, the summands will also have p bit significands provided that x_l, x_h, y_h, ylcan be represented using [p/2] bits. When p is even, it is easy to find a splitting. The number $x_0.x_1 \ldots x_{p-1}$can be written as the sum of $x_0.x_1 \ldots x_{p/2-1}$ and $0.0 \ldots 0x_{p/2} \ldots x_{p-1}$. When p is odd, this simple splitting method will not work. An extra bit can, however, be gained by using negative numbers. For example, if $\beta = 2, p = 5$, and $x = .10111$, x can be split as $x_h = .11$ and $x_l = -.00001$. There is more than one way to split a number. A splitting method that is easy to compute is due to Dekker, but it requires more than a single guard digit.

THEOREM 6

Let p be the floating-point precision, with the restriction that p is even when $\beta > 2$, and assume that floating-point operations are exactly rounded. Then if k = [p/2] is half the precision (rounded up) and $m = \beta^{k} + 1$, x can be split as $x = x_h + x_l$, where

$$x_h = (m \otimes x) \ominus (m \otimes x \ominus x),\ x_l = x \ominus x_h,$$

and each x_i is representable using [p/2] bits of precision. To see how this theorem works in an example, let $\beta = 10$, p = 4, b = 3.476, a = 3.463, and c = 3.479. Thenb2 - ac rounded to the nearest floating-point number is .03480, while b ⊗ b = 12.08, a ⊗ c = 12.05, and so the computed value of b2 - ac is .03. This is an error of 480 ulps. Using Theorem 6 to write b = 3.5 - .024,a = 3.5 - .037, and c = 3.5 - .021, b^2 becomes $3.5^2 - 2 \times 3.5 \times .024 + .0242$. Each summand is exact, sob^2 = 12.25 - .168 + .000576, where the sum is left unevaluated at this point.

Similarly, ac = 3.5^2 - (3.5 ×.037 + 3.5 × .021) + .037 × .021 = 12.25 - .2030 +.000777. Finally, subtracting these two series term by term gives an estimate for b2 - ac of 0 ⊕ .0350 ⊖ .000201 = .03480, which is identical to the exactly rounded result. To show that Theorem 6 really requires exact rounding, consider p = 3, β = 2, and x = 7. Then m = 5, mx = 35, and m ⊗ x = 32. If subtraction is performed with a single guard digit, then (m ⊗ x) ⊖ x= 28. Therefore, x_h = 4 and xl = 3, hence x_l is not represent able with [p/2] = 1 bit.

As a final example of exact rounding, consider dividing m by 10. The result is a floating-point number that will in general not be equal to m/10. When β = 2, multiplying m/10 by 10 will restore m, provided exact rounding is being used. Actually, a more general fact is true.

THEOREM 7

When $\beta = 2$, if m and n are integers with $|m| < 2^{p-1}$ and n has the special form $n = 2^i + 2^j$, then (m% n) ⊗n = m, provided floating-point operations are exactly rounded.

Proof

Scaling by a power of two is harmless, since it changes only the exponent, not the significand. If q = m/n, then scale n so that $2^{p-1} \le n < 2^p$ and scale m so that 1/2 < q < 1. Thus, $2^{p-2} < m < 2^p$. Since m has p significant bits, it has at most one bit to the right of the binary point. Changing the sign of m is harmless, so assume that $q > 0$.

If φ = m% n, to prove the theorem requires showing that

$$\|n\varphi\text{-}n1\|\frac{1}{4}$$

That is because m has at most 1 bit right of the binary point, so $n\varphi$ will round to m. To deal with the halfway case when $|n\varphi - m| = 1/4$, note that since the initial unscaled m had $|m| < 2^{p-1}$, its low-order bit was 0, so the low-order bit of the scaled m is also 0. Thus, halfway cases will round to m.

Suppose that q = .q1q2 ..., and let $\varphi = .q_1q_2 \ldots q_p1$. To estimate $|n\varphi - m|$, first compute

$|\varphi - q| = |N/2p + 1 - m/n|$,

where N is an odd integer. Since $n = 2^i + 2^j$ and $2^{p-1} \le n < 2^p$, it must be that $n = 2^{p-1} + 2^k$ for some $k \le p - 2$, and thus

$$|\varphi - \varphi| = \left|\frac{nN - 2^{p+1}m}{n2^{p+1}}\right| = \left|\frac{(2^{p-1-k}+1)N - 2^{p+1-k}m}{n2^{p+1-k}}\right|.$$

The numerator is an integer, and since N is odd, it is in fact an odd integer. Thus,

$$|\varphi - q| \ge 1/(n2^{p+1-k}).$$

Assume $q < \varphi$ (the case $q > \varphi$ is similar). Then $n\varphi < m$, and

$$(9)\quad |m - n^{\varphi}| = m - n\varphi = n(q - ^{\varphi}) = n(q - (^{\varphi} - 2^{-p-1}n$$

$$\left(2^{-p-1} - \frac{1}{n2^{p+1-k}}\right) = (2p^{-1} + 2^k)2^{-p-1} - 2^{-p-1} + k = \frac{1}{4}$$

This establishes (9) and proves the theorem. 11_z The theorem holds true for any base β, as long as $2^i + 2^j$ is replaced by $\beta^i + \beta^j$. As β gets larger, however, denominators of the form $\beta^i + \beta^j$ are farther and farther apart.

We are now in a position to answer the question, Does it matter if the basic arithmetic operations introduce a little more rounding error than necessary?

The answer is that it does matter, because accurate basic operations enable us to prove that formulas are"correct"in the sense they have a small relative error. The section Cancellation discussed several algorithms that require guard digits to produce correct results in this sense. If the input to those formulas are numbers representing imprecise measurements, however, the bounds of Theorems 3 and 4 become less interesting.

The reason is that the benign cancellation x - y can become catastrophic if x and y are only approximations to some measured quantity.

But accurate operations are useful even in the face of inexact data, because they enable us to establish exact relationships like those discussed in Theorems 6 and 7. These are useful even if every floating-point variable is only an approximation to some actual value.

THE IEEE STANDARD

There are two different IEEE standards for floating-point computation. IEEE 754 is a binary standard that requires $\beta = 2$, $p = 24$ for single precision and $p = 53$ for double precision. It also specifies the precise layout of bits in a single and double precision.

IEEE 854 allows either $\beta = 2$ or $\beta = 10$ and unlike 754, does not specify how floating-point numbers are encoded into bits [Cody et al. 1984]. It does not require a particular value for p, but instead it specifies constraints on the allowable values of p for single and double precision. The term IEEE Standard will be used when discussing properties common to both standards.

This section provides a tour of the IEEE standard. Each subsection discusses one aspect of the standard and why it was included. It is not the purpose of this paper to argue that the IEEE standard is the best possible floating-point standard but rather to accept the standard as given and provide an introduction to its use. For full details consult the standards themselves.

FORMATS AND OPERATIONS

Base

It is clear why IEEE 854 allows $\beta = 10$. Base ten is how humans exchange and think about numbers. Using $\beta = 10$ is especially appropriate for calculators, where the result of each operation is displayed by the calculator in decimal. There are several reasons why IEEE 854 requires that if the base is not 10, it must be 2.

The section Relative Error and Ulps mentioned one reason: the results of error analyses are much tighter when β is 2 because a rounding error of .5 ulp wobbles by a factor of β when computed as a relative error, and error analyses are almost always simpler when based on relative error.

A related reason has to do with the effective precision for large bases. Consider $\beta = 16$, $p = 1$ compared to $\beta = 2$, $p = 4$. Both systems have 4 bits of significand. Consider the computation of 15/8. When $\beta = 2$, 15 is represented as 1.111×2^3, and 15/8 as 1.111×2^0. So 15/8 is exact. However, when $\beta = 16$, 15 is represented as $F \times 16^0$, where F is the hexadecimal digit for 15.

But 15/8 is represented as 1×16^0, which has only one bit correct. In general, base 16 can lose up to 3 bits, so that a precision of p hexadecimal digits can have an effective precision as low as 4p - 3 rather than 4pbinary bits. Since large values of β have these problems, why did IBM choose $\beta = 16$ for its system/370? Only IBM knows for sure, but there are two possible reasons.

The first is increased exponent range. Single precision on the system/370 has $\beta = 16$, $p = 6$. Hence the significand requires 24 bits. Since this must fit into 32 bits, this leaves 7 bits for the exponent and one for the sign bit.

Thus the magnitude of representable numbers ranges from about $16 - 2^6$ to about $16 - 2^6 = 2^8$. To get a similar exponent range when b = 2 would require 9 bits of exponent, leaving only 22 bits for the significand. However, it was just pointed out that when b = 16, the effective precision can be as low as 4p - 3 = 21 bits.

Even worse, when b = 2 it is possible to gain an extra bit of precision (as explained later in this section), so the b = 2 machine has 23 bits of precision to compare with a range of 21 - 24 bits for the b = 16 machine. Another possible explanation for choosing $\beta = 16$ has to do with shifting. When adding two floating-point numbers, if their exponents are different, one of the significands will have to be shifted to make the radix points line up, slowing down the operation.

In the $\beta = 16$, $p = 1$ system, all the numbers between 1 and 15 have the same exponent, and so no shifting is required when adding any of the $(\frac{15}{2}) = 105$ possible pairs of distinct numbers from this set. However, in the $\beta = 2$, $p = 4$ system, these numbers have exponents ranging from 0 to 3, and shifting is required for 70 of the 105 pairs.

In most modern hardware, the performance gained by avoiding a shift for a subset of operands is negligible, and so the small wobble of $\beta = 2$ makes it the preferable base. Another advantage of using $\beta = 2$ is that there is a way to gain an extra bit of significance.

Since floating-point numbers are always normalized, the most significant bit of the significand is always 1, and there is no reason to waste a bit of storage representing it. Formats that use this trick are said to have a hidden bit. It was already pointed out inFloating-point Formats that this requires a special convention for 0.

The method given there was that an exponent of $e_{min} - 1$ and a significand of all zeros represents not $1.0 \times 2^{cmin-1}$, but rather 0.

IEEE 754 single precision is encoded in 32 bits using 1 bit for the sign, 8 bits for the exponent, and 23 bits for the significand. However, it uses a hidden bit, so the significand is 24 bits ($p = 24$), even though it is encoded using only 23 bits.

Precision

The IEEE standard defines four different precisions: single, double, single-extended, and double-extended. In IEEE 754, single and double precision correspond roughly to what most floating-point hardware provides.

Single precision occupies a single 32 bit word, double precision two consecutive 32 bit words. Extended precision is a format that offers at least a little extra precision and exponent range.

Table. D-1 IEEE 754 Format Parametres

Parametre	Format			
	Single	Single-Extended	Double	Double-Extended
p	24	≥ 32	53	≥ 64
e_{max}	+127	≥ 1023	+1023	> 16383
e_{min}	-126	≤ -1022	-1022	≤ -16382
Exponent width in bits	8	≤ 11	11	≥ 15
Format width in bits	32	≥ 43	64	≥ 79

The IEEE standard only specifies a lower bound on how many extra bits extended precision provides. The minimum allowable double-extended format is sometimes referred to as 80-bit format, even though the table shows it using 79 bits. The reason is that hardware implementations of extended precision normally do not use a hidden bit, and so would use 80 rather than 79 bits.

The standard puts the most emphasis on extended precision, making no recommendation concerning double precision, but strongly recommending that Implementations should support the extended format corresponding to the widest basic format supported.

One motivation for extended precision comes from calculators, which will often display 10 digits, but use 13 digits internally. By displaying only 10 of the 13 digits, the calculator appears to the user as a"black box"that computes exponentials, cosines, etc. to 10 digits of accuracy.

For the calculator to compute functions like exp, log and cos to within 10 digits with reasonable efficiency, it needs a few extra digits to work with. It is not hard to find a simple rational expression that approximates log with an error of 500 units in the last place. Thus computing with 13 digits gives an answer correct to 10 digits. By keeping these extra 3 digits hidden, the calculator presents a simple model to the operator. Extended precision in the IEEE standard serves a similar function. It enables libraries to efficiently compute quantities to within about .5 ulp in single (or double) precision, giving the user of those libraries a simple model, namely that each primitive operation, be it a simple multiply or an invocation of log, returns a value accurate to within about .5 ulp. However, when using extended precision, it is important to make sure that its use is transparent to the user.

For example, on a calculator, if the internal representation of a displayed value is not rounded to the same precision as the display, then the result of further operations will depend on the hidden digits and appear unpredictable to the user. To illustrate extended precision further, consider the problem of converting between IEEE 754 single precision and decimal. Ideally, single precision numbers will be printed with enough digits so that when the decimal number is read back in, the single precision number can be recovered.

It turns out that 9 decimal digits are enough to recover a single precision binary number (see the section Binary to Decimal Conversion). When converting a decimal number back to its unique binary representation, a rounding error as small as 1 ulp is fatal, because it will give the wrong answer. Here is a situation where extended precision is vital for an efficient algorithm. When single-extended is available, a very straightforward method exists for converting a decimal number to a single precision binary one.

First read in the 9 decimal digits as an integer N, ignoring the decimal point. From TABLE D-1, $p \geq 32$, and since $10^9 < 2^{32} \approx 4.3 \times 10^9$, N can be represented exactly in single-extended. Next find the appropriate power 10^P necessary to scale N. This will be a combination of the exponent of the decimal number, together with the position of the (up until now) ignored decimal point.

Compute $10^{|P|}$. If $|P| \leq 13$, then this is also represented exactly, because 1013 = 213513, and 513 < 232. Finally multiply (or divide if $p < 0$) N and 10|P|. If this last operation is done exactly, then the closest binary number is recovered. The section Binary to Decimal Conversion shows how to do the last multiply (or divide) exactly. Thus for $|P| \leq 13$, the use of the single-extended format enables 9-digit decimal numbers to be converted to the closest binary number (i.e. exactly rounded). If $|P| > 13$, then single-extended is not enough for the above algorithm to always compute the exactly rounded binary equivalent, but shows that it is enough to guarantee that the conversion of binary to decimal and back will recover the original binary number.

If double precision is supported, then the algorithm above would be run in double precision rather than single-extended, but to convert double precision to a 17-digit decimal number and back would require the double-extended format.

EXPONENT

Since the exponent can be positive or negative, some method must be chosen to represent its sign. Two common methods of representing signed numbers are sign/magnitude and two's complement. Sign/magnitude is the system used for the sign of the significand in the IEEE formats: one bit is used to hold the sign, the rest of the bits represent the magnitude of the number. The two's complement representation is often used in integer arithmetic. In this scheme, a number in the range $[-2^{p-1}, 2^{p-1} - 1]$ is represented by the smallest nonnegative number that is congruent to it modulo 2p.

The IEEE binary standard does not use either of these methods to represent the exponent, but instead uses a biased representation. In the case of single precision, where the exponent is stored in 8 bits, the bias is 127 (for double precision it is 1023). What this means is that if $\bar{K}$ is the value of the exponent bits interpreted as an unsigned integer, then the exponent of the floating-point number is $\bar{K}$ - 127. This is often called the unbiased exponent to distinguish from the biased exponent $\bar{K}$.

Referring to Table D-1, single precision has $e_{max} = 127$ and $e_{min} = -126$. The reason for having $|emin| <$ emaxis so that the reciprocal of the smallest number $(1/2^{e_{min}})$ will not overflow. Although it is true that the reciprocal of the largest number will underflow, underflow is usually less serious than overflow. The section Base explained that e_{min} - 1 is used for representing 0, and Special Quantities will introduce a use for $e_{max} + 1$. In IEEE single precision, this means that the biased exponents range between $e_{min} - 1 = -127$ and $e_{max} + 1 = 128$, whereas the unbiased exponents range between 0 and 255, which are exactly the nonnegative numbers that can be represented using 8 bits.

OPERATIONS

The IEEE standard requires that the result of addition, subtraction, multiplication and division be exactly rounded. That is, the result must be computed exactly and then rounded to the nearest floating-point number (using round to even). The section Guard Digits pointed out that computing the exact difference or sum of two floating-point numbers can be very expensive when their exponents are substantially different.

That section introduced guard digits, which provide a practical way of computing differences while guaranteeing that the relative error is small. However, computing with a single guard digit will not always give the same answer as computing the exact result and then rounding. By introducing a second guard digit and a third sticky bit, differences can be computed at only a little more cost than with a single guard digit, but the result is the same as if the difference were computed exactly and then rounded. Thus the standard can be implemented efficiently.

One reason for completely specifying the results of arithmetic operations is to improve the portability of software. When a programme is moved between two machines and both support IEEE arithmetic, then if any intermediate result differs, it must be because of software bugs, not from differences in arithmetic. Another advantage of precise specification is that it makes it easier to reason about floating-point.

Proofs about floating-point are hard enough, without having to deal with multiple cases arising from multiple kinds of arithmetic. Just as integer programmes can be proven to be correct, so can floating-point programmes, although what is proven in that case is that the rounding error of the result satisfies certain bounds. Theorem 4 is an example of such a proof. These proofs are made much easier when the operations being reasoned about are precisely specified. Once an algorithm is proven to be correct for IEEE arithmetic, it will work correctly on any machine supporting the IEEE standard.

Brown [1981] has proposed axioms for floating-point that include most of the existing floating-point hardware. However, proofs in this system cannot verify the algorithms of sections Cancellation and Exactly Rounded Operations, which require features not present on all hardware. Furthermore, Brown's axioms are more complex than simply defining operations to be performed exactly and then rounded. Thus proving theorems from Brown's axioms is usually more difficult than proving them assuming operations are exactly rounded.

There is not complete agreement on what operations a floating-point standard should cover. In addition to the basic operations +, –, × and/, the IEEE standard also specifies that square root, remainder, and conversion between integer and floating-point be correctly rounded. It also requires that conversion between internal formats and decimal be correctly rounded (except for very large numbers). It is proposed adding inner product to the list of operations that are precisely specified. They note that when inner products are computed in IEEE arithmetic, the final answer can be quite wrong. For example sums are a special case of inner products, and the sum $((2 \times 10^{-30} + 10^{30}) - 10^{30}) - 10^{-30}$ is exactly equal to 10^{-30}, but on a machine with IEEE arithmetic the computed result will be -10^{-30}. It is possible to compute inner products to within 1 ulp with less hardware than it takes to implement a fast multiplier.

All the operations mentioned in the standard are required to be exactly rounded except conversion between decimal and binary. The reason is that efficient algorithms for exactly rounding all the operations are known, except conversion. For conversion, the best known efficient algorithms produce results that are slightly worse than exactly rounded ones.

The IEEE standard does not require transcendental functions to be exactly rounded because of the table maker's dilemma. To illustrate, suppose you are making a table of the exponential function to 4 places. Then exp(1.626) = 5.0835. Should this be rounded to 5.083 or 5.084? If exp(1.626) is computed more carefully, it becomes 5.08350. And then 5.083500. And then 5.0835000. Since exp is transcendental, this could go on arbitrarily long before distinguishing whether exp(1.626) is 5.083500...0ddd or 5.0834999...9ddd. Thus it is not practical to specify that the precision of transcendental functions be the same as if they were computed to infinite precision and then rounded.

Another approach would be to specify transcendental functions algorithmically. But there does not appear to be a single algorithm that works well across all hardware architectures. Rational approximation, CORDIC, and large tables are three different techniques that are used for computing transcendental on contemporary machines. Each is appropriate for a different class of hardware, and at present no single algorithm works acceptably over the wide range of current hardware.

SPECIAL QUANTITIES

On some floating-point hardware every bit pattern represents a valid floating-point number. The IBM System/370 is an example of this. On the other hand, the VAXTM reserves some bit patterns to represent special numbers called reserved operands. This idea goes back to the CDC 6600, which had bit patterns for the special quantities INDEFINITE and INFINITY. The IEEE standard continues in this tradition and has NaNs (Not a Number) and infinities.

Without any special quantities, there is no good way to handle exceptional situations like taking the square root of a negative number, other than aborting computation. Under IBM System/370 FORTRAN, the default action in response to computing the square root of a negative number like -4 results in the printing of an error message. Since every bit pattern represents a valid number, the return value of square root must be some floating-point number. In the case of System/370 FORTRAN, $\sqrt{-4} = 2$ is returned. In IEEE arithmetic, a NaN is returned in this situation.

The IEEE standard specifies the following special values, denormalized numbers, $\pm\infty$ and NaNs (there is more than one NaN, as explained in the next section). These special values are all encoded with exponents of either e_{max} + 1 or e_{min} – 1 (it was already pointed out that 0 has an exponent ofemin – 1).

Table. D-2 IEEE 754 Special Values

Exponent	Fraction	Represents
$e = e_{min} - 1$	$f = 0$	± 0
$e = e_{min} - 1$	$f \neq 0$	$0.f \times 2^{e_{min}}$
$e_{min} \leq e \leq e_{max}$	--	$1.f \times 2^{e}$
$e = e^{max} + 1$	$f = 0$	$\pm\infty$
$e = e_{max} + 1$	$f \neq 0$	NaN

NaNs

Traditionally, the computation of 0/0 or $\sqrt{-1}$ has been treated as an unrecoverable error which causes a computation to halt. However, there are examples where it makes sense for a computation to continue in such a situation. Consider a subroutine that finds the zeros of a function f, say zero(f). Traditionally, zero finders require the user to input an interval [a, b] on which the function is defined and over which the zero finder will search.

That is, the subroutine is called as zero(f, a, b). A more useful zero finder would not require the user to input this extra information. This more general zero finder is especially appropriate for calculators, where it is natural to simply key in a function, and awkward to then have to specify the domain. However, it is easy to see why most zero finders require a domain.

The zero finder does its work by probing the function f at various values. If it probed for a value outside the domain of f, the code for f might well compute 0/0 or $\sqrt{-1}$, and the computation would halt, unnecessarily aborting the zero finding process. This problem can be avoided by introducing a special value called NaN, and specifying that the computation of expressions like 0/0 and $\sqrt{-1}$ produce NaN, rather than halting. A list of some of the situations that can cause a NaN are given in Table D-3. Then when zero(f) probes outside the domain of f, the code for f will return NaN, and the zero finder can continue.

That is, zero(f) is not"punished"for making an incorrect guess. With this example in mind, it is easy to see what the result of combining a NaN with an ordinary floating-point number should be. Suppose that the final statement of f is return(-b + sqrt(d))/(2*a).

If d < 0, then fshould return a NaN. Since d < 0, sqrt(d) is a NaN, and -b + sqrt(d) will be a NaN, if the sum of a NaN and any other number is a NaN. Similarly if one operand of a division operation is a NaN, the quotient should be a NaN. In general, whenever a NaN participates in a floating-point operation, the result is another NaN.

Table. D-3 Operations That Produce a NaN

Operation	NaN Produced By
+	$\infty + (-\infty$
×	$0 \times \infty$
/	$0/0$, ∞ / ∞
REM	x REM 0, ∞ REM y
$\sqrt{\ }$	$\sqrt{x}$ (when $x < 0$)

Another approach to writing a zero solver that doesn't require the user to input a domain is to use signals. The zero-finder could install a signal handler for floating-point exceptions. Then if f was evaluated outside its domain and raised an exception, control would be returned to the zero solver. The problem with this approach is that every language has a different method of handling signals (if it has a method at all), and so it has no hope of portability.

In IEEE 754, NaNs are often represented as floating-point numbers with the exponent $e_{max} + 1$ and nonzero significands. Implementations are free to put system-dependent information into the significand. Thus there is not a unique NaN, but rather a whole family of NaNs. When a NaN and an ordinary floating-point number are combined, the result should be the same as the NaN operand. Thus if the result of a long computation is a NaN, the system-dependent information in the significand will be the information that was generated when the first NaN in the computation was generated. Actually, there is a caveat to the last statement. If both operands are NaNs, then the result will be one of those NaNs, but it might not be the NaN that was generated first.

INFINITY

Just as NaNs provide a way to continue a computation when expressions like 0/0 or $\sqrt{-1}$ are encountered, infinities provide a way to continue when an overflow occurs. This is much safer than simply returning the largest representable number.

As an example, consider computing $\sqrt{x^2 + y^2}$, when b = 10, p = 3, and e_{max} = 98. If $x = 3 \times 10^{70}$ and $y = 4 \times 10^{70}$, then x^2 will overflow, and be replaced by 9.99×10^{98}. Similarly y^2, and $x^2 + y^2$ will each overflow in turn, and be replaced by 9.99×10^{98}. So the final result will be $\sqrt{9.99 \times 10^{98}} = 3.16 \times 10^{49}$, which is drastically wrong: the correct answer is 5 × 1070.

In IEEE arithmetic, the result of x^2 ∞ is, as is y^2, $x^2 + y^2$ and $\sqrt{x^2 + y^2}$. So the final result is ∞, which is safer than returning an ordinary floating-point number that is nowhere near the correct answer.

The division of 0 by 0 results in a NaN. A nonzero number divided by 0, however, returns infinity: $1/0 = \infty$, $-1/0 = -\infty$. The reason for the distinction is this: if $f(x) \to 0$ and $g(x) \to 0$ as x approaches some limit, thenf(x)/g(x) could have any value. For example, when f(x) = sin x and g(x) = x, then $f(x)/g(x) \to 1$ as $x \to 0$. But when $f(x) = 1 - \cos x$, $f(x)/g(x) \to 0$. When thinking of 0/0 as the limiting situation of a quotient of two very small numbers, 0/0 could represent anything.

Thus in the IEEE standard, 0/0 results in a NaN. But when $c > 0$, $f(x) \to c$, and $g(x) \to 0$, then $f(x)/g(x) \to \pm\infty$, for any analytic functions f and g. If $g(x) < 0$ for small x, then f(x)/g(x) $\to -\infty$, otherwise the limit is $+\infty$. So the IEEE standard defines

$c/0 = \pm\infty$, as long as $c \neq 0$. The sign of ∞ depends on the signs of c and 0 in the usual way, so that $-10/0 = -\infty$, and $-10/-0 = +\infty$. You can distinguish between getting ∞ because of overflow and getting ∞ because of division by zero by checking the status flags. The overflow flag will be set in the first case, the division by zero flag in the second.

The rule for determining the result of an operation that has infinity as an operand is simple: replace infinity with a finite number x and take the limit as $x \to \infty$. Thus $3/\infty = 0$, because $\lim_{x\to\infty} 3/x = 0$. Similarly, $4 - \infty = -\infty$, and $\sqrt{\infty} = \infty$. When the limit doesn't exist, the result is a NaN, so ∞/∞ will be a NaN (Table D-3 has additional examples). This agrees with the reasoning used to conclude that 0/0 should be a NaN. When a sub expression evaluates to a NaN, the value of the entire expression is also a NaN. In the case of $\pm\infty$ however, the value of the expression might be an ordinary floating-point number because of rules like $1/\infty = 0$. Here is a practical example that makes use of the rules for infinity arithmetic. Consider computing the function $x/(x^2 + 1)$.

This is a bad formula, because not only will it overflow when x is larger than $\sqrt{\beta}\beta^{e_{min}/2}$, but infinity arithmetic will give the wrong answer because it will yield 0, rather than a number near $1/x$. However, $x/(x^2 + 1)$ can be rewritten as $1/(x + x^{-1})$. This improved expression will not overflow prematurely and because of infinity arithmetic will have the correct value when $x = 0$: $1/(0 + 0^{-1}) = 1/(0 + \infty) = 1/\infty = 0$.

Without infinity arithmetic, the expression $1/(x + x^{-1})$ requires a test for $x = 0$, which not only adds extra instructions, but may also disrupt a pipeline. This example illustrates a general fact, namely that infinity arithmetic often avoids the need for special case checking; however, formulas need to be carefully inspected to make sure they do not have spurious behaviour at infinity (as $x/(x^2 + 1)$ did).

SIGNED ZERO

Zero is represented by the exponent $e_{min} - 1$ and a zero significand. Since the sign bit can take on two different values, there are two zeros, +0 and –0. If a distinction were made when comparing +0 and -0, simple tests like *if (x = 0)* would have very unpredictable behaviour, depending on the sign of x. Thus the IEEE standard defines comparison so that +0 = -0, rather than -0 < +0.

Although it would be possible always to ignore the sign of zero, the IEEE standard does not do so. When a multiplication or division involves a signed zero, the usual sign rules apply in computing the sign of the answer. Thus 3·(+0) = +0, and +0/-3 = -0. If zero did not have a sign, then the relation 1/(1/x) = x would fail to hold when $x = \pm\infty$. The reason is that $1/-\infty$ and $1/+\infty$ both result in 0, and 1/0 results in $+\infty$, the sign information having been lost. One way to restore the identity 1/(1/x) = x is to only have one kind of infinity, however that would result in the disastrous consequence of losing the sign of an overflowed quantity.

Another example of the use of signed zero concerns underflow and functions that have a discontinuity at 0, such as log. In IEEE arithmetic, it is natural to define $\log 0 = -\infty$ and log x to be a NaN when x < 0. Suppose that x represents a small negative number that has under flowed to zero. Thanks to signed zero, x will be negative, so log can return a NaN. However, if there were no signed zero, the log function could not distinguish an under flowed negative number from 0, and would therefore have to return $-\infty$. Another example of a function with a discontinuity at zero is the signum function, which returns the sign of a number.

Probably the most interesting use of signed zero occurs in complex arithmetic. To take a simple example, consider the equation.

$$\sqrt{1/z} = 1/\left(\sqrt{z}\right)$$

This is certainly true when $z \geq 0$. If $z = -1$, the obvious computation gives $\sqrt{1/(-1)} = \sqrt{-1} = i$ and $\sqrt{1/(-1)} = 1/i = -i$. Thus, $\sqrt{1/z} \neq 1/(\sqrt{z})$! The problem can be traced to the fact that square root is multi-valued, and there is no way to select the values so that it is continuous in the entire complex plane.

However, square root is continuous if a branch cut consisting of all negative real numbers is excluded from consideration. This leaves the problem of what to do for the negative real numbers, which are of the form -x+ i0, where x > 0.

Signed zero provides a perfect way to resolve this problem. Numbers of the form x + i(+0) have one sign $(i\sqrt{x})$ and numbers of the form x + i(-0) on the other side of the branch cut have the other sign $(-i\sqrt{x})$. In fact, the natural formulas for computing will give these results.

Back to $\sqrt{1/z} = 1/(\sqrt{z})$. If z =1 = –1 + i0, then 1/z = 1/(–1 + i0) = [(–1– i0)]/[(–1 + i0)(–1 – i0)] = (–1 -- i0)/((–1)2 – 02) = –1 + i(–0), and so $\sqrt{1/z} = \sqrt{-1+i(-0)} = -i$, while $1/(\sqrt{z}) = 1/i = -i$. Thus IEEE arithmetic preserves this identity for all z. Some more sophisticated examples are given by Kahan [1987]. Although distinguishing between +0 and -0 has advantages, it can occasionally be confusing.

For example, signed zero destroys the relation x = y ⇔ 1/x = 1/y, which is false when x = +0 and y = –0. However, the IEEE committee decided that the advantages of utilizing the sign of zero outweighed the disadvantages.

DENORMALIZED NUMBERS

Consider normalized floating-point numbers with β – 10, p = 3, and e_{min} = –98. The numbers x = 6.87 × 10^{-97} and y = 6.81 × 10^{-97} appear to be perfectly ordinary floating-point numbers, which are more than a factor of 10 larger than the smallest floating-point number 1.00 × 10^{-98}. They have a strange property, however: x ⊖ y = 0 even though x ≠ y! The reason is that x – y = .06 × 10^{-97} = 6.0 × 10^{-99} is too small to be represented as a normalized number, and so must be flushed to zero. How important is it to preserve the property

$$(10)\ x = y \Leftrightarrow x - y = 0$$

It's very easy to imagine writing the code fragment, if *(x ≠ y) then z = 1/(x-y)*, and much later having a programme fail due to a spurious division by zero. Tracking down bugs like this is frustrating and time consuming. On a more philosophical level, computer science textbooks often point out that even though it is currently impractical to prove large programmes correct, designing programmes with the idea of proving them often results in better code. For example, introducing invariants is quite useful, even if they aren't going to be used as part of a proof.

Floating-point code is just like any other code: it helps to have provable facts on which to depend. For example, when analyzing formula (6), it was very helpful to know that $x/2 < y < 2x \Rightarrow x \ominus y = x - y$. Similarly, knowing that (10) is true makes writing reliable floating-point code easier. If it is only true for most numbers, it cannot be used to prove anything. The IEEE standard uses denormalized numbers, which guarantee (10), as well as other useful relations.

They are the most controversial part of the standard and probably accounted for the long delay in getting 754 approved. Most high performance hardware that claims to be IEEE compatible does not support denormalized numbers directly, but rather traps when consuming or producing denormals, and leaves it to software to simulate the IEEE standard.

The idea behind denormalized numbers goes back to Goldberg [1967] and is very simple. When the exponent is emin, the significand does not have to be normalized, so that when $\beta = 10$, $p = 3$ and $e_{min} = -98$, 1.00×10^{-98} is no longer the smallest floating-point number, because 0.98 × 10-98is also a floating-point number.

There is a small snag when $\beta = 2$ and a hidden bit is being used, since a number with an exponent of eminwill always have a significand greater than or equal to 1.0 because of the implicit leading bit. The solution is similar to that used to represent 0, and is summarized in Table D-2. The exponent emin is used to represent denormals.

More formally, if the bits in the significand field are b_1, b_2, ..., b_{p-1}, and the value of the exponent is e, then when e > emin - 1, the number being represented is $1.b_1b_2...b_{p-1} \times$ 2e whereas when e =emin - 1, the number being represented is $0.b_1b_2...b_{p-1} \times 2^{e+1}$. The +1 in the exponent is needed because denormals have an exponent of emin, not e^{min} - 1. Recall the example of $\beta = 10$, $p = 3$, $e^{min} = -98$, $x = 6.87 \times$ 10-^{97} and y = 6.81

× 10-97 presented at the beginning of this section. With denormals, x – y does not flush to zero but is instead represented by the denormalized number .6 × 10-98. This behaviour is called gradual underflow. It is easy to verify that always holds when using gradual underflow.

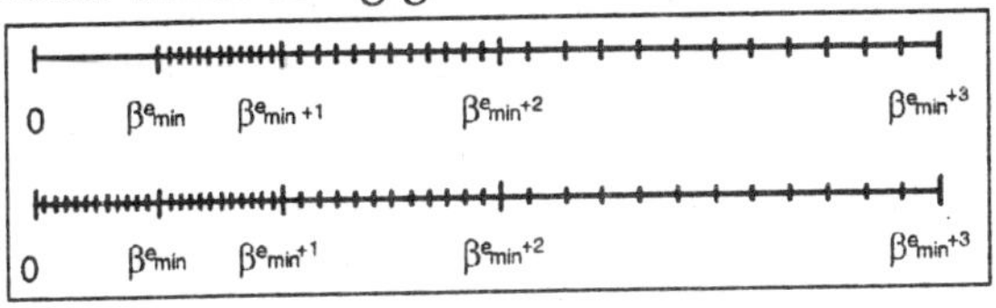

Fig. D-2 Flush To Zero Compared With Gradual Underflow'

Figure D-2 illustrates denormalized numbers. The top number line in the figure shows normalized floating-point numbers. Notice the gap between 0 and the smallest normalized number $1.0 \times \beta^{e_{min}}$. If the result of a floating-point calculation falls into this gulf, it is flushed to zero.

The bottom number line shows what happens when denormals are added to the set of floating-point numbers. The"gulf"is filled in, and when the result of a calculation is less than $1.0 \times \beta^{e_{min}}$, it is represented by the nearest denormal. When denormalized numbers are added to the number line, the spacing between adjacent floating-point numbers varies in a regular way: adjacent spacings are either the same length or differ by a factor of β.

Without denormals, the spacing abruptly changes from $\beta^{-p+1}\beta^{e_{min}}$ to $\beta^{e_{min}}$, which is a factor of β^{p-1}, rather than the orderly change by a factor of β.

Because of this, many algorithms that can have large relative error for normalized numbers close to the underflow threshold are well-behaved in this range when gradual underflow is used. Without gradual underflow, the simple expression x – y can have a very large relative error for normalized inputs, as was seen above for x = 6.87×10^{-97} and y = 6.81×10^{-97}.

Large relative errors can happen even without cancellation, as the following example shows. Consider dividing two complex numbers, a + ib and c + id. The obvious formula

$$\frac{a+ib}{c+id}=\frac{ac+bd}{c^2+d^2}+\frac{bc-ad}{c^2+d^2}\cdot i$$

suffers from the problem that if either component of the denominator c + id is larger than $\sqrt{\beta}\beta^{e_{max}/2}$, the formula will overflow, even though the final result may be well within range. A better method of computing the quotients is to use Smith's formula:

$$(11)\ \frac{a+ib}{c+id}=\begin{cases}\dfrac{a+b(d/c)}{c+d(d/c)}+i\dfrac{b-a(d/c)}{c+d(d/c)} & \text{if}(|d|<|c|)\\[2ex] \dfrac{b+a(c/d)}{d+c(c/d)}+i\dfrac{-a+b(c/d)}{d+c(c/d)} & \text{if}(|d|\geq|c|)\end{cases}$$

Applying Smith's formula to $(2 \cdot 10^{-98} + i10^{-98})/(4 \cdot 10^{-98} + i(2 \cdot 10^{-98}))$ gives the correct answer of 0.5 with gradual underflow. It yields 0.4 with flush to zero, an error of 100 ulps. It is typical for denormalized numbers to guarantee error bounds for arguments all the way down to $1.0 \times \beta^{e_{min}}$.

Exceptions, Flags and Trap Handlers

When an exceptional condition like division by zero or overflow occurs in IEEE arithmetic, the default is to deliver a result and continue. Typical of the default results are NaN for 0/0 and $\sqrt{-1}$, and ∞ for 1/0 and overflow. The preceding sections gave examples where proceeding from an exception with these default values was the reasonable thing to do.

When any exception occurs, a status flag is also set. Implementations of the IEEE standard are required to provide users with a way to read and write the status flags. The flags are"sticky"in that once set, they remain set until explicitly cleared. Testing the flags is the only way to distinguish 1/0, which is a genuine infinity from an overflow.

Sometimes continuing execution in the face of exception conditions is not appropriate. The section Infinity gave the example of $x/(x^2 + 1)$. When $x > \sqrt{\beta}\beta^{e_{min}/2}$, the denominator is infinite, resulting in a final answer of 0, which is totally wrong. Although for this formula the problem can be solved by rewriting it as $1/(x + x^{-1})$, rewriting may not always solve the problem. The IEEE standard strongly recommends that implementations allow trap handlers to be installed. Then when an exception occurs, the trap handler is called instead of setting the flag. The value returned by the trap handler will be used as the result of the operation. It is the responsibility of the trap handler to either clear or set the status flag; otherwise, the value of the flag is allowed to be undefined.

The IEEE standard divides exceptions into 5 classes: overflow, underflow, division by zero, invalid operation and inexact. There is a separate status flag for each class of exception. The meaning of the first three exceptions is self-evident. Invalid operation covers the situations listed in Table D-3, and any comparison that involves a NaN. The default result of an operation that causes an invalid exception is to return a NaN, but the converse is not true. When one of the operands to an operation is a NaN, the result is a NaN but no invalid exception is raised unless the operation also satisfies one of the conditions in Table D-3.

Table D-4 Exceptions in IEEE 754*

Exception	Result when traps disabled	Argument to trap handler
overflow	$\pm\infty$ or $\pm x_{max}$	round(x2- α)
underflow	0, $\pm 2^{e_{min}}$ or denormal	round(x2 α)
divide by zero	$\pm\infty$	operands
invalid	NaN	operands
inexact	round(x)	round(x)

*x is the exact result of the operation, α = 192 for single precision, 1536 for double, and xmax = 1.11 ...11 $\times 2^{e_{max}}$.

The inexact exception is raised when the result of a floating-point operation is not exact. In the $\beta = 10$, $p = 3$ system, $3.5 \otimes 4.2 = 14.7$ is exact, but $3.5 \otimes 4.3 = 15.0$ is not exact (since $3.5 \cdot 4.3 = 15.05$), and raises an inexact exception. Binary to Decimal Conversion discusses an algorithm that uses the inexact exception. A summary of the behaviour of all five exceptions is given in Table D-4.

There is an implementation issue connected with the fact that the inexact exception is raised so often. If floating-point hardware does not have flags of its own, but instead interrupts the operating system to signal a floating-point exception, the cost of inexact exceptions could be prohibitive. This cost can be avoided by having the status flags maintained by software. The first time an exception is raised, set the software flag for the appropriate class, and tell the floating-point hardware to mask off that class of exceptions. Then all further exceptions will run without interrupting the operating system. When a user resets that status flag, the hardware mask is re-enabled.

Trap Handlers

One obvious use for trap handlers is for backward compatibility. Old codes that expect to be aborted when exceptions occur can install a trap handler that aborts the process. This is especially useful for codes with a loop like do S until (x >= 100). Since comparing a NaN to a number with <, ≤, >, ≥, or = (but not ≠) always returns false, this code will go into an infinite loop if x ever becomes a NaN.

There is a more interesting use for trap handlers that comes up when computing products such as,

$$\Pi_{i=1}^{n} x_i$$

that could potentially overflow. One solution is to use logarithms, and compute $\exp(\Sigma \log x_2)$ instead. The problem with this approach is that it is less accurate, and that it costs more than the simple expression Πx_i, even if there is no overflow. There is another solution using trap handlers called over/underflow counting that avoids both of these problems. The idea is as follows.

There is a global counter initialized to zero. Whenever the partial product

$$p_k = \Pi_{i=1}^{k} x_i$$

overflows for some k, the trap handler increments the counter by one and returns the overflowed quantity with the exponent wrapped around. In IEEE 754 single precision, $e_{max} = 127$, so if $p_k = 1.45 \times 2^{130}$, it will overflow and cause the trap handler to be called, which will wrap the exponent back into range, changing pkto 1.45×2^{-62}. Similarly, if p_k underflows, the counter would be decremented, and negative exponent would get wrapped around into a positive one. When all the multiplications are done, if the counter is zero then the final product is p_n.

If the counter is positive, the product overflowed, if the counter is negative, it underflowed. If none of the partial products are out of range, the trap handler is never called and the computation incurs no extra cost. Even if there are over/underflows, the calculation is more accurate than if it had been computed with logarithms, because each p_k was computed from p_{k-1} using a full precision multiply. Barnett discusses a formula where the full accuracy of over/underflow counting turned up an error in earlier tables of that formula.

IEEE 754 specifies that when an overflow or underflow trap handler is called, it is passed the wrapped-around result as an argument. The definition of wrapped-around for overflow is that the result is computed as if to infinite precision, then divided by 2α, and then rounded to the relevant precision. For underflow, the result is multiplied by 2α . The exponent α is 192 for single precision and 1536 for double precision. This is why 1.45×2^{130} was transformed into 1.45×2^{-62} in the example.

ROUNDING MODES

In the IEEE standard, rounding occurs whenever an operation has a result that is not exact, since (with the exception of binary decimal conversion) each operation is computed exactly and then rounded. By default, rounding means round toward nearest. The standard requires that three other rounding modes be provided, namely round toward 0, round toward $+\infty$, and round toward $-\infty$.

When used with the convert to integer operation, round toward $-\infty$ causes the convert to become the floor function, while round toward $+\infty$ is ceiling. The rounding mode affects overflow, because when round toward 0 or round toward $-\infty$ is in effect, an overflow of positive magnitude causes the default result to be the largest representable number, not $+\infty$. Similarly, overflows of negative magnitude will produce the largest negative number when round toward $+\infty$ or round toward 0 is in effect.

When a floating-point calculation is performed using interval arithmetic, the final answer is an interval that contains the exact result of the calculation. This is not very helpful if the interval turns out to be large (as it often does), since the correct answer could be anywhere in that interval.

Interval arithmetic makes more sense when used in conjunction with a multiple precision floating-point package. The calculation is first performed with some precision p. If interval arithmetic suggests that the final answer may be inaccurate, the computation is redone with higher and higher precisions until the final interval is a reasonable size.

FLAGS

The IEEE standard has a number of flags and modes. As discussed above, there is one status flag for each of the five exceptions: underflow, overflow, division by zero, invalid operation and inexact. There are four rounding modes: round toward nearest, round toward $+\infty$, round toward 0, and round toward $-\infty$.

It is strongly recommended that there be an enable mode bit for each of the five exceptions. This section gives some simple examples of how these modes and flags can be put to good use. A more sophisticated example is discussed in the Binary to Decimal Conversion.

Consider writing a subroutine to compute xn, where n is an integer. When n > 0, a simple routine like

```
PositivePower(x,n) {
  while (n is even) {
      x = x*x
      n = n/2
  }
  u = x
  while (true) {
      n = n/2
```

```
        if (n==0) return u
    x = x*x
    if (n is odd) u = u*x
}
```

If n < 0, then a more accurate way to compute x^n is not to call *Positive Power(1/x, -n)* but rather*1/Positive Power(x, -n)*, because the first expression multiplies n quantities each of which have a rounding error from the division (i.e., 1/x). In the second expression these are exact (i.e., x), and the final division commits just one additional rounding error. Unfortunately, these is a slight snag in this strategy.

If Positive Power(x, -n) underflows, then either the underflow trap handler will be called, or else the underflow status flag will be set.

This is incorrect, because if x-n underflows, then xn will either overflow or be in range. But since the IEEE standard gives the user access to all the flags, the subroutine can easily correct for this.

It simply turns off the overflow and underflow trap enable bits and saves the overflow and underflow status bits. It then computes *1/Positive Power(x, -n)*. If neither the overflow nor underflow status bit is set, it restores them together with the trap enable bits.

If one of the status bits is set, it restores the flags and redoes the calculation using Positive Power(1/x, $^{-n}$), which causes the correct exceptions to occur.

Another example of the use of flags occurs when computing arccos via the formula

$$\arccos x = 2 \arctan \sqrt{\frac{1-x}{1+x}} \; .$$

If arctan(∞) evaluates to $\pi/2$, then arccos(-1) will correctly evaluate to 2·arctan(∞) $=\pi$, because of infinity arithmetic. However, there is a small snag, because the computation of (1 - x)/(1 + x) will cause the divide by zero exception flag to be set, even though arccos(-1) is not exceptional.

The solution to this problem is straightforward. Simply save the value of the divide by zero flag before computing arccos, and then restore its old value after the computation.

SYSTEMS ASPECTS

The design of almost every aspect of a computer system requires knowledge about floating-point. Computer architectures usually have floating-point instructions, compilers must generate those floating-point instructions, and the operating system must decide what to do when exception conditions are raised for those floating-point instructions.

Computer system designers rarely get guidance from numerical analysis texts, which are typically aimed at users and writers of software, not at computer designers. As an example of how plausible design decisions can lead to unexpected behaviour, consider the following BASIC programme.

```
q = 3.0/7.0
if q = 3.0/7.0 then print"Equal":
  else print"Not Equal"
```

When compiled and run using Borland's Turbo Basic on an IBM PC, the programme prints Not Equal. This example will be analysed in the next section Incidentally, some people think that the solution to such anomalies is never to compare floating-point numbers for equality, but instead to consider them equal if they are within some error bound E.

This is hardly a cure-all because it raises as many questions as it answers. What should the value of E be? If $x < 0$ and $y > 0$ are within E, should they really be considered to be equal, even though they have different signs? Furthermore, the relation defined by this rule, $a \sim b \Leftrightarrow |a - b| < E$, is not an equivalence relation because $a \sim b$ and $b \sim c$ does not imply that $a \sim c$.

Instruction Sets

It is quite common for an algorithm to require a short burst of higher precision in order to produce accurate results. One example occurs in the quadratic formula

$$\left(-b \pm \sqrt{b^2 - 4ac}\right)/2a$$

As discussed in the section Proof of Theorem 4, when $b^2 \approx 4ac$, rounding error can contaminate up to half the digits in the roots computed with the quadratic formula. By performing the sub calculation of $b^2 - 4ac$ in double precision, half the double precision bits of the root are lost, which means that all the single precision bits are preserved.

The computation of $b^2 - 4ac$ in double precision when each of the quantities a, b, and c are in single precision is easy if there is a multiplication instruction that takes two single precision numbers and produces a double precision result. In order to produce the exactly rounded product of two p-digit numbers, a multiplier needs to generate the entire 2p bits of product, although it may throw bits away as it proceeds. Thus, hardware to compute a double precision product from single precision operands will normally be only a little more expensive than a single precision multiplier, and much cheaper than a double precision multiplier. Despite this, modern instruction sets tend to provide only instructions that produce a result of the same precision as the operands.

If an instruction that combines two single precision operands to produce a double precision product was only useful for the quadratic formula, it wouldn't be worth adding to an instruction set. However, this instruction has many other uses. Consider the problem of solving a system of linear equations,

```
a11x1 + a12x2 + · · · + a1nxn= b1
a21x1 + a22x2 + · · · + a2nxn= b2
 . . .
an1x1 + an2x2 + · · ·+ annxn= bn
```

which can be written in matrix form as Ax = b, where

$$A = \begin{bmatrix} a_{11} & a_{12} & \cdots & a_{1n} \\ a_{21} & a_{22} & \cdots & a_{2(1)n} \\ & & \cdots & \\ a_{n1} & a_{n2} & \cdots & a_{nn} \end{bmatrix}$$

Suppose that a solution $x^{(1)}$ is computed by some method, perhaps Gaussian elimination. There is a simple way to improve the accuracy of the result called iterative improvement. First compute

$$\xi = Ax^{(1)} - b$$

and then solve the system

$$Ay = \xi$$

Note that if $x^{(1)}$ is an exact solution, then ξ is the zero vector, as is y. In general, the computation of ξ andy will incur rounding error, so Ay » ξ » $Ax^{(1)} - b = A(x^{(1)} - x)$, where x is the (unknown) true solution. Then y » $x^{(1)} - x$, so an improved estimate for the solution is

$$x^{(2)} = x^{(1)} - y$$

The three steps can be repeated, replacing $x^{(1)}$ with $x^{(2)}$, and $x^{(2)}$ with $x^{(3)}$. This argument that $x^{(i+1)}$ is more accurate than $x^{(i)}$ is only informal.

When performing iterative improvement, ξ is a vector whose elements are the difference of nearby inexact floating-point numbers, and so can suffer from catastrophic cancellation. Thus iterative improvement is not very useful unless $\xi = Ax^{(1)} - b$ is computed in double precision.

Once again, this is a case of computing the product of two single precision numbers (A and $x^{(1)}$), where the full double precision result is needed. To summarize, instructions that multiply two floating-point numbers and return a product with twice the precision of the operands make a useful addition to a floating-point instruction set. Some of the implications of this for compilers are discussed in the next section.

LANGUAGES AND COMPILERS

The interaction of compilers and floating-point and much of the discussion in this chapter is taken from that paper.

Ambiguity

Ideally, a language definition should define the semantics of the language precisely enough to prove statements about programmes. While this is usually true for the integer part of a language, language definitions often have a large grey area when it comes to floating-point. Perhaps this is due to the fact that many language designers believe that nothing can be proven about floating-point, since it entails rounding error. If so, the previous sections have demonstrated the fallacy in this reasoning. This section discusses some common grey areas in language definitions, including suggestions about how to deal with them. Remarkably enough, some languages don't clearly specify that if x is a floating-point variable (with say a value of *3.0/10.0)*, then every occurrence of (say) *10.0*x* must have the same value.

For example Ada, which is based on Brown's model, seems to imply that floating-point arithmetic only has to satisfy Brown's axioms, and thus expressions can have one of many possible values. Thinking about floating-point in this fuzzy way stands in sharp contrast to the IEEE model, where the result of each floating-point operation is precisely defined. In the IEEE model, we can prove that *(3.0/10.0)*10.0* evaluates to 3. Another ambiguity in most language definitions concerns what happens on overflow, underflow and other exceptions. The IEEE standard precisely specifies the behaviour of exceptions, and so languages that use the standard as a model can avoid any ambiguity on this point.

Another grey area concerns the interpretation of parentheses. Due to roundoff errors, the associative laws of algebra do not necessarily hold for floating-point numbers. For example, the expression (x+y)+z has a totally different answer than *x+(y+z)* when $x = 10^{30}$, $y = -10^{30}$ and z = 1 (it is 1 in the former case, 0 in the latter). The importance of preserving parentheses cannot be overemphasized. The algorithms presented in theorems 3, 4 and 6 all depend on it. For example, in Theorem 6, the formula xh = mx – (mx – x) would reduce to xh = xif it weren't for parentheses, thereby destroying the entire algorithm. A language definition that does not require parentheses to be honoured is useless for floating-point calculations.

Sub expression evaluation is imprecisely defined in many languages. Suppose that ds is double precision, but x and y are single precision. Then in the expression *ds + x*y* is the product performed in single or double precision? Another example: in *x + m/n* where m and n are integers, is the division an integer operation or a floating-point. There are two ways to deal with this problem, neither of which is completely satisfactory. The first is to require that all variables in an expression have the same type. This is the simplest solution, but has some drawbacks. First of all, languages like Pascal that have sub range types allow mixing sub range variables with integer variables, so it is somewhat bizarre to prohibit mixing single and double precision variables.

Another problem concerns constants. In the expression 0.1*x, most languages interpret 0.1 to be a single precision constant. Now suppose the programmer decides to change the declaration of all the floating-point variables from single to double precision. If 0.1 is still treated as a single precision constant, then there will be a compile time error. The programmer will have to hunt down and change every floating-point constant.

The second approach is to allow mixed expressions, in which case rules for sub expression evaluation must be provided. There are a number of guiding examples. The original definition of C required that every floating-point expression be computed in double precision.

This leads to anomalies like the example at the beginning of this section. The expression *3.0/7.0* is computed in double precision, but if qis a single-precision variable, the quotient is rounded to single precision for storage. Since *3/7* is a repeating binary fraction, its computed value in double precision is different from its stored value in single precision. Thus the comparison q = 3/7 fails.

This suggests that computing every expression in the highest precision available is not a good rule. Another guiding example is inner products. If the inner product has thousands of terms, the rounding error in the sum can become substantial. One way to reduce this rounding error is to accumulate the sums in double precision. If d is a double precision variable, and *x[]* and *y[]* are single precision arrays, then the inner product loop will look like *d = d + x[i]*y[i]*.

If the multiplication is done in single precision, than much of the advantage of double precision accumulation is lost, because the product is truncated to single precision just before being added to a double precision variable. A rule that covers both of the previous two examples is to compute an expression in the highest precision of any variable that occurs in that expression. Then *q = 3.0/7.0* will be computed entirely in single precision and will have the boolean value true, whereas *d = d + x[i]*y[i]* will be computed in double precision, gaining the full advantage of double precision accumulation. However, this rule is too simplistic to cover all cases cleanly.

If dx and dy are double precision variables, the expression y = x + single(dx-dy) contains a double precision variable, but performing the sum in double precision would be pointless, because both operands are single precision, as is the result.A more sophisticated sub expression evaluation rule is as follows. First assign each operation a tentative precision, which is the maximum of the precisions of its operands. This assignment has to be carried out from the leaves to the root of the expression tree.

Then perform a second pass from the root to the leaves. In this pass, assign to each operation the maximum of the tentative precision and the precision expected by the parent. In the case of *q = 3.0/7.0*, every leaf is single precision, so all the operations are done in single precision. In the case of *d = d + x[i]*y[i]*, the tentative precision of the multiply operation is single precision, but in the second pass it gets promoted to double precision, because its parent operation expects a double precision operand. And in *y = x +* single*(dx-dy)*, the addition is done in single precision.

The disadvantage of this rule is that the evaluation of a sub expression depends on the expression in which it is embedded. This can have some annoying consequences. For example, suppose you are debugging a programme and want to know the value of a sub expression. You cannot simply type the sub expression to the debugger and ask it to be evaluated, because the value of the sub expression in the programme depends on the expression it is embedded in. A final comment on sub expressions: since converting decimal constants to binary is an operation, the evaluation rule also affects the interpretation of decimal constants. This is especially important for constants like 0.1 which are not exactly representable in binary.

Another potential grey area occurs when a language includes exponentiation as one of its built-in operations. Unlike the basic arithmetic operations, the value of exponentiation is not always obvious.

If ** is the exponentiation operator, then *(–3)**3* certainly has the value *–27*. However, *(–3.0)**3.0* is problematical. If the ** operator checks for integer powers, it would compute *(–3.0)**3.0* as *–3.03 = –27*.

On the other hand, if the formula xy = eylogx is used to define ** for real arguments, then depending on the log function, the result could be a NaN (using the natural definition of log(x) = NaN when x < 0). If the FORTRANCLOG function is used however, then the answer will be –27, because the ANSI FORTRAN standard defines CLOG(-3.0) to be $i\pi$ + log 3. The programming language Ada avoids this problem by only defining exponentiation for integer powers, while ANSI FORTRAN prohibits raising a negative number to a real power.

In fact, the FORTRAN standard says that Any arithmetic operation whose result is not mathematically defined is prohibited... Unfortunately, with the introduction of $\pm\infty$ by the IEEE standard, the meaning of not mathematically defined is no longer totally clear cut.

One definition might be to use the method shown in section Infinity. For example, to determine the value of a^b, consider non-constant analytic functions f and g with the property thatf(x) $\rightarrow$ a and g(x) $\rightarrow$b as x $\rightarrow$ 0. If $f(x)^{g(x)}$ always approaches the same limit, then this should be the value of a^b. This definition would set $2^{\infty} = \infty$ which seems quite reasonable.

In the case of 1.0^{∞}, when f(x) = 1 and g(x) = 1/x the limit approaches 1, but when f(x) = 1 – x and g(x) = 1/x the limit is e-1. So 1.0^{∞}, should be a NaN. In the case of 0^0, $f(x)^{g(x)} = e^{g(x)\log f(x)}$. Since f and g are analytic and take on the value 0 at 0, f(x) $=a_1^{x1} + a_2^{x2} + \ldots$ and $g(x) = b_1^{x1} + b_2^{x2} + \ldots$. Thus $\lim_x \rightarrow {}_0 g(x) \log f(x) = \lim_x \rightarrow {}_0 x \log(x(a_1 + a_2x + \ldots)) = \lim_x \rightarrow {}_0 x \log(a_1x) = 0$. So $f(x)^{g(x)} \rightarrow e^0 = 1$ for all f and g, which means that $0^0 = 1$. Using this definition would unambiguously define the exponential function for all arguments, and in particular would define *(–3.0)**3.0* to be –27.

IEEE STANDARD

This chapter explains many of the features of the IEEE standard. However, the IEEE standard says nothing about how these features are to be accessed from a programming language. Thus, there is usually a mismatch between floating-point hardware that supports the standard and programming languages like C, Pascal or FORTRAN. Some of the IEEE capabilities can be accessed through a library of subroutine calls. For example the IEEE standard requires that square root be exactly rounded, and the square root function is often implemented directly in hardware.

This functionality is easily accessed via a library square root routine. However, other aspects of the standard are not so easily implemented as subroutines. For example, most computer languages specify at most two floating-point types, while the IEEE standard has four different precisions (although the recommended configurations are single plus single-extended or single, double, and double-extended). Infinity provides another example. Constants to represent $\pm\infty$ could be supplied by a subroutine. But that might make them unusable in places that require constant expressions, such as the initializer of a constant variable.

A more subtle situation is manipulating the state associated with a computation, where the state consists of the rounding modes, trap enable bits, trap handlers and exception flags. One approach is to provide subroutines for reading and writing the state. In addition, a single call that can atomically set a new value and return the old value is often useful. As the examples in the section Flags show, a very common pattern of modifying IEEE state is to change it only within the scope of a block or subroutine.

Thus the burden is on the programmer to find each exit from the block, and make sure the state is restored. Language support for setting the state precisely in the scope of a block would be very useful here. Modula-3 is one language that implements this idea for trap handlers [Nelson 1991]. There are a number of minor points that need to be considered when implementing the IEEE standard in a language. Since x – x = +0 for all x, (+0) – (+0) = +0.

However, –(+0) = –0, thus –x should not be defined as 0 – x. The introduction of NaNs can be confusing, because a NaN is never equal to any other number (including another NaN), so x = x is no longer always true. In fact, the expression x ≠ x is the simplest way to test for a NaN if the IEEE recommended function *Isnan* is not provided. Furthermore, NaNs are unordered with respect to all other numbers, so x ≤ y cannot be defined as not x > y. Since the introduction of NaNs causes floating-point numbers to become partially ordered, a *compare* function that returns one of <, =, >, or unordered can make it easier for the programmer to deal with comparisons.

Although the IEEE standard defines the basic floating-point operations to return a NaN if any operand is a NaN, this might not always be the best definition for compound operations. For example when computing the appropriate scale factor to use in plotting a graph, the maximum of a set of values must be computed. In this case it makes sense for the max operation to simply ignore NaNs.

Finally, rounding can be a problem. The IEEE standard defines rounding very precisely, and it depends on the current value of the rounding modes. This sometimes conflicts with the definition of implicit rounding in type conversions or the explicit *round* function in languages. This means that programmes which wish to use IEEE rounding can't use the natural language primitives, and conversely the language primitives will be inefficient to implement on the ever increasing number of IEEE machines.

OPTIMIZERS

Compiler texts tend to ignore the subject of floating-point. For example Aho et al. [1986] mentions replacing *x/2.0* with *x*0.5*, leading the reader to assume that *x/10.0* should be replaced by *0.1*x*. However, these two expressions do not have the same semantics on a binary machine, because 0.1 cannot be represented exactly in binary. This textbook also suggests replacing *x*y–x*z by x*(y–z)*, even though we have seen that these two expressions can have quite different values when y ≈ z. Although it does qualify the statement that any algebraic identity can be used when optimizing code by noting that optimizers should not violate the language definition, it leaves the impression that floating-point semantics are not very important.

Whether or not the language standard specifies that parenthesis must be honoured, *(x+y)+z* can have a totally different answer than *x+(y+z)*, as discussed above. There is a problem closely related to preserving parentheses that is illustrated by the following code

```
eps = 1;
do eps = 0.5*eps; while (eps + 1 > 1);
```

This is designed to give an estimate for machine epsilon. If an optimizing compiler notices that eps + 1 > 1 Û eps > 0, the programme will be changed completely.

Instead of computing the smallest number x such that 1Å x is still greater than x (x » e » β^{-p}), it will compute the largest number x for which x/2 is rounded to 0 (x » $\beta^{e_{min}}$). Avoiding this kind of"optimization"is so important that it is worth presenting one more very useful algorithm that is totally ruined by it.

Many problems, such as numerical integration and the numerical solution of differential equations involve computing sums with many terms. Because each addition can potentially introduce an error as large as .5 ulp, a sum involving thousands of terms can have quite a bit of rounding error.

A simple way to correct for this is to store the partial summand in a double precision variable and to perform each addition using double precision. If the calculation is being done in single precision, performing the sum in double precision is easy on most computer systems.

However, if the calculation is already being done in double precision, doubling the precision is not so simple. One method that is sometimes advocated is to sort the numbers and add them from smallest to largest. However, there is a much more efficient method which dramatically improves the accuracy of sums, namely

THEOREM 8 (KAHAN SUMMATION FORMULA)

Suppose that $\Sigma_{j=1}^{N} x_j$ is computed using the following algorithm

```
S = X[1];
C = 0;
for j = 2 to N {
        Y = X[j] - C;
        T = S + Y;
        C = (T - S) - Y;
        S = T;
}
```

Then the computed sum S is equalto

$$\Sigma x_j(1+\delta_j) + 0(N\varepsilon^2)\Sigma|x_j| \text{ where } (|\delta_j| \le 2\varepsilon).$$

Using the naive formula $\Sigma\, x_j$, the computed sum is equal to

$$\Sigma x_j (1+\delta_j) \text{ where } |\, \delta_j \,| < (n-j)e.$$

Comparing this with the error in the Kahan summation formula shows a dramatic improvement. Each summand is perturbed by only 2e, instead of perturbations as large as ne in the simple formula. Details are in, Errors In Summation.

An optimizer that believed floating-point arithmetic obeyed the laws of algebra would conclude that C = [T-S] – Y = [(S+Y)–S] – Y = 0, rendering the algorithm completely useless. These examples can be summarized by saying that optimizers should be extremely cautious when applying algebraic identities that hold for the mathematical real numbers to expressions involving floating-point variables.

Another way that optimizers can change the semantics of floating-point code involves constants. In the expression *1.0E–40*x*, there is an implicit decimal to binary conversion operation that converts the decimal number to a binary constant. Because this constant cannot be represented exactly in binary, the inexact exception should be raised. In addition, the underflow flag should to be set if the expression is evaluated in single precision. Since the constant is inexact, its exact conversion to binary depends on the current value of the IEEE rounding modes.

Thus an optimizer that converts *1.0E-40* to binary at compile time would be changing the semantics of the programme. However, constants like 27.5 which are exactly representable in the smallest available precision can be safely converted at compile time, since they are always exact, cannot raise any exception, and are unaffected by the rounding modes.

Constants that are intended to be converted at compile time should be done with a constant declaration, such as *const pi = 3.14159265*. Common sub expression elimination is another example of an optimization that can change floating-point semantics, as illustrated by the following code

```
C = A*B;
RndMode = Up
D = A*B;
```

Although *A*B* can appear to be a common sub expression, it is not because the rounding mode is different at the two evaluation sites. Three final examples: x = x cannot be replaced by the boolean constant *true*, because it fails when x is a NaN; -x = 0 − x fails for x = +0; and x < y is not the opposite of x ≥ y, because NaNs are neither greater than nor less than ordinary floating-point numbers.

Despite these examples, there are useful optimizations that can be done on floating-point code. First of all, there are algebraic identities that are valid for floating-point numbers. Some examples in IEEE arithmetic are x + y = y + x, 2 × x = x + x, 1 × x = x, and 0.5× x = x/2. However, even these simple identities can fail on a few machines such as CDC and Cray supercomputers. Instruction scheduling and in-line procedure substitution are two other potentially useful optimizations.

As a final example, consider the expression *dx = x*y*, where x and y are single precision variables, and dx is double precision. On machines that have an instruction that multiplies two single precision numbers to produce a double precision number, *dx = x*y* can get mapped to that instruction, rather than compiled to a series of instructions that convert the operands to double and then perform a double to double precision multiply.

Some compiler writers view restrictions which prohibit converting (x + y) + z to x + (y + z) as irrelevant, of interest only to programmers who use unportable tricks. Perhaps they have in mind that floating-point numbers model real numbers and should obey the same laws that real numbers do. The problem with real number semantics is that they are extremely expensive to implement.

Every time two n bit numbers are multiplied, the product will have 2n bits. Every time two n bit numbers with widely spaced exponents are added, the number of bits in the sum is n + the space between the exponents.

The sum could have up to $(e_{max} - e_{min}) + n$ bits, or roughly 2·emax + n bits. An algorithm that involves thousands of operations (such as solving a linear system) will soon be operating on numbers with many significant bits, and be hopelessly slow. The implementation of library functions such as sin and cos is even more difficult, because the value of these transcendental functions isn't rational numbers. Exact integer arithmetic is often provided by lisp systems and is handy for some problems. However, exact floating-point arithmetic is rarely useful.

The fact is that there are useful algorithms (like the Kahan summation formula) that exploit the fact that $(x+ y) + z \neq x + (y + z)$, and work whenever the bound

$$a \oplus b = (a + b)(1 + d)$$

holds (as well as similar bounds for –, × and/). Since these bounds hold for almost all commercial hardware, it would be foolish for numerical programmers to ignore such algorithms, and it would be irresponsible for compiler writers to destroy these algorithms by pretending that floating-point variables have real number semantics.

EXCEPTION HANDLING

The topics discussed up to now have primarily concerned systems implications of accuracy and precision. Trap handlers also raise some interesting systems issues. The IEEE standard strongly recommends that users be able to specify a trap handler for each of the five classes of exceptions, and the section Trap Handlers, gave some applications of user defined trap handlers. In the case of invalid operation and division by zero exceptions, the handler should be provided with the operands, otherwise, with the exactly rounded result. Depending on the programming language being used, the trap handler might be able to access other variables in the programme as well.

For all exceptions, the trap handler must be able to identify what operation was being performed and the precision of its destination. The IEEE standard assumes that operations are conceptually serial and that when an interrupt occurs, it is possible to identify the operation and its operands.

On machines which have pipelining or multiple arithmetic units, when an exception occurs, it may not be enough to simply have the trap handler examine the programme counter. Hardware support for identifying exactly which operation trapped may be necessary.

Another problem is illustrated by the following programme fragment.

```
x = y*z;
z = x*w;
a = b + c;
d = a/x;
```

Suppose the second multiply raises an exception, and the trap handler wants to use the value of a. On hardware that can do an add and multiply in parallel, an optimizer would probably move the addition operation ahead of the second multiply, so that the add can proceed in parallel with the first multiply. Thus when the second multiply traps, $a = b + c$ has already been executed, potentially changing the result of a.

It would not be reasonable for a compiler to avoid this kind of optimization, because every floating-point operation can potentially trap, and thus virtually all instruction scheduling optimizations would be eliminated. This problem can be avoided by prohibiting trap handlers from accessing any variables of the programme directly. Instead, the handler can be given the operands or result as an argument.

But there are still problems. In the fragment

```
x = y*z;
z = a + b;
```

the two instructions might well be executed in parallel. If the multiply traps, its argument z could already have been overwritten by the addition, especially since addition is usually faster than multiply. Computer systems that support the IEEE standard must provide some way to save the value of z, either in hardware or by having the compiler avoid such a situation in the first place.

W. Kahan has proposed using pre substitution instead of trap handlers to avoid these problems. In this method, the user specifies an exception and the value he wants to be used as the result when the exception occurs. As an example, suppose that in code for computing (sin x)/x, the user decides that x = 0 is so rare that it would improve performance to avoid a test for x = 0, and instead handle this case when a 0/0 trap occurs. Using IEEE trap handlers, the user would write a handler that returns a value of 1 and install it before computing sin x/x. Using pre substitution, the user would specify that when an invalid operation occurs, the value 1 should be used.

Kahan calls this pre substitution, because the value to be used must be specified before the exception occurs. When using trap handlers, the value to be returned can be computed when the trap occurs. The advantage of pre substitution is that it has a straightforward hardware implementation. As soon as the type of exception has been determined, it can be used to index a table which contains the desired result of the operation. Although pre substitution has some attractive attributes, the widespread acceptance of the IEEE standard makes it unlikely to be widely implemented by hardware manufacturers.

The Details

A number of claims have been made in this paper concerning properties of floating-point arithmetic. We now proceed to show that floating-point is not black magic, but rather is a straightforward subject whose claims can be verified mathematically. This section is divided into three parts. The first part presents an introduction to error analysis, and provides the details for the section Rounding Error. The second part explores binary to decimal conversion, filling in some gaps from the section The IEEE Standard.

Rounding Error

In the discussion of rounding error, it was stated that a single guard digit is enough to guarantee that addition and subtraction will always be accurate (Theorem 2). We now proceed to verify this fact. Theorem 2 has two parts, one for subtraction and one for addition. The part for subtraction is

THEOREM 9

If x and y are positive floating-point numbers in a format with parametres β and p, and if subtraction is done with p + 1 digits (i.e. one guard digit), then the relative rounding error in the result is less than

$$\left(\frac{\beta}{2}+1\right)\beta^{-p}=\left(1+\frac{2}{\beta}\right)$$

e £ 2e.

Proof

Interchange x and y if necessary so that x > y. It is also harmless to scale x and y so that x is represented by $x_0.x_1 \ldots x_p - 1 \times \beta^0$. If y is represented as $y_0.y_1 \ldots y_{p-1}$, then the difference is exact. If y is represented as $0.y_1 \ldots y_p$, then the guard digit ensures that the computed difference will be the exact difference rounded to a floating-point number, so the rounding error is at most e. In general, let $y = 0.0 \ldots 0y_{k+1} \ldots y_{k+p}$ and $\tilde{y}$ be y truncated to p + 1 digits. Then

$$y-\tilde{y} < (b-1)(b^{-p-1}+b^{-p-2}+\ldots+b^{-p-k}).$$

From the definition of guard digit, the computed value of x – y is $x-\tilde{y}$ rounded to be a floating-point number, that is, $(x-\tilde{y}) + d$, where the rounding error d satisfies.

$$|\delta| \le (\beta/2)\beta^{-P}.$$

The exact difference is x – y, so the error is $(x - y) - (x - \tilde{y} + \delta) = \tilde{y} - y + \delta$. There are three cases. If $x - y \geq 1$ then the relative error is bounded by

$$\frac{y - \tilde{y} + \delta}{1}$$

$$\le \beta^{-p} [(\beta - 1)(\beta - 1 + \ldots + \beta^{-k}) + \beta/2] < \beta^{-p}(1 + \beta/2).$$

Secondly, if $x - \tilde{y} < 1$, then $\delta = 0$. Since the smallest that x - y can be is,

$$\cdot\ 1.0 - 0.\left(\overbrace{0\cdots0}^{k}\right)\left(\overbrace{\rho\cdots\rho}^{\rho}\right)$$

$$> (\beta - 1)(\beta^{-1} + \ldots + \beta^{-k}),\ \text{where } \rho = \beta - 1,$$

in this case the relative error is bounded by

$$\frac{y - \tilde{y} + \delta}{(\beta-1)(\beta^{-1} + \cdots + \beta^{-k})} < \frac{(\beta-1)\beta^{-\rho}(\beta^{-1} + \cdots + \beta^{-k})}{(\beta-1)(\beta^{-1} + \cdots + \beta^{-k})} = \beta^{-\rho}.$$

The final case is when $x - y < 1$ but $x - \tilde{y} \geq 1$. The only way this could happen is if $x - \tilde{y} = 1$, in which case $\delta = 0$. But if $\delta = 0$, then (18) applies, so that again the relative error is bounded by $\beta^{-p} < \beta^{-p}(1 + \beta/2)$.

When $\beta = 2$, the bound is exactly 2e, and this bound is achieved for $x = 1 + 2^{2-p}$ and $y = 2^{1-p} - 2^{1-2p}$ in the limit as $p \to \infty$. When adding numbers of the same sign, a guard digit is not necessary to achieve good accuracy, as the following result shows.

THEOREM 10

If $x \geq 0$ and $y \geq 0$, then the relative error in computing x + y is at most 2ε, even if no guard digits are used.

Proof

The algorithm for addition with k guard digits is similar to that for subtraction. If $x \geq y$, shift y right until the radix points of x and y are aligned. Discard any digits shifted past the p + k position. Compute the sum of these two p + k digit numbers exactly. Then round to p digits. We will verify the theorem when no guard digits are used; the general case is similar. There is no loss of generality in assuming that $x \geq y \geq 0$ and that x is scaled to be of the form d.dd...d × β^0. First, assume there is no carry out. Then the digits shifted off the end of y have a value less than β^{-p+1}, and the sum is at least 1, so the relative error is less than $\beta^{-p+1}/1 = 2e$. If there is a carry out, then the error from shifting must be added to the rounding error of

$$\frac{1}{2}\beta^{-p+2}.$$

The sum is at least β, so the relative error is less than

$$\left(\beta^{-p+1} + \frac{1}{2}\beta^{-p+2}\right)/\beta = (1 + \beta/2)\beta^{-p} \leq 2\varepsilon. \; z$$

It is obvious that combining these two theorems gives Theorem 2. Theorem 2 gives the relative error for performing one operation. Comparing the rounding error of $x^2 - y^2$ and $(x + y)(x - y)$ requires knowing the relative error of multiple operations.

The relative error of $x \ominus y$ is $\delta 1 = [(x \ominus y) - (x - y)]/(x - y)$, which satisfies $|\delta 1| \leq 2e$. Or to write it another way

$$x \ominus y = (x - y)(1 + \delta 1), \; |\delta 1| \leq 2e$$

Similarly

$$x \oplus y = (x + y)(1 + \delta_2), \; |\delta_2| \leq 2e$$

Assuming that multiplication is performed by computing the exact product and then rounding, the relative error is at most .5 ulp, so

$$u \otimes v = uv(1 + \delta_3), \; |\delta_3| \leq e$$

for any floating-point numbers u and v. Putting these three equations together (letting $u = x \ominus y$ and $v = x \oplus y$) gives

$$(x \ominus y) \otimes (x \oplus y) = (x - y)(1 + \delta_1)(x + y)(1 + \delta_2)(1 + \delta_3)$$

So the relative error incurred when computing $(x - y)(x + y)$ is

$$\frac{(x - y)\theta(x + y) - (x^2 - y^2)}{(x^2 - y^2)} = (1 + \delta_1)(1 + \delta_2)(1 + \delta_3) - 1$$

This relative error is equal to $\delta_1 + \delta_2 + \delta_3 + \delta_1\delta_2 + \delta_1\delta_3 + \delta_2\delta_3 + \delta_1\delta_2\delta_3$, which is bounded by $5\varepsilon + 8\varepsilon^2$. In other words, the maximum relative error is about 5 rounding errors (since e is a small number, e^2 is almost negligible). A similar analysis of $(x \otimes x) \ominus (y \otimes y)$ cannot result in a small value for the relative error, because when two nearby values of x and y are plugged into $x^2 - y^2$, the relative error will usually be quite large. Another way to see this is to try and duplicate the analysis that worked on $(x \ominus y) \otimes (x \oplus y)$, yielding

$$(x \otimes x) \ominus (y \otimes y) = [x^2(1 + \delta_1) - y^2(1 + \delta_2)]\,(1 + \delta_3)$$
$$= ((x^2 - y^2)\,(1 + \delta_1) + (\delta_1 - \delta_2)y^2)\,(1 + \delta_3)$$

When x and y are nearby, the error term $(\delta_1 - \delta_2)y^2$ can be as large as the result $x^2 - y^2$. These computations formally justify our claim that $(x - y)(x + y)$ is more accurate than $x^2 - y^2$. We next turn to an analysis of the formula for the area of a triangle. In order to estimate the maximum error that can occur when computing with (7), the following fact will be needed.

THEOREM 11

If subtraction is performed with a guard digit, and $y/2 \le x \le 2y$, then $x - y$ is computed exactly.

Proof

Note that if x and y have the same exponent, then certainly $x \ominus y$ is exact. Otherwise, from the condition of the theorem, the exponents can differ by at most 1. Scale and interchange x and y if necessary so that $0 \le y \le x$, and x is represented as $x_0.x_1 \ldots x_{p-1}$ and y as $0.y_1 \ldots yp$.

Then the algorithm for computing $x \ominus y$ will compute $x - y$ exactly and round to a floating-point number. If the difference is of the form $0.d_1 \ldots d_p$, the difference will already be p digits long, and no rounding is necessary. Since $x \le 2y$, $x - y \le y$, and since y is of the form $0.d_1 \ldots d_p$, so is $x - y$. z

When $\beta > 2$, the hypothesis of Theorem 11 cannot be replaced by $y/\beta \le x \le \beta y$; the stronger condition $y/2 \le x \le 2y$ is still necessary. The analysis of the error in $(x - y)(x + y)$, immediately following the proof of Theorem 10, used the fact that the relative error in the basic operations of addition and subtraction is small (namely equations (19) and (20)). This is the most common kind of error analysis. However, analyzing formula (7) requires something more, namely Theorem 11, as the following proof will show.

THEOREM 12

If subtraction uses a guard digit, and if a, b and c are the sides of a triangle ($a \geq b \geq c$), then the relative error in computing $(a + (b + c))(c - (a - b))(c + (a - b))(a +(b - c))$ is at most 16ε, provided $e < .005$.

Proof

Let's examine the factors one by one. From Theorem 10, $b \oplus c = (b + c)(1 + \delta_1)$, where$\delta_1$ is the relative error, and $|\delta_1| \leq 2\varepsilon$. Then the value of the first factor is,

$$(a \oplus (b \oplus c)) = (a + (b \oplus c))(1 + \delta_2) = (a + (b + c)(1 + \delta_1))(1 + \delta_2),$$

and thus,

$$\begin{aligned}(a + b + c)(1 - 2\varepsilon)2 &\leq [a + (b + c)(1 - 2\varepsilon)] \cdot (1-2\varepsilon) \\ &\leq a \oplus (b \oplus c) \\ &\leq [a + (b + c)(1 + 2\varepsilon)](1 + 2\varepsilon) \\ &\leq (a + b + c)(1 + 2\varepsilon)^2\end{aligned}$$

This means that there is an η1 so that

$$(a \oplus (b \oplus c)) = (a + b + c)(1 + \eta_1)2, \ |\eta_1| \leq 2\varepsilon.$$

The next term involves the potentially catastrophic subtraction of c and $a \ominus b$, because $a \ominus b$ may have rounding error. Because a, b and c are the sides of a triangle, $a \leq b+ c$, and combining this with the ordering $c \leq b \leq a$ gives $a \leq b + c \leq 2b \leq 2a$.

So $a - b$ satisfies the conditions of Theorem 11. This means that $a - b= a \ominus b$ is exact, hence $c \ominus (a - b)$ is a harmless subtraction which can be estimated from Theorem 9 to be

$$(c \ominus (a \ominus b)) = (c - (a - b))(1 + \eta_2), \ |\eta_2| \leq 2\varepsilon$$

The third term is the sum of two exact positive quantities, so

$$(c \oplus (a \ominus b)) = (c + (a - b))(1 + \eta_3), \ |\eta_3| \leq 2\varepsilon$$

Finally, the last term is,

$$(a \oplus (b \ominus c)) = (a + (b - c))(1 + \eta_4)2, \ |\eta_4| \leq 2\varepsilon,$$

using both Theorem 9 and Theorem 10. If multiplication is assumed to be exactly rounded, so that $x \otimes y = xy(1 + \zeta)$ with $|\zeta| \leq \varepsilon$, then combining gives

$$(a \oplus (b \oplus c))\ (c \ominus (a \ominus b))\ (c \oplus (a \ominus b))\ (a \oplus (b \ominus c))$$
$$\leq (a + (b + c))\ (c - (a - b))\ (c + (a - b))\ (a + (b - c))\ E$$

where

$$E = (1 + \eta_1)^2\ (1 + \eta_2)\ (1 + \eta_3)\ (1 + \eta_4)^2\ (1 + \zeta_1)(1 + \zeta_2)\ (1 + \zeta_3)$$

An upper bound for E is $(1 + 2\varepsilon)^6(1 + \varepsilon)^3$, which expands out to $1 + 15\varepsilon + O(\varepsilon^2)$. Some writers simply ignore the $O(e^2)$ term, but it is easy to account for it. Writing $(1 + 2\varepsilon)^6(1 + \varepsilon)^3 = 1 + 15\varepsilon + \varepsilon R(\varepsilon)$, $R(\varepsilon)$ is a polynomial in e with positive coefficients, so it is an increasing function of ε. Since $R(.005) = .505$, $R(\varepsilon) < 1$ for all $\varepsilon < .005$, and hence $E \leq (1 + 2\varepsilon)^6(1 + \varepsilon)^3 < 1 + 16\varepsilon$.

To get a lower bound on E, note that $1 - 15\varepsilon - \varepsilon R(\varepsilon) < E$, and so when $\varepsilon < .005$, $1 - 16\varepsilon < (1 - 2\varepsilon)^6(1 - \varepsilon)^3$. Combining these two bounds yields $1 - 16\varepsilon < E < 1 + 16\varepsilon$. Thus the relative error is at most 16ε. z

Theorem 12 certainly shows that there is no catastrophic cancellation in formula (7). So although it is not necessary to show formula (7) is numerically stable, it is satisfying to have a bound for the entire formula, which is what Theorem 3 of Cancellation gives.

Proof of Theorem 3

Let

$$q = (a + (b + c))\ (c - (a - b))\ (c + (a - b))\ (a + (b - c))$$

and

$$Q = (a \oplus (b \oplus c)) \otimes (c \ominus (a \ominus b)) \otimes (c \oplus (a \ominus b)) \otimes (a \oplus (b \ominus c)).$$

Then, Theorem 12 shows that $Q = q(1 + \delta)$, with $\delta \leq 16\varepsilon$. It is easy to check that

$$1 - 0.52|\delta| \leq \sqrt{1 - |\delta|} \leq \sqrt{1 + |\delta|} \leq 1 + 0.52|\delta|$$

provided $\delta \leq .04/(.52)^2 \approx .15$, and since $|\delta| \leq 16\varepsilon \leq 16(.005) = .08$, δ does satisfy the condition. Thus

$$\sqrt{Q} = \sqrt{q(1+\delta)} = \sqrt{q}(1 + \delta_1),$$

with $|\delta_1| \leq .52|\delta| \leq 8.5\varepsilon$. If square roots are computed to within .5 ulp, then the error when computing $\sqrt{Q}$ is $(1 + \delta_1)(1 + \delta_2)$, with $|\delta_2| \leq \varepsilon$. If $\beta = 2$, then there is no further error committed when dividing by 4. Otherwise, one more factor $1 + \delta_3$ with $|\delta_3| \leq \varepsilon$ is necessary for the division, and using the method in the proof of Theorem 12, the final error bound of $(1 + \delta_1)(1 + \delta_2)(1 + \delta_3)$ is dominated by $1 + \delta_4$, with $|\delta_4| \leq 11\varepsilon$.

To make the heuristic explanation immediately following the statement of Theorem 4 precise, the next theorem describes just how closely $\mu(x)$ approximates a constant.

THEOREM 13

If $\mu(x) = \ln(1 + x)/x$, then for $0 \leq x \leq 1$ and $0 \leq \mu(x) \leq 1$ and the derivative satisfies $|\mu'(x)| \leq x$.

Proof

Note that $\mu(x) = 1 - x/2 + x2/3 - \ldots$ is an alternating series with decreasing terms, so for $x \leq 1$, $\mu(x) \geq 1 - x/2 \geq 1/2$. It is even easier to see that because the series for μ is alternating, $\mu(x) \leq 1$.

Proof of Theorem 4

Since the Taylor series for ln

$$\ln(1+x) = x - \frac{x^2}{2} + \frac{x^3}{3} - \cdots$$

is an alternating series, $0 < x - \ln(1 + x) < x^2/2$, the relative error incurred when approximating $\ln(1 + x)$ by xis bounded by $x/2$. If $1 \oplus x = 1$, then $|x| < \varepsilon$, so the relative error is bounded by $\varepsilon/2$.

When $1 \oplus x \neq 1$, define $\tilde{x}$ via $1 \oplus x = 1 + \tilde{x}$. Then since $0 \leq x < 1$, $(1 \oplus x) \ominus 1 = \tilde{x}$. If division and logarithms are computed to within, then the computed value of the expression ln

$$(1 + x)/((1 + x) - 1) \text{ is } \frac{\ln(1 \oplus x)}{(1 \oplus x) \odot 1}$$

$$(1 + \delta_1)(1 + \delta_2) = \frac{\ln(1 + \tilde{x})}{\tilde{x}}(1 + \delta_1)(1 + \delta_2)$$

$$= \mu(\tilde{x})(1 + \delta_1)(1 + \delta_2)$$

where $|\delta_1| \leq \varepsilon$ and $|\delta_2| \leq \varepsilon$. To estimate $\mu(\tilde{x})$, use the mean value theorem, which says that

$$\mu(\tilde{x}) - \mu(x) = \tilde{x}(-x)\mu'(\xi)$$

for some ξ between x and $\tilde{x}$. From the definition of $\tilde{x}$, it follows that $|\tilde{x} - x| \le \varepsilon$, and combining this with Theorem 13 gives $|\mu(\tilde{x}) - \mu(x)| \le \varepsilon/2$, or $|\mu(\tilde{x})/\mu(x) - 1| \le \varepsilon/(2|\mu(x)|) \le \varepsilon$ which means that $\mu(\tilde{x}) = \mu(x)(1 + \delta_3)$, with $|\delta_3| \le \varepsilon$.

Finally, multiplying by x introduces a final δ_4, so the computed value of

$$x \cdot \ln(1 \oplus x)/((1 \oplus x) \ominus 1)$$

is

$$\frac{x\ln(1+x)}{(1+x)-1}(1+\delta_1)(1+\delta_2)(1+\delta_3)(1+\delta_4), |\delta_i \le \varepsilon|$$

It is easy to check that if $\varepsilon < 0.1$, then

$$(1 + \delta_1)(1 + \delta_2)(1 + \delta_3)(1 + \delta_4) = 1 + \delta,$$

with $|\delta| \le 5\varepsilon$. z

An interesting example of error analysis using formulas occurs in the quadratic formula

$$(-b \pm \sqrt{b^2 - 4ac})/2a \cdot$$

The section Cancellation, explained how rewriting the equation will eliminate the potential cancellation caused by the ± operation. But there is another potential cancellation that can occur when computing $d = b_2 - 4ac$. This one cannot be eliminated by a simple rearrangement of the formula. Roughly speaking, when $b^2 \approx 4ac$, rounding error can contaminate up to half the digits in the roots computed with the quadratic formula.

If $b^2 \approx 4ac$, rounding error can contaminate up to half the digits in the roots computed with the quadratic formula

$$(-b \pm \sqrt{b^2 - 4ac})/2a \cdot$$

Proof: Write $(b \otimes b) \ominus (4a \otimes c) = (b^2(1 + \delta_1) - 4ac(1 + \delta_2))(1 + \delta_3)$, where $|\delta_i| \le \varepsilon$. 30 Using $d = b^2 - 4ac$, this can be rewritten as $(d(1 + \delta 1) - 4ac(\delta_2 - \delta_1))(1 + \delta_3)$. To get an estimate for the size of this error, ignore second order terms in δ_i, in which case the absolute error is $d(\delta_1 + \delta_3) - 4ac\delta_4$, where $|\delta_4| = |\delta_1 - \delta_2| \le 2\varepsilon$.

Since $d \ll 4ac$, the first term $d(\delta_1 + \delta_3)$ can be ignored. To estimate the second term, use the fact that $ax2 + bx + c = a(x -$

$r_1)$ $(x - r_2)$, so ar1r_2 = c. Since $b^2 \approx 4ac$, then $r_1 \approx r_2$, so the second error term is $4ac\delta_4 \approx 4a^2 r_1 \delta_4{}^2$.

Thus the computed value of $\sqrt{d}$ is

$$\sqrt{d + 4a^2 r_1^2 \delta_4}.$$

The inequality

$$p - q \le \sqrt{p^2 - q^2} \le \sqrt{p^2 + q^2} \le p + q, p \ge q > 0$$

shows that

$$\sqrt{d + 4a^2 r_1^2 \delta_4} = \sqrt{d} + E,$$

where

$$|E| \le \sqrt{4a^2 r_1^2 |\delta_4|},$$

so the absolute error in $\sqrt{d}/2$ a is about $r_1\sqrt{\delta_4}$.

Since

$$\delta_4 \approx \beta^{-p}, \sqrt{\delta_4} \approx \beta^{-p/2},$$

and thus the absolute error of $r_1\sqrt{\delta_4}$ destroys the bottom half of the bits of the roots $r_1 \approx r_2$. In other words, since the calculation of the roots involves computing with $(\sqrt{d})/(2a)$, and this expression does not have meaningful bits in the position corresponding to the lower order half of ri, then the lower order bits of ri cannot be meaningful. z

Finally, we turn to the proof of Theorem 6. It is based on the following fact, which is proven in the Theorem 14 and Theorem 8.

THEOREM 14

Let $0 < k < p$, and set $m = \beta k + 1$, and assume that floating-point operations are exactly rounded. Then $(m \otimes x) \ominus (m \otimes x \ominus x)$ is exactly equal to x rounded to p – k significant digits. More precisely, x is rounded by taking the significand of x, imagining a radix point just left of the k least significant digits and rounding to an integer.

Proof of Theorem 6

By Theorem 14, x_h is x rounded to $p - k = \lfloor p/2 \rfloor$ places.

If there is no carry out, then certainly x_h can be represented with $\lfloor p/2 \rfloor$ significant digits. Suppose there is a carry-out. If $x = x_0.x_1 \ldots x_{p-1} \times \beta^e$, then rounding adds 1 to x_{p-k-1}, and the only way there can be a carry-out is if $x_{p-k-1} = \beta - 1$, but then the low order digit of xh is $1 + x_{p-k-1} = 0$, and so again xh is representable in $\lfloor p/2 \rfloor$ digits.

To deal with x_l, scale x to be an integer satisfying $\beta^{p-1} \leq x \leq \beta^{p-1}$. Let $x = \tilde{x}_k + \tilde{x}_1$ where $\tilde{x}_k$ is the p – k high order digits of x, and $\tilde{x}_1$ is the k low order digits. There are three cases to consider. If $\tilde{x}_1 < (\beta/2)\beta^{k-1}$, then rounding x to p – k places is the same as chopping and $x_h = \tilde{x}_h$, and $x_1 = \tilde{x}_1$.

Since $\tilde{x}_1$ has at most k digits, if p is even, then $\tilde{x}_1$ has at most $k = \lceil p/2 \rceil = \lfloor p/2 \rfloor$ digits. Otherwise, $\beta = 2$ and $\tilde{x}_1 < 2^{k-1}$ is representable with $k - 1 \leq \lfloor p/2 \rfloor$ significant bits. The second case is when $\tilde{x}_1 > (\beta/2)\beta^{k-1}$, and then computing xh involves rounding up, so $x_h = \tilde{x}_h + \beta^k$, and $x_l = x - x_h = x - \tilde{x}_h - \beta k = \tilde{x}_1 - \beta^k$. Once again, $\tilde{x}_1$ has at most k digits, so is representable with $\lfloor p/2 \rfloor$ digits.

Finally, if $\tilde{x}_1 = (\beta/2)\beta k - 1$, then $x_h = \tilde{x}_h$ or $\tilde{x}_h + \beta^k$ depending on whether there is a round up. Soxl is either $(\beta/2)\beta^{k-1}$ or $(\beta/2)\beta^{k-1} - \beta k = -\beta k/2$, both of which are represented with 1 digit. Theorem 6 gives a way to express the product of two working precision numbers exactly as a sum. There is a companion formula for expressing a sum exactly. If $|x| \geq |y|$ then $x + y = (x \oplus y) + (x \ominus (x \oplus y)) \oplus y$.

However, when using exactly rounded operations, this formula is only true for $\beta = 2$, and not for $\beta = 10$ as the example x = .99998, y = .99997 shows.

BINARY TO DECIMAL CONVERSION

Since single precision has p = 24, and $2^{24} < 10^8$, you might expect that converting a binary number to 8 decimal digits would be sufficient to recover the original binary number. However, this is not the case.

THEOREM 15

When a binary IEEE single precision number is converted to the closest eight digit decimal number, it is not always possible to uniquely recover the binary number from the decimal one. However, if nine decimal digits are used, then converting the decimal number to the closest binary number will recover the original floating-point number.

Proof

Binary single precision numbers lying in the half open interval $[10^3, 2^{10}) = [1000, 1024)$ have 10 bits to the left of the binary point, and 14 bits to the right of the binary point. Thus there are (210 - 103)214 = 393,216 different binary numbers in that interval.

If decimal numbers are represented with 8 digits, then there are $(2^{10} - 10^3)10^4 = 240{,}000$ decimal numbers in the same interval. There is no way that 240,000 decimal numbers could represent 393,216 different binary numbers. So 8 decimal digits are not enough to uniquely represent each single precision binary number.

To show that 9 digits are sufficient, it is enough to show that the spacing between binary numbers is always greater than the spacing between decimal numbers. This will ensure that for each decimal number N, the interval,

$$\left[N - \frac{1}{2}\,\text{ulp}, N + \frac{1}{2}\,\text{ulp}\right]$$

contains at most one binary number. Thus each binary number rounds to a unique decimal number which in turn rounds to a unique binary number.

To show that the spacing between binary numbers is always greater than the spacing between decimal numbers, consider an interval $[10^n, 10^{n+1}]$. On this interval, the spacing between consecutive decimal numbers is $10^{(n+1)-9}$.

On $[10^n, 2^m]$, where m is the smallest integer so that $10^n < 2^m$, the spacing of binary numbers is 2^{m-24}, and the spacing gets larger further on in the interval. Thus it is enough to check that $10^{(n+1)-9} < 2^m - 24$. But in fact, since 10n < 2m, then 10(n

+ 1) - 9 = $10^n 10^{-8} < 2^m 10^{-8} < 2^m 2^{-24}$. The same argument applied to double precision shows that 17 decimal digits are required to recover a double precision number.

Binary-decimal conversion also provides another example of the use of flags. Recall from the section Precision, that to recover a binary number from its decimal expansion, the decimal to binary conversion must be computed exactly. That conversion is performed by multiplying the quantities N and $10^{|P|}$ (which are both exact if $p < 13$) in single-extended precision and then rounding this to single precision (or dividing if $p < 0$; both cases are similar).

Of course the computation of $N \cdot 10^{|P|}$ cannot be exact; it is the combined operation round($N \cdot 10^{|P|}$) that must be exact, where the rounding is from single-extended to single precision. To see why it might fail to be exact, take the simple case of $\beta = 10$, $p = 2$ for single, and $p = 3$ for single-extended. If the product is to be 12.51, then this would be rounded to 12.5 as part of the single-extended multiply operation. Rounding to single precision would give 12. But that answer is not correct, because rounding the product to single precision should give 13. The error is due to double rounding.

By using the IEEE flags, double rounding can be avoided as follows. Save the current value of the inexact flag, and then reset it. Set the rounding mode to round-to-zero. Then perform the multiplication N · 10 | P |. Store the new value of the inexact flag in $_{ixflag}$, and restore the rounding mode and inexact flag. If $_{ixflag}$ is 0, then $N \cdot 10^{|P|}$ is exact, so round($N \cdot 10^{|P|}$) will be correct down to the last bit. If $_{ixflag}$ is 1, then some digits were truncated, since round-to-zero always truncates. The significand of the product will look like $1.b_1...b_{22}b_{23}...b_{31}$. A double rounding error may occur if b23 ...b31 = 10...0. A simple way to account for both cases is to perform a logical $_{OR}$ of $_{ixflag}$ with b_{31}. Then round($N \cdot 10^{|P|}$) will be computed correctly in all cases.

ERRORS IN SUMMATION

This chapter Optimizers, mentioned the problem of accurately computing very long sums. The simplest approach to improving accuracy is to double the precision. To get a rough estimate of how much doubling the precision improves the accuracy of a sum, let $s_1 = x_1$, $s_2 = s1 \oplus x_2 \ldots$, $s_i = s_i - 1 \oplus x_i$. Then $s_i = (1 + \delta_i)(s_i - 1 + x_i)$, where $|\delta_i| \leq \varepsilon$, and ignoring second order terms in δ_i gives

$$s_n = \sum_{j=1}^{n} x_j \left(1 + \sum_{k=j}^{n} \delta_k \right) = \sum_{j=1}^{n} x_j + \sum_{j=1}^{n} x_j \left(\sum_{k=j}^{n} \delta_k \right)$$

The first equality of (31) shows that the computed value of Σx_j is the same as if an exact summation was performed on perturbed values of xj. The first term x_1 is perturbed by $n\varepsilon$, the last term xn by only ε. The second equality in (31) shows that error term is bounded by,

$$n\varepsilon\Sigma|x_j|$$

Doubling the precision has the effect of squaring ε. If the sum is being done in an IEEE double precision format, $1/\varepsilon \approx$ 1016, so that $n\varepsilon \ll 1$ for any reasonable value of n. Thus, doubling the precision takes the maximum perturbation of n ε and changes it to $n\varepsilon^2 \ll \varepsilon$.

Thus the 2 ε error bound for summation formula (Theorem 8) is not as good as using double precision, even though it is much better than single precision. For an intuitive explanation of why the summation formula works, consider the following diagram of the procedure.

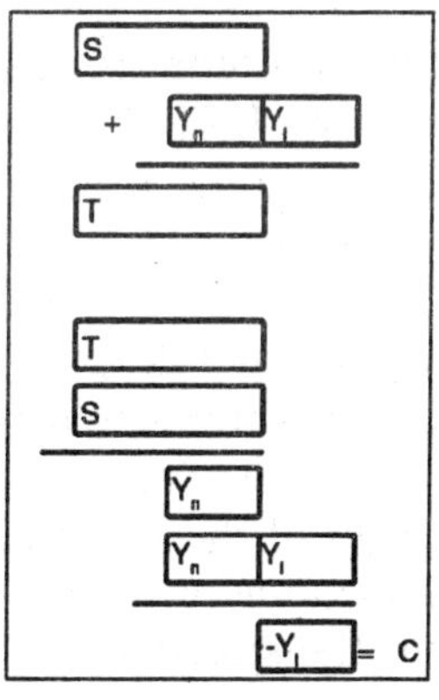

Each time a summand is added, there is a correction factor C which will be applied on the next loop. So first subtract the correction C computed in the previous loop from X_j, giving the corrected summand Y. Then add this summand to the running sum S. The low order bits of Y (namely Y_l) are lost in the sum. Next compute the high order bits of Y by computing T – S. When Y is subtracted from this, the low order bits of Y will be recovered. These are the bits that were lost in the first sum in the diagram. They become the correction factor for the next loop.

FLOATING-POINT OPERATION

In C, an operation is the effect of an operator on an expression. Specific to floating-point numbers, a floating-point operation is any mathematical operation (such as +, –, *,/) or assignment that involves floating-point numbers (as opposed to binary integer operations).

Floating-point numbers have decimal points in them. The number 2.0 is a floating-point number because it has a decimal in it. The number 2 (without a decimal point) is a binary integer. Floating-point operations involve floating-point numbers and typically take longer to execute than simple binary integer operations. For this reason, most embedded applications avoid wide-spread usage of floating-point math in favour of faster, smaller integer operations.

FLOATING-POINT NUMBERS

Scalars of type float are stored using four bytes (32-bits). The format used follows the IEEE-754 standard. A floating-point number is expressed as the product of two parts: the mantissa and a power of two.

For example:

±mantissa × 2exponent

The mantissa represents the actual binary digits of the floating-point number. The power of two is represented by the exponent. The stored form of the exponent is an 8-bit value from 0 to 255. The actual value of the exponent is calculated by subtracting 127 from the stored value (0 to 255) giving a range of -127 to +128. The mantissa is a 24-bit value (representing about seven decimal digits) whose most significant bit (MSB) is always 1 and is, therefore, not stored. There is also a sign bit that indicates whether the floating-point number is positive or negative.

Floating-point numbers are stored on byte boundaries in the following format:

	Address+0	Address+1	Address+2	Address+3
Contents	SEEE EEEE	EMMM MMMM	MMMM MMMM	MMMM MMMM

Where,

S	Represents the sign bit where 1 is negative and 0 is positive.
E	Is the exponent with an offset of 127.
M	Is the 24-bit mantissa (stored in 23 bits).

Zero is a special value denoted with an exponent field of 0 and a mantissa of 0.

Using the above format, the floating-point number -12.5 is stored as a hexadecimal value of 0xC1480000. In memory, this value appears as follows:

	Address+0	Address+1	Address+2	Address+3
Contents	0xC1	0x48	0x00	0x00

It is fairly simple to convert floating-point numbers to and from their hexadecimal storage equivalents. The following example demonstrates how this is done for the value –12.5 shown above. The floating-point storage representation is not an intuitive format. To convert this to a floating-point number, the bits must be separated as specified in the floating-point number storage format table shown above. For example:

	Address+0	Address+1	Address+2	Address+3
Format	SEEEEEEE	EMMM MMMM	MMMM MMMM	MMMM MMMM
Binary	11000001	01001000	00000000	00000000
Hex	C1	48	00	00

From this illustration, you can determine the following:

- The sign bit is 1, indicating a negative number.
- The exponent value is 10000010 binary or 130 decimal. Subtracting 127 from 130 leaves 3, which is the actual exponent.
- The mantissa appears as the following binary number:

Here is an understood binary point at the left of the mantissa that is always preceded by a 1. This digit is omitted from the stored form of the floating-point number. Adding 1 and the binary point to the beginning of the mantissa gives the following value:

```
1.10010000000000000000000
```

To adjust the mantissa for the exponent, move the decimal point to the left for negative exponent values or right for positive exponent values. Since the exponent is three, the mantissa is adjusted as follows:

```
1100.10000000000000000000
```

The result is a binary floating-point number. Binary digits to the left of the decimal point represent the power of two corresponding to their position. For example, 1100 represents $(1 \times 2^3) + (1 \times 2^2) + (0 \times 2^1) + (0 \times 2^0)$, which is 12.

Binary digits to the right of the decimal point also represent the power of two corresponding to their position. However, the powers are negative. For example, .100... represents $(1 \times 2^{-1}) + (0 \times 2^{-2}) + (0 \times 2^{-3}) + \ldots$ which equals .

The sum of these values is 12.5. Because the sign bit was set, this number should be negative.

Chapter 5

Control Unit

INSTRUCTION

INSTRUCTION DECODER

For executing software, the very job of a processor, each CPU begins with the decoding of the program's machine instructions,'translating'it into operations or OPs that the microprocessor can handle internally. Loosely comparable, AMD calls those OPs'MOps', for Macro Operations; Intel calls them micro-OPs or short μ–OPs.

In fact, AMD's MOp actually contains two operations compared to Intel's one for one uOP. Modern processors can directly decode common and frequently used instructions extremely fast into these OPs, and execute very quickly as well (typically in one clock).

Less common or very complex instructions need to be decoded in a slower process, which involves looking up the OPs in a ROM within the CPU, and the amount of resulting OPs is often more than only two. The part of the Athlon decoder that deals with the directly decodable instructions is called'direct path', the part for the complex instructions is called'vector path'The P6 architecture (PentiumPro, Pentium-II and Pentium III) is similar but less flexible, using only one path for both types of decodes.

Why is all this done? For Athlon it is speed! For the P6, it's design simplicity. Let's compare the Athlon's decoders to the well known P6 decoders. Intel's Pentium III has three parallel decoding units, they are known as complex and simple and simple. Without going into the boring super technical detail, Intel has strict rules in using these decoders. This means that ideally three instructions can be decoded at the same time, if and only if one of them is a complex instruction and the other two are simple instructions.

Intel defines complex as an instruction that can be represented by no more that 4 uOPs. Simple is defined as an instruction that can be translated in to a single uOP. Athlon can also only decode three instructions at the same time, but it comes with three fully capable decoders.

This means that Athlon will decode virtually any combination of instructions with any of its decoders. It has no special rules like the P6 architecture. Let's say that this is performance advantage No.1.

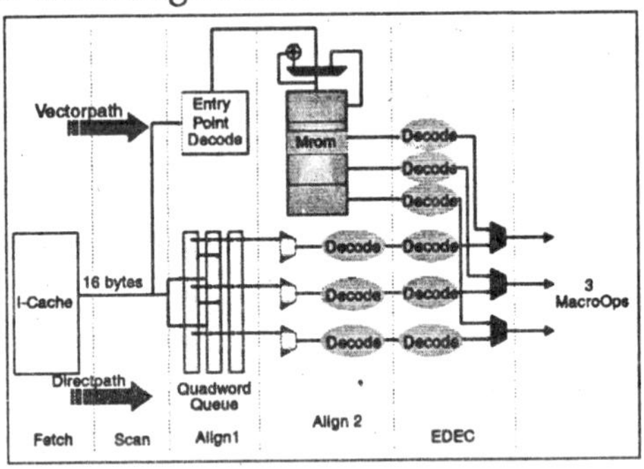

INSTRUCTION CONTROL UNIT

As you can see from the processor block diagrams, the next stage, once an instruction is decoded, is in Athlon's case the Instruction Control Unit. This Unit can hold up to 72 MOps (because a MOp can equal an x86 instruction, this means Athlon can have up to 72 in-flight instructions) before they're dispatched to the schedulers.

This is a lot more than the 20 μ-Ops (if you take an average of say 1.5 uOPs per instructions, then the P6 archtecture has approximately 13 in-flight instructions) that can be held in Intel's Reservation Station, which is already the next advantage of Athlon over PIII, but let's not even count that. The next step is where it gets really interesting.

THE EXECUTION PORTS

You certainly agree that the most important thing a microprocessor has to do is to actually execute the instructions of the software it's running. Thus it's about time that we are getting to this stage. You cannot really see it in the block diagrams, but Pentium III has 11 (+1) parallel execution units, Athlon has even more. Those units are executing the OPs, and since it's so many in parallel, you can imagine why we are talking of'out-of-order'execution here.

Executing one OP after another would obviously not make any use of parallel execution units. To make sure that the out-of-order execution is actually working, Intel is using the'Renamer & Allocator'as well as the'Reorder-Unit'. The'Integer/FP Renamer/Allocator'is found before the Reservation Station, and as the name already says it, this unit is responsible for integer as well as FP and multimedia OPs. Athlon does this work a bit more sophisticated. The units that take care of the out-of-order execution are the Integer Scheduler and the FP Scheduler, both able to hold a quite impressive number of OPs (18/36).

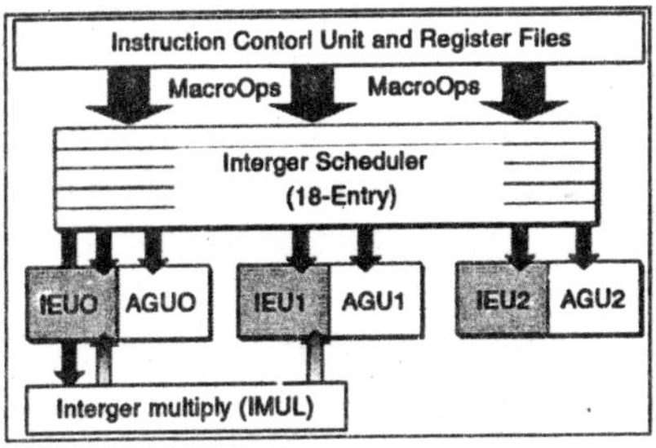

Athlon's Integer Execution Path

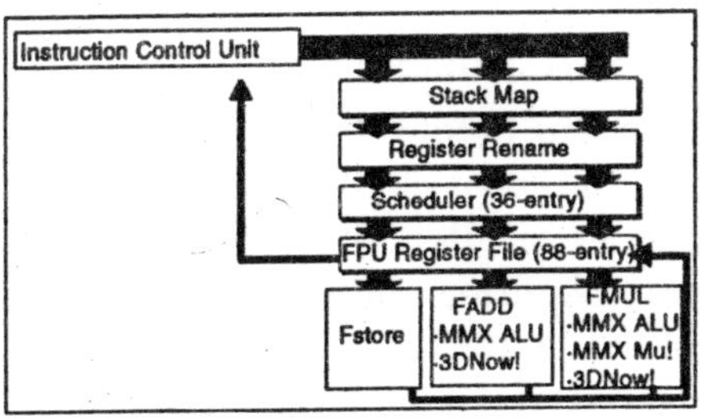

FORMATS

The control unit is a finite state machine that takes as its inputs the IR, the status register (which is partly filled by the status output from the ALU), and the current major state of the cycle. Its rules are encoded either in random logic, a Programmable Logic Array (PLA), or Read-Only Memory (ROM), and its outputs are sent across the processor to each point requiring coordination or direction for the control unit.

For example the outputs needed for the portion of the instruction/data path shown in Discussion 13 are Jump/Branch/Next PC, IR Latch, Read Control, Load Control, ALU Function Select, Load/Reg-Reg, Reg R/W.

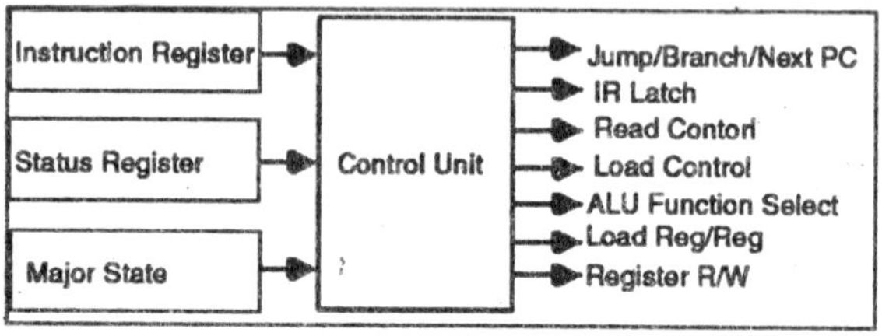

The ALU function select takes the instruction op code and translates it into a given function of the ALU (either one line per ALU function or a compact binary code for the function). The Jump/Branch/PC depends on the instruction type and in a RISC architecture these may be directly coded in the op code. Read control occurs at the start of an instruction cycle.

IR latch and occurs at the end of the fetch state. Load control happens at the end of the data fetch state of a load instruction. Load Reg/Reg again depends on the op-code. Register R/W is in the start of the data fetch stage and at the write back stage of an operation. It thus depends on the major state and the instruction.

A CISC architecture typically uses a more complex control unit. As we've noted before, the IR is often multiple words, and the control unit has to look at different parts of the IR at different stages of execution. In fact, the entire IR may not be available at once, requiring interlocks with fetch logic to ensure the contents of the IR are valid. There are many more control signals coming out of a CISC control unit, partly to control the more complex addressing logic, but also to directly connect to the many special purpose registers. In a RISC architecture, the registers are accessed uniformly in a block so a simple decoder in the register file can select the particular register. In a CISC architecture, there are restrictions on the particular registers that can be used by a given instruction and these are enforced by the control unit.

To begin the design of a control unit, we start by listing every control signal in the instruction/data path of the processor. This becomes a list of the control unit's outputs. As input, it has the instruction register, any status information (such as branch flags, interrupts, etc.) from the processor, and a"major state"which simply keeps track of where we are in the execution of an instruction.

We always begin an instruction with state 0, which corresponds to Fetch. During that state, the control unit outputs the necessary signals to route the contents of the PC to the memory address port, to select and clock the memory until it responds with data from that location, and then cause this data to be latched into the IR>

In a CISC architecture, the Fetch may only retrieve the first part of an instruction, and (depending on bits in the IR that are then decoded by the control unit) more words may need to be fetched. In a RISC architecture, a single Fetch retrieves a complete instruction, so we may proceed to the next major state, which is usually to begin fetching data from the registers, while we decode the instruction.

In a RISC architecture,"decoding an instruction"mainly means that the instruction type field determines what the control unit will do for the remainder of the instructions. If you think of the CU as a finite state machine, the bits in the type field select the next state following the decode.

In terms of a program's logic, this is like selecting a branch in a Switch statement - each branch of the Switch contains the series of steps to be performed for one type of instruction. For example, after decoding a Jump instruction, the control unit outputs the signals required to combine the address portion of the instruction with the upper bits of the PC and load the result back into the PC. The CU then returns to the Fetch step. Thus, a Jump has three major states (Fetch, Decode, Complete). For a memory Load instruction, the CU first sends one of the selected register values (the address) to the address port of the memory (via a multiplexer) and signals the memory to fetch this location.

When the memory returns the value, then the CU sends signals to the necessary multiplexer(s) and the register file so that the memory data goes over the Dest bus and is stored in the designated register. So, for each type of instruction, and for each major state in each type of instruction, we look at the list of control signals and decide what value each signal must have.

In some cases, the value doesn't matter (e.g., if memory isn't selected, it doesn't matter whether it is set to read or write, because it simply won't do anything in either case). You can think of this as a large 2-dimensional table indexed by instruction type and major state. Within each cell of the table is a list of the control signal and their values.

One last bit of control output that we've neglected is the control of the major state itself. This is usually a register, as shown above, that is input to the CU. But it also receives its next value on each clock from the CU. In the above example, the Jump proceeds from State 0 (Fetch) to State 1 (Decode) to State 3 (Complete) and then goes back to State 0. While a Load adds a State 4. In some designs, the state register also encodes the instruction type.

Thus, it is really referring to the different states of the finite state machine (FSM) rather than the major steps of the instructions. So, for example, the FSM states for a Load might be the sequence 0, 1, 12, 13. The latter two distinguish Memory and Write Back from the Complete stage of the Jump. In other designs, we might see Jump going through states 0, 1, 2, and Load going through 0, 1, 2, 3, with the type field used to distinguish the different behaviour of the latter states. This is all just a matter of using somewhat different ways of naming the same things. The important point is just that the CU has the inputs it needs to know what it is supposed to be doing on the present clock and what it will do next. In the CU design process, this translate to ensuring that one of the control signals on the list is the"next state"signal, and that we always specify this in every cell of our table.

CONTROL FOR THE MULTICYCLE DATA PATH

Unlike the way this is drawn in the text, it is quite obvious here that each level of the controller's finite state machine corresponds to a clock cycle (or major state). This view clearly shows the commonality of the first two major states, prior to the decoding of the instruction. The third stage is a typical fanning out of the finite state machine to deal with the different cases of the instruction types. Thus, we can see that the machine is arranged in a table where the rows are major states, and the columns are major instruction types. Because the new PC values have been computed, the Jump and Branch types can be finished early. The memory read takes the longest (5 major states).

Each of these states produces a set of control signals that cause the multiplexers to select the appropriate inputs, and the various registers to latch at the proper time. This is determined by looking at each device requiring control and determining for each state whether it is necessary to issue a signal on that particular control line.

Note that in the text, the circuitry controlled by the status from the ALU is shown external to the control for simplicity. But in a more general controller that must handle multiple conditions, this logic would not be separated. Because there are ten distinct states, and the book chooses to encode the instruction type in the major state (really the FSM state number) the state register for this machine must have four bits.

One common approach to implementing a controller is to have the major state be implemented by a counter register and within each of these states the different columns are represented by the state register (which in a RISC architecture could just be the instruction type code). The major state counter simply increments on each clock cycle, and when a column of states finishes early, its last state generates a reset signal to the major state counter. Another issue that is not addressed here is what happens when there is a memory delay. We are still assuming that memory returns in a single cycle. The simplest case is to stall the finite state machine until the fetch is complete. This is done by having a memory wait signal that is input to the finite state machine. Each memory fetch state has a next state arc that loops back to itself whenever memory wait is asserted.

MICROCODE

In many CISC architectures the control unit can feed back to the major (and minor) states and has internal registers and a ROM. It can thus cause portions of an instruction to be extended or repeated as necessary. The minor states, registers. additional control logic, and ROM form a finite state machine called a microcode engine. In the microcode engine, the op-code from the IR becomes a jump address into the ROM. A micro-PC can be used to step through a series of fetches from the ROM starting at that point, with each fetch resulting in control signals being sent out and providing feedback to the major and minor state values.

An alternative to using a micro-PC is to have each instruction explicitly specify the address of its successor. Thus, one of the fields in the micro-op may be the address of the next instruction. This allows jumps to be used anywhere in the microcode with no time penalty -- consider that if a separate instruction had to be employed for a jump, it would add a cycle to the execution of the ISA instruction.

The microcode instruction set can contain a subroutine jump so that common sequences of control outputs can be reused. This is typically present in systems that employ a microPC rather than a next instruction field. There is typically just one subroutine return register, so nesting of subroutines is not allowed.

Thus, the subroutine jump may be implemented as a normal jump with a signal issued that stores the current micro-PC value into the return register. And the subroutine ends with a Return operation rather than a jump to another location. The

Return operation issues a signal that loads the return register back into the micro-PC. In a system with an explicit next instruction field, the current address plus one is stored into the return register and it is implicit that the next location holds the next instruction following the subroutine call.

An alternative is to have both a subroutine jump address and a next instruction address, and simply return to the same instruction, but this requires the instruction format to be larger than necessary for most operations.

MICROINSTRUCTION FORMAT DESIGN

From the preceding discussion of how sequential execution, jumps, and calls are executed we can gather that the microinstruction needs to include control information for the microengine itself. But what else does it store?

In the simplest microinstruction formats, each bit represents a control signal that is sent out to the datapath. Thus, when a microinstruction is fetched, the bits in the instruction are connected to control wires and cause actions to occur in the datapath.

For example, in our PDP-8 example, there are 14 control signals that are driven by a single bit, and three others that each require multiple bits, for a total of 23 bits. Thus, we might use a microinstruction format such as:

Control Signal Output	Next Instruction
0 23	24 31

Each of the first 20 bits of this microinstruction corresponds to a control signal in the PDP-8. For example, bit 0 might be the Halt, bit 1 the No defer, bit 2 the Max St., bit 3 Acc. Load, bit 4 Acc. clear, etc. This simple representation is effective but inefficient. For example, it uses 4 bits to select the ALU function but only one of those bits should be asserted at any time.

Thus, we can save some memory by storing the number of the active bit and using an external"decoder"circuit to translate the two bits into the four lines that control the ALU.

In a simple design such as the PDP-8, it may seem that this (two bit) savings is trivial, but in a CISC ISA, the number of control signals can be quite large and it is important to minimize the number of bits in the microinstruction format. Every location in the microcode memory has to store the same set of bits, so any waste of bits is multiplied by the number of words. Microinstruction format designs are often classified by the width of the word employed.

One approach is to have a very wide word that contains all of the control signals necessary to drive the system. Such a design is referred to as a"horizontal"microinstruction format. Another approach is to use a narrower word, with a sequence of microinstructions being required to drive all of the control signals. This is called a"vertical"microinstruction format. At first glance, it appears that a vertical microinstruction is inherently slower -- it takes a sequence of operations to accomplish what the horizontal microinstruction can do in a single cycle.

But consider that in many cases, individual control lines are asserted only in certain minor states. If all of these are grouped together by minor state, then they can reuse some of the bits of the microword by having their outputs first fed to a"demultiplexer"that steers them to the proper signal lines according to the current minor state (which may itself be part of the instruction). In effect the microinstruction format is using multiple instruction formats to reduce redundancy.

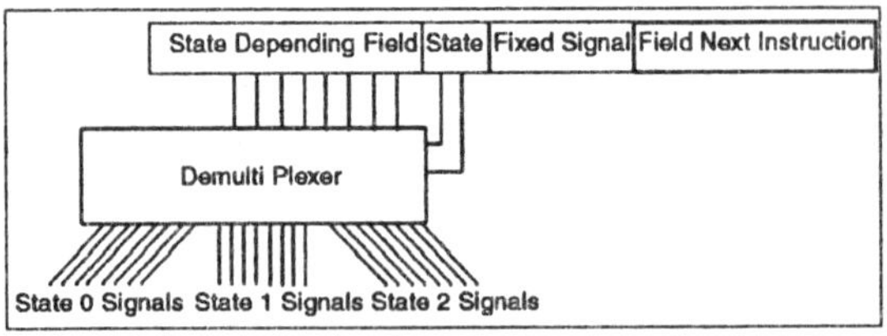

Horizontal microcode has been employed in massively parallel array processors where every processor in the system shares a single controller. Often the controller is itself a full-fledged computer, and so the microinstruction both contains traditional machine code for the controller itself as well as the control signals that are distributed to the processors that make up the array. A typical horizontal microinstruction for this type of machine is 128 bits wide (16 bytes). Thus, every effort is made to reduce the number of words required. It is important to note, however, that this is an unusual application of microcode.

One other problem with horizontal microcode is that it is difficult to drive such a large number of signals simultaneously. The switching of so many drivers at once can cause the power supply voltage to sag momentarily (the same as when your lights dim as you turn on a big appliance). This in turn causes noise to appear on signal lines that can cause erroneous behaviour in other parts of the computer. Avoiding this requires careful circuit design and sometimes clever tricks, such as ensuring that the signals are asserted in a series of slightly offset time steps.

Why Microcode?

Of course, the whole reason for using microcode is to manage the complexity of a CISC ISA's control unit. Most RISC designs, even those that have fairly complex implementations, are still sufficiently regular that their control units can be directly constructed from a FSM built with combinational logic. (The advantage of using combinational logic is that it is easier to build a fast decoder with it than with a microcode ROM.)

However, for a CISC ISA, the speed decrease resulting from the use of microcode is often outweighted by the need to manage the complexity of controlling the architecture (a slow processor is, after all, more useful than a faster one that doesn't work). In a CISC architecture there may be a large number of instruction types, each with different fields referring to a wide range of registers that have asymmetrical functions, or referring to one or more memory operands with as many as 20 different addressing modes. (The DEC VAX, Intel 80X86/ Pentium, and Intel iAPX 432 are prime examples).

A control unit for a CISC ISA can thus have to deal with instructions that involve tens and even hundreds of minor states. There would thus be thousands of logic expressions to generate the control signals. CAD tools can simplify and minimize these and even lay them out on the silicon automatically, but it is still a large block of irregular logic on the chip. More importantly, if a mistake is discovered later (i.e., one of the logic expressions is wrong), then it may be necessary to resimplify the entire design and lay it out again, which could mean a redesign of the rest of the chip to accommodate a change in the size of the control unit. This is obviously a very costly error.

Unfortunately, it is also common. Even with the best design and simulation tools, several commercial chips have gone into production with errors that were discovered later. An early 68000 design had a bug that would cause the processor to hang in certain cases, Intel shipped half a million Pentium processors with an error in the floating-point division instruction before it was caught, and has had bugs in earlier processors.

Since errors do occur, manufacturers of CISC processors use microcode to reduce the cost of correcting the errors (and to help simplify the initial design, which in itself helps to reduce errors). A bug-fix in a micro coded controller is just a matter of changing the ROM, which does not affect the size of the controller at all. It is a very low-cost correction. In addition, a micro coded design is easier to enhance because unused op-codes can be turned into new machine instructions by simply extending the microcode. This simplicity of extension may be another factor that has lead to the increasingly complex ISAs produced by CISC manufacturers.

At one point, it was even thought that allowing the user to add to the microcode was a good idea. If a user has a particular operation that they want to accelerate, they can code it up as a new instruction in the microcode. Such machines were said to have"writeable control stores."The VAX 11/780, the first model in the VAX line, was one of the most widely sold of these machines. However, the feature was rarely used for two reasons: first, the compilers could not take advantage of the custom instructions so the user had to programme in assembly language; second, the microcode is tied to the machine implementation (it refers to the particular control signals in the design) so it is not even portable to another model of the same architecture.

NANOCODE

In some cases, such as the Motorola 68000, there is also a nano code engine. The 68000 uses 544 17-bit words in its micro engine and 336 68-bit words in its nano code engine. It thus has 32,096 bits of ROM. If everything had been done with 68-bit words, it would have required 36,992 bits.

The M68000 microcode is very unusual in that the microcode implicitly calls the nano code. Each microcode instruction causes a corresponding nano code engine instruction to be fetched automatically. The nano code bits are actually the control signals that get distributed across the machine. The microcode instructions thus have only to determine what the next instruction will be.

They have two formats, one for an unconditional jump (perhaps just to the next location) or a conditional jump (two bits of the jump address are reserved for the result of the conditional test). This would seem to imply that there are as many nano code instructions as microcode instructions. Yet we can see that there are 208 fewer. This is accomplished by carefully assigning the addresses so that common nano code operations can have multiple microcode locations corresponding to them.

The address space allows for 1024 instructions, and they are arranged so that if a bit (or several) is ignored, the same nano code address is produced. Essentially the engineers mapped the microcode operations into locations so that certain of the address bits are"don't cares"and all of those locations are then mapped to the same nano code address. The don't cares are achieved by removing selected transistors in the address decoders of the nano code ROM.

REGISTERS

Registers are fast memory, almost always connected to circuitry that allows various arithmetic, logical, control, and other manipulations, as well as possibly setting internal flags. Most early computers had only one data register that could be used for arithmetic and logic instructions. Often there would be additional special purpose registers set aside either for temporary fast internal storage or assigned to logic circuits to implement certain instructions.

Some early computers had one or two address registers that pointed to a memory location for memory accesses (a pair of address registers typically would act as source and destination pointers for memory operations). Computers soon had multiple data registers, address registers, and sometimes other special purpose registers. Some computers have general purpose registers that can be used for both data and address operations.

Every digital computer using a von Neumann architecture has a register (called the programme counter) that points to the next executable instruction. Many computers have additional control registers for implementing various control capabilities. Often some or all of the internal flags are combined into a flag or status register.

ACCUMULATORS

Accumulators are registers that can be used for arithmetic, logical, shift, rotate, or other similar operations. The first computers typically only had one accumulator. Many times there were related special purpose registers that contained the source data for an accumulator.

Accumulators were replaced with data registers and general purpose registers. Accumulators reappeared in the first microprocessors.

- *Intel 8086/80286*: one word (16 bit) accumulator; named AX (high order byte of the AX register is named AH and low order byte of the AX register is named AL)
- *Intel 80386*: one doubleword (32 bit) accumulator; named EAX (low order word uses the same names as the accumulator on the Intel 8086 and 80286 [AX] and low order and high order bytes of the low order

words of four of the registers use the same names as the accumulator on the Intel 8086 and 80286 [AH and AL])

- *Mix*: one accumulator; named A-register; five bytes plus sign

DATA REGISTERS

Data registers are used for temporary scratch storage of data, as well as for data manipulations (arithmetic, logic, etc.). In some processors, all data registers act in the same manner, while in other processors different operations are performed are specific registers.

- *Mix*: one extension register; named X-register; five bytes plus sign; can be concatenated on the right hand side of the A-register (accumulator)
- *Motorola 680x0, 68300*: 8 longword (32 bit) data registers; named D0, D1, D2, D3, D4, D5, D6, and D7

ADDRESS REGISTERS

Address registers store the addresses of specific memory locations. Often many integer and logic operations can be performed on address registers directly (to allow for computation of addresses). Sometimes the contents of address register(s) are combined with other special purpose registers to compute the actual physical address. This allows for the hardware implementation of dynamic memory pages, virtual memory, and protected memory.

The number of bits of an address register (possibly combined with information from other registers) limits the maximum amount of addressable memory. A 16-bit address register can address 64K of physical memory. A 24-bit address register can address address 16 MB of physical memory. A 32-bit address register can address 4 GB of physical memory. A 64-bit address register can address 1.8446744×10^{19} of physical memory. Addresses are always unsigned binary numbers.

- *Mix*: one jump registers; named J-register; two bytes and sign is always positive

- *Motorola 680x0, 68300*: 8 longword (32 bit) address registers; named A0, A1, A2, A3, A4, A5, A6, and A7 (also called the stack pointer)

GENERAL PURPOSE REGISTERS

General purpose registers can be used as either data or address registers:

- DEC VAX: 16 word (32 bit) general purpose registers; named R0 through R15
- IBM 360/370: 16 full word (32 bit) general purpose registers; named 0, 1, 2, 3, 4, 5, 6, 7, 8, 9, A (or 10), B (or 11), C (or 12), D (or 13), E (or 14), and F (or 15)
- Intel 8086/80286: 8 word (16 bit) general purpose registers; named AX, BX, CX, DX, BP, SP, SI, and DI (high order bytes of the AX, BX, CX, and DX registers have the names AH, BH, CH, and DH and low order bytes of the AX, BX, CX, and DX registers have the names AL, BL, CL, and DL)
- Intel 80386: 8 doubleword (32 bit) general purpose registers; named EAX, EBX, ECX, EDX, EBP, ESP, ESI, and EDI (low order words use the same names as the general purpose registers on the Intel 8086 and 80286 and low order and high order bytes of the low order words of four of the registers use the same names as the general purpose registers on the Intel 8086 and 80286)
- Motorola 88100: 32 word (32 bit) general purpose registers; named r0 through r31

CONSTANT REGISTERS

Constant registers are special read-only registers that store a constant. Attempts to write to a constant register are illegal or ignored. In some RISC processors, constant registers are used to store commonly used values (such as zero, one, or negative one) — for example, a constant register containing zero can be used in register to register data moves, providing the equivalent of a clear instruction without adding one to the instruction set. Constant registers are also often used in floating point units to provide such value as pi or e with additional hidden bits for greater accuracy in computations.

- Motorola 88100: r0 (general purpose register 0) contains the constant 32 bit integer zero

FLOATING POINT REGISTERS

Floating point registers are special registers set aside for floating point math.

INDEX REGISTERS

Index registers are used to provide more flexibility in addressing modes, allowing the programmer to create a memory address by combining the contents of an address register with the contents of an index register (with displacements, increments, decrements, and other options).

In some processors, there are specific index registers (or just one index register) that can only be used only for that purpose. In some processors, any data register, address register, or general register (or some combination of the three) can be used as an index register.

- *IBM 360/370*: any of the 16 general purpose registers may be used as an index register
- *Intel 80x86*: 7 of the 8 general purpose registers may be used as an index register (the ESP is the exception)
- *Mix*: five index registers; named I-registers I1, I2, I3, I4, and I5; five bytes plus sign
- *Motorola 680x0, 68300*: any of the 8 data registers or the 8 address registers may be used as an index register

BASE REGISTERS

Base registers or segment registers are used to segment memory. Effective addresses are computed by adding the contents of the base or segment register to the rest of the effective address computation. In some processors, any register can serve as a base register. In some processors, there are specific base or segment registers (one or more) that can only be used for that purpose. In some processors with multiple base or segment registers, each base or segment register is used for different kinds of memory accesses (such as a segment register for data accesses and a different segment register for programme accesses).

- *IBM 360/370*: Any of the 16 general purpose registers may be used as a base register
- *Intel 80x86*: 6 dedicated segment registers: CS (code segment), SS (stack segment), DS (data segment), ES (extra segment, a second data segment register), FS (third data segment register), and GS (fourth data segment register)
- *Motorola 680x0, 68300*: any of the 8 address registers may be used as a base register

CONTROL REGISTERS

Control registers control some aspect of processor operation. The most universal control register is the programme counter.

PROGRAMME COUNTER

Almost every digital computer ever made uses a programme counter. The programme counter points to the memory location that stores the next executable instruction. Branching is implemented by making changes to the programme counter. Some processor designs allow software to directly change the programme counter, but usually software only indirectly changes the programme counter (for example, a JUMP instruction will insert the operand into the programme counter).

An assembler has a location counter, which is an internal pointer to the address (first byte) of the next location in storage (for instructions, data areas, constants, etc.) while the source code is being converted into object code. The VAX uses the 16th of 16 general purpose registers as the programme counter (PC). Almost the entire instruction set can directly manipulate the programme counter, allowing a very rich set of possible kinds of branching. The programme counter in System/360 and 370 machines is contained in bits 40-63 of the programme status word (PSW), which is directly accessible by some instructions.

- *IBM 360/370*: Programme counter is bits 40-63 of the programme status word (PSW)
- *Intel 8086/80286*: 16-bit instruction pointer (IP)
- *Intel 80386*: 32-bit instruction pointer (EIP)
- *Motorola 680x0, 68300*: 32-bit programme counter (PC)

PROCESSOR FLAGS

Processor flags store information about specific processor functions. The processor flags are usually kept in a flag register or a general status register. This can include result flags that record the results of certain kinds of testing, information about data that is moved; certain kinds of information about the results of compations or transformations, and information about some processor states.

Closely related and often stored in the same processor word or status register (although often in a privileged portion) are control flags that control processor actions or processor states or the actions of certain instructions.

- *IBM 360/370*: programme status word (PSW)
- *Intel 8086/80286*: 16-bit flag register (FLAGS); system flags, control flag, and status flags)
- *Intel 80386*: 32-bit flag register (EFLAGS); system flags, control flag, and status flags)
- *Mix*: an overflow toggle and a comparison indicator
- *Motorola 680x0, 68300*: 16-bit status register (SR); high byte is system byte and requires privileged access, low byte is user byte or condition code register (CCR)

STACK POINTER

Stack pointers are used to implement a processor stack in memory. In many processors, address registers can be used as generic data stack pointers and queue pointers.

A specific stack pointer or address register may be hardwired for certain instructions. The most common use is to store return addresses, processor state information, and temporary variables for subroutines.

- IBM 360/370: any of the 16 general purpose registers may be used as a stack pointer
- Intel 8086/80286: dedicated stack pointer (SP) combined with stack segment pointer (SS) to create address of stack
- Intel 80386: dedicated stack pointer (ESP) combined with stack segment pointer (SS) and the stack-frame base pointer (EBP) to create address of stack
- Motorola 680x0, 68300: dedicated user stack pointer (USP, A7) and system stack pointer (SSP, A7) for implicit stack pointer operations, as well as allowing any of the 8 address registers to be as explicit stack pointers

SUBROUTINE RETURN POINTER

Some RISC processors include a special subroutine return pointer rather than using a stack in memory. The return address for subroutine calls is stored in this register rather than in memory. More than one level of subroutine calls requires storing and saving the contents of this register to and from memory.

- Motorola 88100: r1 is a 32 bit register containing the return pointer generated by bsr and jsr instructions; the register can be read or overwritten by software and can even be used as a temporary general purpose data register

Chapter 6

Hardwire and Microprogrammed Control

HARDWIRED CONTROL

To execute instructions, a computer's processor must generate the control signals used to perform the processor's actions in the proper sequence. This sequence of actions can either be executed by another processor's software (for example in software emulation or simulation of a processor) or in hardware. Hardware methods fall into two categories: the processor's hardware signals are generated either by hardwired control, in which the instruction bits directly generate the signals, or by micro programmed control in which a dedicated microcontroller executes a microprogram to generate the signals. Before microprocessors, hardwired control usually was implemented using discrete components, flip-chips, or even rotating discs or drums. This can be generally done by two methods.

METHODS

Method1

The classical method of sequential circuit design. It attempts to minimize the amount of hardwire, in particular, by using only log2p flip flops to realise a p state circuit.

Method2

An approach that uses one flip flop per state. While expensive in terms of flip flops, this method simplifies controller unit design and debugging. In practice, processor control units are often so complex that no one design method by itself can yield a satisfactory circuit at an acceptable cost. The most acceptable design may consist of several linked, but independently designed, sequential circuits.

Microprogramming made it possible to re-wire, as it were, a computer by simply downloading a new micro programme to it. This required dedicated hardware or an external processor. For example, some of DEC's PDP-10 processors used aPDP-11 as a front-end which uploaded a microprogram to the main processor at boot time.

Traditionally, sewing machines'stitch patterns and a washing machine's wash programmes were implemented as hardwired, usually mechanical, controls. In modern machines, these are instead implemented as software which controls a computer which controls the machine hardware. This makes it possible, for example, to download additional stitch patterns for a small fee[citation needed]or upgrade a machine without having to buy a complete new machine. It also opens up for intellectual property rights issues.

The term hardwired is also used in a biological context to denote behaviour that is innately determined by an organism's genetically determined neurophysiology. Such hardwired behaviour would include the well-known knee-jerk reflex. Non-hardwired behaviour is dependent upon learning during the lifetime of the individual organism. As such the term is used in a way that is directly analogous to its use in computing.

MICRO PROGRAMMED CONTROL

MICROCODE

Microcode is a layer of hardware-level instructions and/ or data structures involved in the implementation of higher level machine code instructions in many computers and other processors; it resides in a special high-speed memory and translates machine instructions into sequences of detailed circuit-level operations. It helps separate the machine instructions from the underlying electronics so that instructions can be designed and altered more freely. It also makes it feasible to build complex multi-step instructions while still reducing the complexity of the electronic circuitry compared to other methods. Writing microcode is often called microprogramming and the microcode in a particular processor implementation is sometimes called a micro programme.

Modern microcode is normally written by an engineer during the processor design phase and stored in a ROM and/ or PLA structure, although machines exist which have some writable microcode in SRAM or flash memory. Microcode is generally not visible or changeable by a normal programmer, not even by an assembly programmer.

Unlike machine code which often retains some compatibility among different processors in a family, microcode only runs on the exact electronic circuitry for which it's designed, as it constitutes an inherent part of the particular processor design itself.

More extensive micro coding has also been used to allow small and simple micro architectures to emulate more powerful architectures with wider word length, more execution units and so on; a relatively simple way to achieve software compatibility between different products in a processor family.

Some hardware vendors, especially IBM, use the term as a synonym for firmware, so that all code in a device, whether microcode or machine code, is termed microcode (such as in a hard drive for instance, which typically contain both).

OVERVIEW

The elements composing a microprogram exist on a lower conceptual level than a normal application programme. Each element is differentiated by the"micro"prefix to avoid Confusion: microinstruction,microassembler, microprogrammer, micro-architecture, etc. The microcode usually does not reside in the main memory, but in a special high speed memory, called the control store. It might be either read-only or read-write memory. In the latter case the microcode would be loaded into the control store from some other storage medium as part of the initialization of the CPU, and it could be altered to correct bugs in the instruction set, or to implement new machine instructions.

Microprograms consist of series of microinstructions. These microinstructions control the CPU at a very fundamental level of hardware circuitry.

For example, a single typical microinstruction might specify the following operations:

- Connect Register 1 to the"A"side of the ALU
- Connect Register 7 to the"B"side of the ALU
- Set the ALU to perform two's-complement addition
- Set the ALU's carry input to zero
- Store the result value in Register 8
- Update the"condition codes"with the ALU status flags ("Negative","Zero","Overflow", and"Carry")
- Microjump to MicroPC nnn for the next microinstruction

To simultaneously control all processor's features in one cycle, the microinstruction is often as wide as 50 or more bits. Micro programmes are carefully designed and optimized for the fastest possible execution, since a slow micro programme would yield a slow machine instruction which would in turn cause all programmes using that instruction to be slow.

REASON FOR MICROPROGRAMMING

Microcode was originally developed as a simpler method of developing the control logic for a computer. Initially CPU instruction sets were"hard wired". Each step needed to fetch, decode and execute the machine instructions (including any operand address calculations, reads and writes) was controlled directly bycombinatorial logic and rather minimal sequential state machine circuitry.

While very efficient, the need for powerful instruction sets with multi-step addressing and complex operations (see below) made such"hard-wired"processors difficult to design and debug; highly encoded and varied-length instructions can contribute to this as well, especially when very irregular encodings are used. Microcode simplified the job by allowing much of the processor's behaviour and programming model be defined via microprogram routines rather than by dedicated circuitry.

Even late in the design process, microcode could easily be changed, whereas hard wired CPU designs were very cumbersome to change, so this greatly facilitated CPU design. In the 1940s through the late 1970s, much programming was done in assembly language; higher level instructions meant greater programmer productivity, so an important advantage of microcode was the relative ease by which powerful machine instructions could be defined.

During the 1970s, CPU speeds grew more quickly than memory speeds and numerous techniques such as memory block transfer, memory pre-fetch and multi-level caches were used to alleviate this. High level machine instructions, made possible by microcode, helped further, as fewer more complex machine instructions require less memory bandwidth. For example, an operation on a character string could be done as a single machine instruction, thus avoiding multiple instruction fetches.

Architectures with instruction sets implemented by complex microprograms included the IBM System/360 and Digital Equipment Corporation VAX. The approach of increasingly complex microcode-implemented instruction sets was later called CISC. A middle way, used in many microprocessors, is to use PLAs and/or ROMs (instead of combinatorial logic) mainly for instruction decoding, and let a simple state machine (without much, or any, microcode) do most of the sequencing. The various practical uses of microcode and related techniques (such as PLAs) have been numerous over the years, as well as approaches to where, and to which extent, it should be used. It is still used in modern CPU designs.

BENEFITS

A processor's microprograms operate on a more primitive, totally different and much more hardware-oriented architecture than the assembly instructions visible to normal programmers. In coordination with the hardware, the microcode implements the programmer-visible architecture. The underlying hardware need not have a fixed relationship to the visible architecture. This makes it possible to implement a given instruction set architecture on a wide variety of underlying hardware micro-architectures.

Doing so is important if binary programme compatibility is a priority. Those way previously existing programmes can run on totally new hardware without requiring revision and recompilation. However there may be a performance penalty for this approach. The tradeoffs between application backward compatibility vs CPU performance are hotly debated by CPU design engineers.

The IBM System/360 has a 32-bit architecture with 16 general-purpose registers, but most of the System/360 implementations actually use hardware that implemented a much simpler underlying micro architecture; for example, the System/360 Model 30 had 8-bit data paths to the arithmetic logic unit (ALU) and main memory and implemented the general-purpose registers in a special unit of higher-speed core memory, and the System/360 Model 40 had 8-bit data paths to the ALU and 16-bit data paths to main memory and also implemented the general-purpose registers in a special unit of higher-speed core memory.

The Model 50 and Model 65 had full 32-bit data paths and implemented the general-purpose registers in faster transistor circuits. In this way, microprogramming enabled IBM to design many System/360 models with substantially different hardware and spanning a wide range of cost and performance, while making them all architecturally compatible. This dramatically reduced the amount of unique system software that had to be written for each model.

A similar approach was used by Digital Equipment Corporation in their VAX family of computers. Initially a 32-bit TTL processor in conjunction with supporting microcode implemented the programmer-visible architecture. Later VAX versions used different micro architectures, yet the programmer-visible architecture didn't change. Microprogramming also reduced the cost of field changes to correct defects (bugs) in the processor; a bug could often be fixed by replacing a portion of the microprogram rather than by changes being made to hardware logic and wiring.

HISTORY

In 1947, the design of the MIT Whirlwind introduced the concept of a control store as a way to simplify computer design and move beyond ad hoc methods. The control store was a two-dimensional lattice: one dimension accepted"control time pulses"from the CPU's internal clock, and the other connected to control signals on gates and other circuits.

A"pulse distributor"would take the pulses generated by the CPU clock and break them up into eight separate time pulses, each of which would activate a different row of the lattice. When the row was activated, it would activate the control signals connected to it.

Described another way, the signals transmitted by the control store are being played much like a player piano roll. That is, they are controlled by a sequence of very wide words constructed of bits, and they are"played"sequentially. In a control store, however, the"song"is short and repeated continuously.

In 1951 Maurice Wilkes enhanced this concept by adding conditional execution, a concept akin to a conditional in computer software. His initial implementation consisted of a pair of matrices, the first one generated signals in the manner of the Whirlwind control store, while the second matrix selected which row of signals (the microprogram instruction word, as it were) to invoke on the next cycle.

Conditionals were implemented by providing a way that a single line in the control store could choose from alternatives in the second matrix. This made the control signals conditional on the detected internal signal. Wilkes coined the term micro programming to describe this feature and distinguish it from a simple control store.

MICRO PROGRAMMED SYSTEMS

- In common with many other complex mechanical devices, Charles Babbage's analytical engine used banks of cams to control each operation, i.e. it had a read-only control store. As such it deserves to be recognised as the first microprogrammed computer to be designed, even if it has not yet been realised in hardware.
- The EMIDEC 1100 reputedly used a hard-wired control store consisting of wires threaded through ferrite cores, known as'the laces'.
- Most models of the IBM System/360 series were microprogrammed:
- The Model 25 was unique among System/360 models in using the top 16k bytes of core storage to hold the control storage for the microprogram. The 2025 used a 16-bit microarchitecture with seven control words (or microinstructions). At power up, or full system reset, the microcode was loaded from the card reader. The IBM 1410 emulation for this model was loaded this way.
- The Model 30, the slowest model in the line, used an 8-bit microarchitecture with only a few hardware registers; everything that the programmer saw was emulated by the microprogram. The microcode for this model was also held on special punched cards, which were stored inside the machine in a dedicated reader per card, called"CROS"units (Capacitor Read-Only Storage). A second CROS reader was installed for machines ordered with 1620 emulation.
- The Model 40 used 56-bit control words. The 2040 box implements both the System/360 main processor and the multiplex channel (the I/O processor). This model used"TROS"dedicated readers similar to"CROS"units, but with an inductive pickup (Transformer Read-only Store).
- The Model 50 had two internal datapaths which

operated in parallel: a 32-bit datapath used for arithmetic operations, and an 8-bit data path used in some logical operations. The control store used 90-bit microinstructions.

- The Model 85 had separate instruction fetch (I-unit) and execution (E-unit) to provide high performance. The I-unit is hardware controlled. The E-unit is microprogrammed with 108-bit control words.
- The NCR 315 was © with hand wired ferrite cores (aROM) pulsed by a sequencer with conditional execution. Wires routed through the cores were enabled for various data and logic elements in the processor.
- The Digital Equipment Corporation PDP-11 processors, with the exception of the PDP-11/20, were microprogrammed.
- Many systems from the Burroughs were microprogrammed
- The B700"microprocessor"executed application-level opcodes using sequences of 16-bit microinstructions stored in main memory, each of these was either a register-load operation or mapped to a single 56-bit"nanocode"instruction stored in read-only memory. This allowed comparatively simple hardware to act either as a mainframe peripheral controller or to be packaged as a standalone computer.
- The B1700 was implemented with radically different hardware including bit-addressable main memory but had a similar multi-layer organisation. The operating system would preload the interpreter for whatever language was required. These interpreters presented different virtual machines for COBOL, Fortran, etc.
- Microdata produced computers in which the microcode was accessible to the user; this allowed the creation of custom assembler level instructions. Microdata's Reality operating system design made extensive use of this capability.

- The Nintendo 64's Reality Co-Processor, which serves as the console'sgraphics processing unit and audio processor, utilized microcode; it is possible to implement new effects or tweak the processor to achieve the desired output. Some well-known examples of custom microcode includeFactor 5's N64 port of the Indiana Jones and the Infernal Machine, Star Wars: Rogue Squadron and Star Wars: Battle for Naboo.
- The VU0 and VU1 vector units in the Sony PlayStation 2 are microprogrammable; in fact, VU1 was only accessible via microcode for the first several generations of the SDK.

IMPLEMENTATION

Each microinstruction in a microprogram provides the bits which control the functional elements that internally compose a CPU. The advantage over a hard-wired CPU is that internal CPU control becomes a specialized form of a computer programme. Microcode thus transforms a complex electronic design challenge (the control of a CPU) into a less-complex programming challenge.

To take advantage of this, computers were divided into several parts: A micro sequencer picked the next word of the control store. A sequencer is mostly a counter, but usually also has some way to jump to a different part of the control store depending on some data, usually data from the instruction registerand always some part of the control store.

The simplest sequencer is just a register loaded from a few bits of the control store. A register set is a fast memory containing the data of the central processing unit. It may include the programme counter, stack pointer, and other numbers that are not easily accessible to the application programmer.

Often the register set is a triple-ported register file, that is, two registers can be read, and a third written at the same time. An arithmetic and logic unit performs calculations, usually addition, logical negation, a right shift, and logical AND. It often performs other functions, as well. There may also be a memory address register and a memory data register, used to access the main computer storage. Together, these elements form an"execution unit."Most modern CPUs have several execution units. Even simple computers usually have one unit to read and write memory, and another to execute user code. These elements could often be bought together as a single chip. This chip came in a fixed width which would form a'slice'through the execution unit. These were known as'bit slice'chips. The AMD Am2900 family is one of the best known examples of bit slice elements. The parts of the execution units, and the execution units themselves are interconnected by a bundle of wires called a bus.

Programmers develop microprograms. The basic tools are software: Amicroassembler allows a programmer to define the table of bits symbolically. Asimulator programme executes the bits in the same way as the eléctronics (hopefully), and allows much more freedom to debug the microprogram. After the microprogram is finalized, and extensively tested, it is sometimes used as the input to a computer programme that constructs logic to produce the same data. This programme is similar to those used to optimize a programmable logic array. No known computer programme can produce optimal logic, but even pretty good logic can vastly reduce the number of transistors from the number required for a ROM control store. This reduces the cost and power used by a CPU.

Microcode can be characterized as horizontal or vertical. This refers primarily to whether each microinstruction directly controls CPU elements (horizontal microcode), or requires subsequent decoding by combinational logic before doing so (vertical microcode). Consequently each horizontal microinstruction is wider (contains more bits) and occupies more storage space than a vertical microinstruction.

ARITHMETIC TECHNIQUES

ADDITION AND SUBTRACTION

The table for binary addition is:

```
+ 0 1
```

```
0 0 1
1 1 10
```

thus, when two binary bits A and B are added, the bit of the sum in the same place is A XOR B, and the carry is A AND B. The exclusive OR function needs to be built from the fundamental AND, OR, and NOT operations in most forms of logic, and A XOR B is the same as (A OR B) AND (NOT (A AND B)). Of course, A AND B has already been calculated, since it is required as the carry. *Thus, a binary adder has the following logic diagram*:

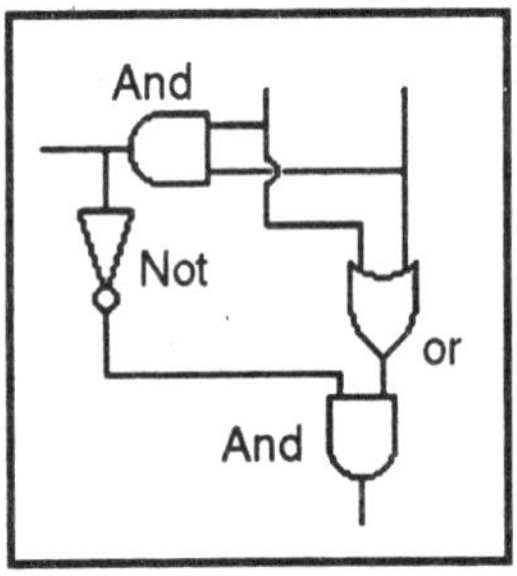

This involves just three gate delays: But addition requires the propagation of carries, and thus the time required to add two long numbers is proportional to their length in the simplest type of adder. This can be speeded up by calculating sums in advance with either input value of the carry, and then selecting the right one, so that carries propagate at a higher level over many bits at a time:

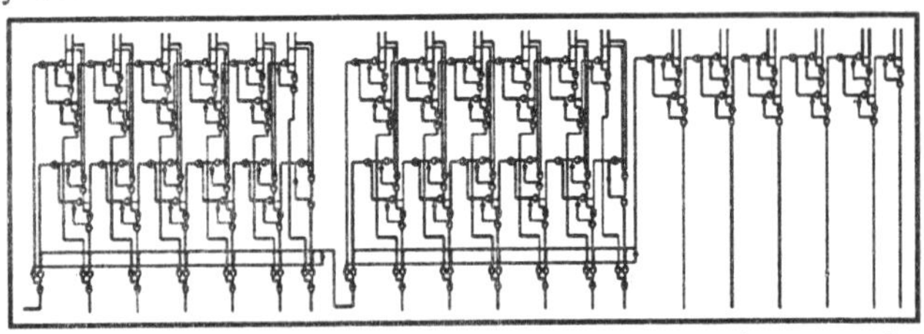

Here, a circuit that adds two binary 18-bit numbers is shown. It is divided into three groups of six bits. Except for the least significant group, each is added together in two ways in parallel, one assuming no carry in, one assuming that a carry in is present; the carry then selects the right result without having to propagate through the six bits of the next group. If we take this kind of architecture to its ultimate conclusion, the form of carry-select adder we obtain is also known as the Sklansky adder, shown in a more schematic form below:

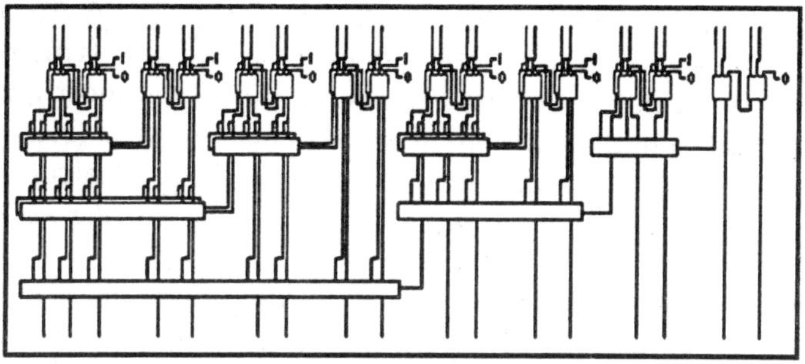

Newer designs for addition units belonging to the *parallel prefix* and *flagged prefix* classes have since been developed. Parallel-prefix adders include the Brent-Kung adder, the Kogge-Stone adder, and the Han-Carlson adder. Although they do not improve on the speed of the Sklansky adder, they address a limitation of real logic circuits which that design ignores, the fact that logic gates have a limited fan-out.

MULTIPLICATION

Binary multiplication does not require much of a multiplication table; all that is required is to make a decision to add or not add a copy of one factor to the result, based on whether the corresponding bit of the other factor is a one or a zero. One straightforward, although expensive in terms of the number of gates required, way to speed up multiplication is to perform all the multiplications of one factor by the individual bits of the other in parallel, and then add the results in pairs, and then the sums in pairs, so that the number of addition stages required is proportional to the logarithm to the base 2 of the length of the second factor.

If, at the beginning of a multiplication, one calculated three times the multiplicand, then two bits of the multiplier at a time, which can only have the values 00, 01, 10, or 11, could each be used to create a partial product; this would trim away the top layer of the addition tree, cutting the amount of circuitry required almost in half. (It may be noted that the

NORC computer by IBM, an ambitious vacuum-tube computer which used decimal arithmetic, calculated multiples up to nine times the multiplicand in advance to speed multiplication.) A special type of adder, called a *carry-save adder*, can be used in multiplication circuits, so that carry propagation can be avoided for all but the last addition in the additions required to perform a multiplication. In order to use this kind of adder, instead of adding numbers in pairs, speed can be increased by adding numbers in groups of three.

This is because one can turn three numbers into two numbers, having the same sum, without propagating carries through the number. This is because a full adder, which takes two bits and an incoming carry bit, and outputs a result bit and a carry bit, can also be used as a 3-2 compressor, one type of carry-save adder. The carry bits move to the left, but since these bits are all shifted left independently, the delays of carry propagation are not required. The diagram below shows the difference between a conventional addition circuit with carry propagation, shown in the top half,

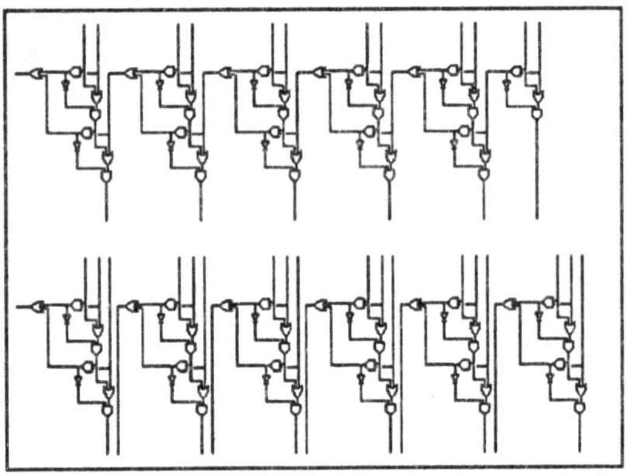

and the 3-2 compressor form of carry-save adder, shown in the bottom half, and involving arguments the same number of bits in length. As the diagram attempts to illustrate, although carries do not propagate in the sense of being added in to the previous digit, they do still move one place to the left. One can then add the two resulting numbers by means of a conventional adder with accelerated carry propagation, such as a carry-select adder as depicted above, or, because carry propagation, even when accelerated, causes such a large delay, one can simply use successive stages of 3-2 compression, performing conventional addition only at the very last stage. This technique was used to speed multiplication in the IBM 7030 computer known as STRETCH.

Instead of simply using one carry-save adder over and over to add one partial product after another, or to have a single line of carry-save adders if it is desired to do successive steps from different multiplications at once in a pipelined fashion, if maximum speed is desired and the cost of hardware and the number of transistors used is no object, one could, as shown above, use several carry-save adders in parallel to produce two results from three partial products, and then repeat the process in successive layers until there are only two numbers left to add in a fast carry-propagate adder. This type of multiplication circuit is called a Wallace Tree adder, after its inventor. The diagram below:

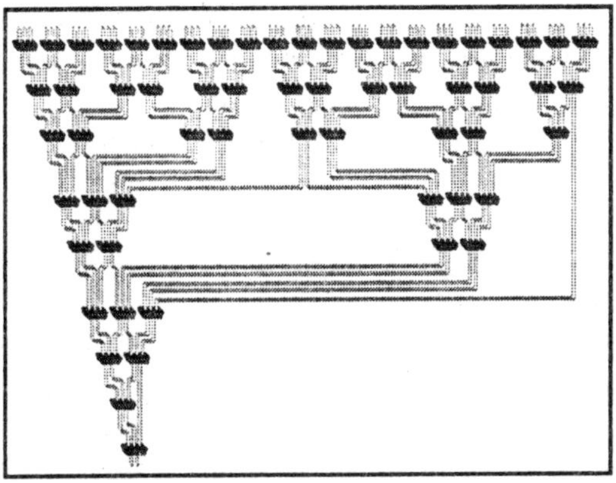

illustrates how, with only two inputs left to go into a carry-propagate adder at the end, successive layers of carry-save adders increase the maximum number of possible partial products that can be included to 3, then 4, and then 6, 9, 13, 19, 28, 42, and 63. The sequence continues: 94, 141, 211... In the IBM System/360 Model 91, a Wallace Tree of limited size was used, as it was necessary to be somewhat concerned with the number of transistors to use.

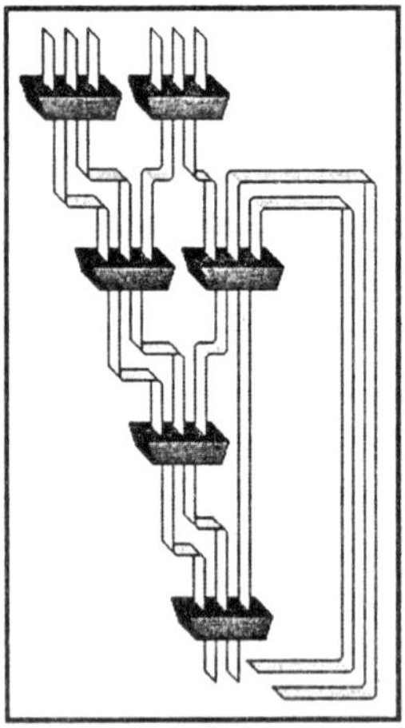

Six partial products were handled by this unit, but only twelve bits of these products were handled at a time. Thus, it would add these six numbers together, sending the least significant twelve bits of the final two results to a carry-propagate adder, while the more significant bits were sent back to be combined with the next more significant twelve bits of the partial products being worked on.

The half adder, although it takes two inputs and provides two outputs, has been used to improve the Wallace Tree adder slightly. One way this has been done is: when there are two left-over values at a given stage to be added, then, they might be put into a half adder.

Although this produces two outputs, one of those outputs will consist of carries, and will therefore be shifted one place to the left. If the number of terms to be added in the next stage is still not an even multiple of three, then, at least at the beginning and end of the part added in the half adders, the number of left-over bits will be reduced by one. This is called a Dadda tree multiplier.

More recently, in U.S. Patent 6,065,033, assigned to the Digital Equipment Corporation, the fact that half the input bits are moved to the left as carry bits was noted explicitly as a way to replace the larger tree generating the middle of the final product by multiple trees of more equal size starting from the middle and proceeding to the left. As noted above, one could trim away a considerable portion of the addition tree by using two digits of the multiplier at a time to create one partial product. But doing this in the naive way described above requires calculating three times the multiplicand, which requires carry propagation.

Another idea that suggests itself is to note that either less than half of the bits in a multiplier are 1, or less than half of the bits in a multiplier are zero, so that in the former case, one could include only the nonzero partial products, and in the latter case, one would multiply by the one's complement of the multiplier and then make a correction.

But this would require an elaborate arrangement for routing the partial products that would more than consume any benefits. Fortunately, there is a method of achieving the same result without having to wait for carries, known as Booth encoding. The goal is to make it possible for each pair of bits in the multiplier to introduce only one partial product that needs to be added. Normally, each pair of bits calls for 0, 1, 2, or 3 times the multiplicand, and the last possibility requires carry propagation to calculate.

Knowing that –1 is represented by a string of ones in two's complement arithmetic, the troublesome number 3 presents itself to us as being equal to 4 minus 1. Four times the multiplicand can be instantly generated by a shift. The two's complement of the multiplicand would require carry propagation to produce, but just inverting all the bits of the multiplicand gives us one less than its additive inverse. It is possible to combine bits representing these errors, since each time this happened, it would be in a different digit, in a single term that could be entered into the addition tree like a partial product.

But that, alone, doesn't eliminate carry propagation. If we code 3 as –1 with +1 to carry into the next pair of bits in the multiplier, then, if we find 2 there, once again we will be stuck with 3. As it happens, though, we have one other possible value that can be produced without carry propagation from the multiplicand that is useful. We can also produce –2 times the multiplicand by both inverting it and shifting it; this time, the result will be too small by two, and that, too, can be accounted for in the error term.

Using the fact that –2 is also available to us in our representation of pairs of bits, we can modify the pairs of digits in the multiplier like this:

```
00         0
01  +  1
10  +  1  -2
11  +  1  -1
```

Since only –2, –1, 0, and +1 are initially and directly used to code a pair of bits, a carry of +1 from the pair of bits to the right will result in the possible values -1, 0, +1, and +2; no troublesome value results that requires an additional carry.

A second step is not really needed, since one just has to peek at the first digit of the following pair of bits to see if a carry out would be coming; thus, Booth coding is often simply presented in the manner in which it would be most efficient when implemented, as a coding that goes directly from three input bits to a signed base-4 digit:

```
00.0     0
00.1  +  1
01.0  +  1
01.1  +  2
10.0  -  2
10.1  -  1
11.0  -  1
11.1     0
```

In the table as shown here, I place a binary point between the two bits for which a substitution is being made and the bit that belongs to the preceding group on the right. This serves as a reminder that the last bit encoded is to the right of the place value of the result of the code, and also that the rightmost pair of bits is encoded on the basis of a 0 lying to their right. Of course, the final carry out, not apparent in this form of the table, should not be forgotten; but it can also be found by coding an additional leading two zero bits appended to the multiplier.

And the digits of the multiplier as converted can be used to determine the value of the error term. In addition to the error term, it is also necessary to remember that the partial products can be negative, and so their signs will need to be extended; this can be done by means of extending the various carry-save adders in the Wallace tree only one additional bit to the left with proper organization. An alternative version of Booth encoding that does require generating three times the multiplicand, in return for converting three bits of the multiplier at a time into a term from the set {–4, –3, –2, –1, 0, +1, +2, +3, +4} has also been used.

However, if one is going to allow *hard multiples* of the multiplicand, that is, multiples which require a carry-propagate addition to produce, then, one could also generate five times the multiplicand (5 = 4 + 1), nine times the multiplicand (9 = 8 + 1), and even, through the use of the same principle as underlies Booth encoding, seven times the multiplicand (7 = 8 – 1); three times, of course, gives six and twelve times by a shift, so, if one is willing to build three carry-propagate adders working in parallel, one can produce all the multiples in the set {–8, –7, –6, –5, –4, –3, –2, –1, 0, +1, +2, +3, +4, +5, +6, +7, +8}, and encode four bits of the multiplier at a time. If the multiples of the multiplicand are generated in advance, and the multiplier is long enough, then one can retire four bits of the multiplier and, using a pre-generated multiple, following the principle used in the NORC, do so with only a single carry-save addition.

If the multiples are not generated in advance, or when a full-width Wallace Tree is used, it would seem that multi-bit Booth encoding could not provide a gain in speed, because an addition requiring carries would take as long as several stages of carry-save addition.

DIVISION

Division is the most difficult of the basic arithmetic operations. For a simple computer that uses a single adder circuit for its arithmetic operations, a variant of the conventional long division method used manually, called *nonrestoring division* provides greater simplicity and speed. This method proceeds as follows, assuming without loss of generality (which means we can fix things by complementing the operands and remembering what we've done, if it isn't so) that both operands are positive:

If the divisor is less than the dividend, then the quotient is zero, the remainder is the dividend, and one is finished.

Otherwise, shift the divisor as many places left as is necessary for its first one bit to be in the same position as the first one bit in the dividend. Also, shift the number one the same number of places left; the result is called the quotient term.

The quotient value starts at zero: Then, do the following until the divisor is shifted right back to its original position:

If the current value in the dividend register is positive, and it has a one bit corresponding to the starting one bit of the value in the divisor register (initially, the divisor as shifted left), subtract the divisor register contents from the dividend register, and add the quotient term to the quotient register.

If the current value in the dividend register is negative, and it has a zero bit corresponding to the starting one bit of the value in the divisor register, add the divisor register contents to the dividend reigster, and subtract the quotient term from the quotient register.

Shift the divisor register and the quotient term one place to the right, then repeat until finished (when the quotient term becomes zero at this step, do not repeat).

If, after the final step, the contents of the dividend register are negative, add the original divisor to the dividend register and subtract one from the quotient register. The dividend register will contain the remainder, and the quotient register the quotient.

An example of this is shown below:

Divide 10010100011 by 101101.

```
00010010100011 DD          0000000    Q
10110100000   DR          100000     QT
11111100000011 DD          0100000    Q
1011010000    DR          10000      QT
```

```
1111110000011 DD          0100000    Q
101101000     DR          1000       QT
1111110000011 DD          0100000    Q
10110100      DR          100        QT
1111110110111 DD          0011100    Q
1011010       DR          10         QT
0000000010001 DD          0011010    Q
101101        DR          1          QT
0000000010001 remainder   11010      quotient
```

which produces the correct result; 1187 divided by 45 gives 26 with 17 as the remainder.

Speeding up division further is also possible: One approach would be to begin with the divisor, from which 8, 4, and 2 times the divisor can be immediately derived, and then with one layer of addition stages, derive 3 (and hence 6 and 12) times the divisor, 5 (and hence 10) times the divisor, and 9 times the divisor, and then with a second layer of addition stages, derive the remaining multiples from 1 to 15 of the divisor.

Then an assembly of adders working in parallel to determine the largest multiple that could be subtracted from the dividend or the remaining part of it without causing it to go negative could generate four bits of the quotient in the time a conventional division algorithm could generate one.

The decimal version of this technique was used in the NORC computer, a vacuum tube computer designed for very high-speed calculation.

Another method of division is known as SRT division. In its original form, it was a development of nonrestoring division. Instead of choosing, at each bit position, to add or subtract the divisor, the option of doing nothing, and skipping quickly over several bits in the partial remainder, is also included.

Starting from the same example as given above for nonrestoring division:

Divide 10010100011 by 101101.

```
0001001010011      DD          0000000    Q
10110100000        DR          100000     QT
```

```
1111110000011    DD           0100000    Q
10110100         DR           100        QT
1111110110111    DD           0011100    Q
1011010          DR           10         QT
0000000010001    remainder    11010      quotient
```

Thus, when the partial remainder is positive, we align the divisor so that its first 1 bit is under the first one bit of the partial remainder, and subtract; we add a similarly shifted 1 to the quotient.

When the partial remainder is negative, we align the divisor so that its first 1 bit is under the first zero bit of the partial remainder,and add; we subtract a similarly shifted 1 from the quotient.

In the example, an immediate stop is shown when the right answer was achieved; normally, two additional steps would take place; first, a subtraction of the divisor, and then, since the result is negative, an addition in the same digit position; this is the same second chance without shifting as is used to terminate nonrestoring division.

The property of shifting at once over multiple zeroes is no longer present in the high-radix forms of SRT division.

Thus, in radix 4 SRT division, one might, at each step, either do nothing, add or subtract the divisor at its current shifted position, or add or subtract twice the divisor at its current shifted position. Instead of a simple rule of adding to a zero, and subtracting from a 1, a table of the first few bits of both the partial remainder and the divisor is needed to determine the appropriate action at each step.

To achieve time proportional to the logarithm of the length of the numbers involved, a method is required that attempts to refine an approximation of the reciprocal of the divisor. This basic method, which uses the recurrence relation

```
r' = r * (2 - r*x)
```

where x is the number whose reciprocal is to be found, and r and r′ are two successive approximations to its reciprocal, is known as Goldschmidt division, and is described in U.S. patent 3,508,038 with inventors Goldschmidt and Powers, assigned to IBM, and was developed for the IBM System/360 Model 91 computer. In the Model 91 computer, the results of floating-point divisions were rounded instead of truncated; this was an improvement on the behaviour of the other computers in the System/360 line, but it was still an incompatibility; one page claims that this was corrected in the Model 195 by prescaling, but refers to the characteristic of the Model 91 as though it were a serious bug, producing genuinely wrong answers, which it was not.

The recurrence relation can be made more understandable by splitting it into two parts. Given that r is an approximation to the reciprocal of x, then we can consider r*x to be 1+e, where e is a small error term reflecting the proportion by which r differs from the real reciprocal.

Thus, we can have as our first equation, containing one multiplication,

```
e = r*x - 1
```

If r is (1+e) times the real reciprocal, (1-e) times q will be a much closer approximation to the reciprocal, since the result will be (1-e^2) times the real reciprocal. Thus, the second multiplication can be part of the equation:

```
r' = (1 - e)*r
```

An advantage of leaving the recurrence relation in the form from which it was originally derived is that e is a small quantity compared to 1+e, and so significance can be preserved. We will see how this can be used below. One difficulty with the use of iterative methods for division is that they do not naturally lend themselves to producing the most accurate result in every case, as required by the IEEE 754 standard.

The obvious way of dealing with this is as follows: If one is calculating a/b, one begins by approximating the reciprocal of b. Because the accuracy of that approximation doubles with each iteration, there will be some excess precision available at the final iteration. Obtain an approximation to a/b by multiplying this result by a at the full working precision of the calculation. If the part of that result that needs to be rounded off to fit the quotient into the desired format is close enough to.4999... or.5000... to create concern (thinking of the mantissa as being scaled so as to become an integer in its ultimate destination), then, first replace that part by an exact.5. Multiply it by b, the divisor.

If the result is greater than a, then.5 is too high, so round down. If the result is less than a.5 is too low, so round up. Because allowing a division to take a variable amount of time could interfere with pipelining in some computer designs, work has been done on finding improved algorithms for IEEE 754 compliant Goldschmidt division.

A table-driven method of division for arguments of limited width, described in a paper by Hung, Fahmy, Mencer, and Flynn, can also be used to obtain an excellent initial approximation to the reciprocal in the time required for two multiplications; conventional techniques can then double the precision of the approximation in each additional multiplication time used.

To divide A by B: B will be normalized before starting, so that its value is between 1 and 2. The first few bits of B will be used to obtain two values from a table; one value will be an approximation to 1/B, and the other will be the derivative of the function 1/B with respect to B at the point indicated by the first few bits of B.

In the first multiplication time, multiply, in parallel, both A and B by the approximation to 1/B found in the table, and also multiply 1 plus the remaining bits of B, not used to find a table entry, by the second table entry. In the second multiplication time, multiply, in parallel, both the modified A and the modified B by the product involving the remaining bits of B. In subsequent steps, where the modified B is 1 + epsilon, multiply both the modified A and the modified B by 1 – epsilon. Since 1.001 times.999 is.999999, this doubles the precision in each step.

Basically, what is being done here is: as the reciprocal of the divisor is being determined by repeatedly multiplying the divisor by numbers that will bring it closer to 1, the dividend is being multiplied, in parallel, by these numbers, so that it does not need to be multiplied by the reciprocal of the divisor separately, at the end of the computation. Is one exchanging one multiplier for several? Not really, as the reciprocal of the divisor would have to be constructed from several individual multiplications if it were used explicitly. The need for several multipliers, instead of just two, comes from the desire to allow full pipelining.

It is the high-precision starting approximation obtained in the first two steps that was the unique contribution of this paper. Producing the quotient in parallel with the reciprocal as outlined above is also a potential feature of hardware implementations of the methods of producing accurate quotients by the iterative method outlined in the IBM and Intel patents referred to above.

Thus, the procedure given in the IBM patent involves a recurrence relation with four operations; the reciprocal of b, approximated by r, is improved by the two-step recurrence relation:

```
m  =  1  -  b*r
r'  =  r  +  m*r
```

(note that m stands for minus epsilon) and the quotient is improved in parallel by the operations:

```
s  =  a  -  b*q
q  =  q  +  s*r
```

By choosing an initial approximation to the reciprocal of b that is guaranteed to be greater than 1/b rather than less than 1/b for a divisor b whose mantissa consists entirely of ones, the final step is guaranteed to produce a result that will round properly.

Once enough approximation steps are performed so that the final r has the precision required, the two steps to improve the quotient are performed one extra time, with the second of the two steps also used to set the condition codes for the division operation as a whole. (All the preceding steps must be performed as round to nearest regardless of the rounding mode that is selected.)

In the Intel improvement of this method, it is noted that once epsilon, the error in an approximation to the reciprocal of b, is known, epsilon squared can be computed directly, instead of being discovered as the error in a subsequent step.

Thus, instead of approximating 1/(1+e) as 1-e, one can directly calculate an infinite product yielding the reciprocal,

$$(1 - e) * (1 + e^2) * (1 + e^4) * (1 + e^8) \ldots,$$

since,

$$(1 + e) * (1 - e) = 1 - e^2$$
$$(1 - e^2) * (1 + e^2) = 1 - e^4$$
$$(1 - e^4) * (1 + e^4) = 1 - e^8$$
$$(1 - e^8) * (1 + e^8) = 1 - e^{16}$$

and so on: if one thinks of the first term as 1-e insted of 1+e, then all the corrections are in the same direction. A method to obtain a further improvement in efficiency in this type of calculation is discussed in a paper by Ercegovac, Imbert, Matula, Muller, and Wei from Inria.

It can happen that the initial approximation to the reciprocal of the divisor is such that as it doubles in accuracy in each step, instead of having half the required accuracy just before the final step, it may be short of the required accuracy by only a few bits. In that case, instead of squaring e^n to obtain e^(2n), one could simply look up 1 + e^(2n) in a table using the first few bits of e, and this could be done at an early point in the computation.

Although it still takes two multiplies per iteration, it is also still an improvement, because it now takes only one add.

SQUARE ROOT

Using the formula (a+b)^2 = a^2 + 2ab + b^2, a method for calculating square roots by hand was devised that resembles long division:

```
8. 4 2 6 1 4 9
----------------------
71. 00 00 00 00 00 00   |
64                      |
---------------------   |
  7.00                  | 1 6
  6.56                  | 4
  --------------------- |
  44 00                 | 16 8
  33 64                 | 2
```

```
-----------------------|
 10 36 00              | 1 68 4
 10 10 76              | 6
 ----------------------|
    25 24 00           | 16 85 2
    16 85 21           | 1
    -------------------|
      8 38 79 00       | 1 68 52 2
      6 73 29 44       | 4
      -----------------|
      1 55 49 56 00    | 16 85 22 8
      1 51 67 06 01    | 9
      -----------------|
         3 82 49 99    |
```

To find the square root of 71, first, it is noted that 71 is between 64 and 81. Thus, we subtract 8 squared, or 64, from 71, and note that our square root will be 8 point something. In subsequent steps, what has gone before will play the role of a in the formula above, and the next digit in the square root will play the role of b. And, as with 8, a^2 has already been subtracted, so, for whatever digit we choose as b, we must be able to subtract 2ab + b^2 from what remains.

Thus, let us choose 4 as the next digit in the square root. We will subtract 2 * 8 *.4 plus.4 squared, which is 6.56, from the number. On the next line, what we are dividing by (with the allowance that the b^2 term may change what we use) is 2 * 8.4, which is 16.8. This goes into.44 a bit more than.02 times, so we get 33 60 plus 04, or 33 64 to subtract.

8.42 times 2 is 16.84; this goes into.1036.006 times, and so we get 10 10 76 to subtract. Finally, we start with 8.426 * 2, which is 16.852, and divide.002524 by it, to get 1, and so we subtract 16 85 21. As the last decimal place of a is one position ahead of b, if we treat both terms as integers instead of as real numbers, the formula becomes 20*ab+b^2, which is what is used when this is done in a more mechanical fashion.

Other than noting that as the numbers involved keep growing, this is not useful as a method of pseudorandom number generation, not much more need be said.

The resemblance between this method of calculating square roots and long division is sufficiently close that it is possible to adapt, for example, high-radix SRT division to calculating square roots. If the first part of the square root is determined from a table, the 2ab term will be large enough, compared to the b^2 term, that a modified table, giving the value of b to try from 2a and the current remainder will keep the error small enough so that it is always possible to proceed to the next digit on the next step.

Another method of approximating the square root of a number is available for computers, which is much faster for sufficiently large numbers, or when performed in software, known as Newton-Raphson iteration. In fact, the method of approximating the reciprocal of a number shown above is another example of Newton-Raphson iteration.

If r is our existing approximation, and r′ is the improved approximation, for 1/x, the recurrence relation was:

```
r' = r * (2 - r*x)
```

since if r = (1/x)*(1+e), for some small e, 2 - x*r is 1-e, and (1+e)*(1-e) is 1 - e^2, which is much closer to one.

For square root, we get the recurrence relation:

```
        1  x
r'  =-    (— + r)
        2  r
```

and, as x/r and r have, to the first order, equal and opposite discrepancies from the square root of x, r′ is once again much closer to the right answer than r.

This is the classic Newton-Raphson iteration for square root. Given that division is slower than multiplication, can it be improved upon?

One simple-minded approach might be to start with an approximation to the square root, r, and an approximation to the reciprocal of the square root, q, and also calculate y, the reciprocal of x, at the beginning.

Then, use the pair of recurrence relations:

```
         1
r'  =    -   (qx + r)
         2
```

```
          1
q'  =  -   (q + ry)
          2
```

If q is initially the reciprocal of r, then r′ and q′ are better approximations than r and q after the first step. Perhaps they will continue to improve in later steps, a less elaborate iteration which simply improves q that apparently has been used in practice both on Burroughs and Cray machines (my source, which claimed that, had a typographical error, and omitted the factor of 1/2), is the following:

```
          1
q'  =  -   q * (3 - x * q * q)
          2
```

Let us suppose that q is equal to the true reciprocal of the square root of x, which we will call p, times (1 + e). Since e is small, 1/(1+e) is approximately 1-e. Then, q * (3 - x * q * q) becomes, approximately, p * (1 + e) * (3 – (1 + 2e)), which is p * (1 + e) * (2 – 2e), which is approximately 2p, and, thus, half of that is a new approximation in which the new error is of the order of the square of the old error.

LOG AND TRIG FUNCTIONS:

A fast method of calculating trigonometric functions using only shifts and adds was described in a paper which described how it was applied to a device bearing the acronym CORDIC as its name.

A vector (x,y) can be rotated through an angle theta by means of the equations:

```
x' = x cos(theta) - y sin(theta)
y' = y cos(theta) + x sin(theta)
```

In the CORDIC algorithm, a table is required whose contents are:

```
arctangent(1/2)
arctangent(1/4)
arctangent(1/8)
arctangent(1/16)
...
```

Beginning with suitable starting values of x and y, one

iterates through a fixed number of steps wherein one performs either

```
x' = x - y M
y' = y + x M
```

or

```
x' = x + y M
y' = y - x M
```

M starts as 1/2, and is divided by two at each step, so multiplying x and y by M is simply a shift. This enlarges the vector (x,y) in addition to rotating it by plus or minus the arctangent of M.

If one is calculating the sine or cosine of an angle, one adds or subtracts the table value from the angle to bring the result closer to zero, to decide which operation is to be performed. Then, the starting values of x and y are chosen so that the successive enlargements will lead, at the end, to a vector whose length is exactly 1.

If one is trying to find an inverse trigonometric function, the goal is instead to make y equal to zero, although striving to make x equal to y will also work, provided one adds 45 degrees to the angle one uses as the starting point.

In that case, one wishes to find theta, so the scaling of x and y are irrelevant; therefore, the rule about performing either a clockwise or counterclockwise rotation at each step is no longer required.

To find either the arcsine or arccosine, one has to first modify the input by a calculation involving a square root, as due to the scaling at each step, only the arctangent can be found directly by this method.

For that method, one requires a table containing the values:

```
log(1 1/2)
log(1 1/2)
log(1 1/4)
log(1 1/8)
log(1 1/16)
...
```

and to find the logarithm of a number between 1 and 2, one at each step chooses either to leave it alone, or add it to itself shifted right by the number of places N that is also the number of the step; the latter is done if its result is less than or equal to 2.

Since, in this method, we don't have to worry about always having to perform a clockwise or counterclockwise rotation in each step, so that the scaling factor is not altered, it is easy to adapt this method to decimal arithmetic. One can have a table of log(2), log(1.1), log(1.01), and so on, and just repeat the steps at each level up to nine times. This was indeed how logarithms were calculated on the HP-35 calculator, for example.

Could one just always go through five steps for each digit? Or six steps? That won't quite work, since however many steps one uses, the total number of steps is either even or odd. So one would have to go through ten steps for each digit instead; after using arctan(0.001), the error going into using arctan(0.0001) would be up to a factor of 1.002, not 1.001.

Given that, there is no loss using a simpler method; when it is necessary to worry about the scale factor (it is not for inverse trig functions, or for calculating the tangent, it is only a concern for sine and cosine) one still can simply either perform the calculation with the arctangent of decimal 0.1, 0.01, 0.001, 0.0001 and so on or not in up to five steps in either direction. At the end, just calculate sqrt(x*x+y*y) to obtain the scale factor.

Although these methods are quite rapid compared to the conventional method of using the Taylor series to approximate a function, they are not the fastest methods known, at least asymptotically for numbers with very high precision. It is possible to evaluate these elementary transcendental functions, as it is possible to perform division, in a time comparable to that required for multiplication; that is, in a number of addition times proportional to the logarithm of the length of the number.

Originally, CORDIC methods were applied to small computer systems with limited hardware resources, to which they are very well suited, but despite the possibility of better methods in theory for the case of very high precisions, the

CORDIC methods are still useful in large computers as well, if they calculate transcendental functions in hardware instead of software. They are superseded by other methods, though, for multi-precision arithmetic, particularly in the régimes where one would use Schönhage-Strassen multiplication. These algorithms, as described here, require comparisons to be made at each step, on the basis of which decisions are made.

While it would not be possible to make the exact comparisons noted here without completing the additions, and performing carry propagation, can comparisons of a limited type be performed on numbers in the raw redundant form used with carry-save adders, and, if so, can these algorithms be modified to make use of such comparisons? One encouraging factor is that, since multiplication is not used, we do not necessarily have to contend with the negative values that are required for Booth encoding.

If instead of having one binary number, we have two binary numbers that we wish to avoid adding, and we want to say something about their combined value by looking only at their first few bits, we can indeed say that if both numbers are of the form 000xxxxx, their sum is of the form 00xxxxxx.

But some pairs of numbers not of the form 000xxxxx will also have sums of the form 00xxxxxx.

The modification of the CORDIC algorithms for this situation that suggests itself is something based on using twice as many steps, involving changes to the numbers of half the size at each step.

The hyperbolic functions sinh and cosh are defined as:

$$\mathrm{sinh}(x) = \frac{e^{x} - e^{-x}}{2}$$

$$\mathrm{coshx)} = \frac{e^{x} + e^{-x}}{2}$$

We know that:

```
x + y x y
e = e * e
```

and so we can derive the equations,

```
sinh(x+y) = sinh(x)cosh(y) + cosh(x)sinh(y)
cosh(x+y) = sinh(x)sinh(y) + cosh(x)cosh(y)
```

Here, since cosh(x) is always greater than sinh(x), we can choose values of y such that 1/(tanh(y)) is equal to 2, 1 1/2, 1 1/4, 1 1/8, and so on to produce sinh(x) and cosh(x) for arbitrary values of x, starting from some fixed value of x.

Thus, for each step, we once again have:

$$K_n * \sinh(x + y_n) = \sinh(x)\ (1 + 2^{-n}) + \cosh(x)$$

$$K_n * \cosh(x + y_n) = \sinh(x) + \cosh(x)\ (1 + 2^{-n})$$

where K[n] is 1/sinh(y[n]), where (1 + 2^(–n)) = 1/tanh(y[n]).

As with the trigonometric functions, sinh(–x) = -sinh(x) and cosh(-x) = cosh(x), so, once again, we can "rotate" either clockwise or counterclockwise at each step, and we need to do so to keep the scaling consistent at the end *if it is sinh, cosh, or the exponential function we are calculating.*

Since cosh(x) + sinh(x) = e^x, this can be used as an alternative method of calculating the exponential function, or even logarithms. To calculate logarithms, we would start from a value for x based on the number whose logarithm we wish, so that the test performed in each round on the current approximation would not require scaling. Again, if the logarithm is desired, scaling ceases to be an issue.

Logarithms

Since addition is quicker and requires less circuitry than multiplication, some systems convert numbers to their logarithms at the time of input, retaining them in this form only in memory.

Occasionally, though, one has to add and subtract as well as multiply and divide. A paper by S. C. Lee and A. D. Edgar, "The FOCUS number system", described a way to do this using a relatively short look-up table.

Given two numbers a and b, and assuming without loss of generality that a is less than b, one can easily calculate r=a/b.

If one then uses r to find (r+1)/r in a table, the value from the table can be multiplied by b to give a+b. This table is shorter than a lookup table for converting to or from a logarithmic representation, because cases where a is negligible compared to b can be omitted. A table of (r-1)/r is also needed for subtraction. Unfortunately, there does not seem to be a good way to prevent errors from accumulating, so that one could adapt this to multi-precision arithmetic. However, floating-point numbers are used in implementations of Schönhage-Strassen arithmetic, and so there may be possibilities in that direction.

Chapter 7

Memory

CONCEPTS OF HIERARCHY

In principle, for a simple single processor machine, the memory architecture is quite simple -- the memory is connected to the memory address lines and the memory data lines so that whenever an address is presented to the memory the data corresponding to that address appears on the data lines. This is adequate for processors which can address a relatively small address space. However, for larger systems with 32-64 address lines these machines can address 2^{32} (4000 M) bytes to 2^{64} (16×1018) bytes of memory it is not practical to provide all the memory that the machine can address. Logically, memory is structured as a linear array of locations, with addresses from 0 to the maximum memory size for the processor.

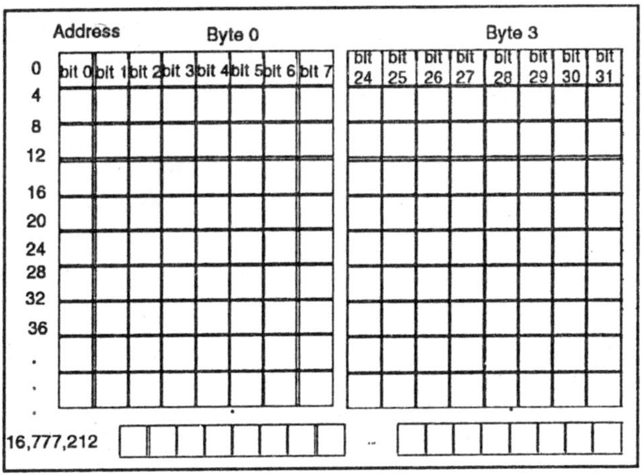

Fig. Memory Organization.

Note that the position of each word in the linear array is indicated by an address. Each byte can be addressed individually (although a whole word is read from memory at one time.) Consequently, word addresses increase by 4, starting from 0. In general, the faster a memory is in general the more expensive it is per bit of storage.

On systems which have a large amount of memory, there is usually a hierarchy of memories, each with different access speeds and storage capacities. Typically, a large system has a small amount of very high speed memory, called a cache where data from frequently used memory locations may be temporarily stored.

This cache is connected to a much larger ``main memory"which is a medium speed memory, currently likely to be ``dynamic memory"with access time from 100-1000 ns. Cache memory access times are typically 10 to 20 times faster than main memory access times, typically from 5 - 40 ns. (In some very large computer systems, the main memory is organized into two or more ``banks", each of which contains adjacent memory words which can be addressed individually and simultaneously. A memory organized in this way is called an ``interleaved"memory.)

The largest block of ``memory"in a modern computer system is usually one or more large magnetic disks, on which data is stored in fixed size blocks of from 256 to 8192 bytes. This disk memory is usually connected directly to the main memory, and has a variable access time depending on how far the disk head must move to reach the appropriate track, and how much the disk must rotate to reach the appropriate sector for the data.

(Some very large systems have multiple head disks which can read from several tracks at once). A modern Winchester disk has a track-to-track latency of about 1-2 ms., and the disk rotates at a speed of 3600 RPM. The disk therefore makes one revolution in 1/60th of a second, or 16.7 ms. The average rotational latency is therefore about 8.4 ms. Faster disks (using smaller diametre disk plates) can rotate even faster. A typical memory system, connected to a medium-to-large size computer (a desktop or server configuration) might consist of the following:

128K-2M bytes of cache memory (5-50ns)
64-256 M bytes of main memory (400-2000ns)
2000-20,000 M bytes of disk storage

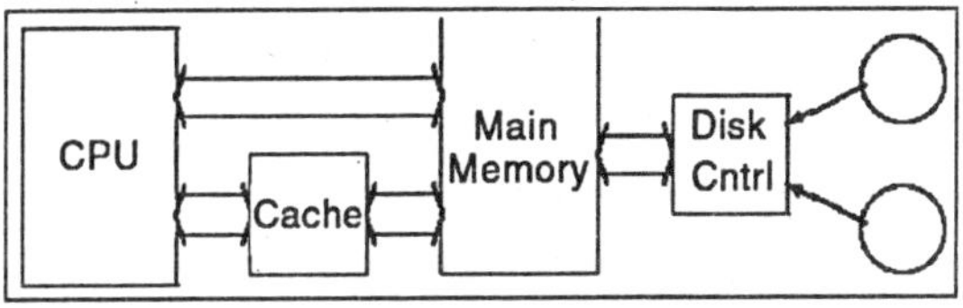

Fig. A Typical Memory Configuration.

THE JET CONCEPT HIERARCHY

The Jet system includes a concept hierarchy. This hierarchy is basically a set of concepts arranged in a tree structure. Associated with each concept are zero or more words which are instances of that concept.

The Concept Hierarchy File

The concept hierarchy is defined by a concept hierarchy file. The file contains lines of the form

```
human isa thing
human words person, man
```

where human and thing are concepts, and person and man are words; isa and words are the only two keywords. This file indicates that human is a subtype of thing, and human is associated with the words person and man. Concept names should begin with a lower-case letter, and may contain lower and upper case letters; a word is normally all lower case. No two concepts in the hierarchy can have the same name, and no two words in the hierarchy can be the same. A concept name and a word can be the same though. Concept hierarchy files should typically have the file extension .hrc.

Loading the concepts

A concept file can be loaded into the system by including a line of the form

Concepts.fileName = filename

Using the Concepts

In an annotation pattern element, in place of a feature test of the form feature=value, one can have a test of the form feature ?isa(concept) This feature test succeeds if the value of feature is a word associated with concept, or associated with some concept'which is a descendant of concept in the hierarchy.

Using the Concept Hierarchy UI

The Concept Hierarchy UI is an editor for concept hierarchy (.hrc) files. You start the Concept Hierarchy UI by selecting"Concept Window"in the Jet File menu. If a hierarchy has been specified in the Jet properties file, it will appear. The Concept Hierarchy UI has the basic features of an editor such as those for a text editor.

File Open, Save, SaveAs and Exit do the standard file IO (note that Exit quits Jet, not just the UI). If a concept hierarchy file is changed after it was last saved, it is marked as dirty with an asterisk after the file name in the window caption. A dialog message will pop up asking if the current file is to be saved. There is a bug here: if the window is being closed when the file is dirty, a dialog pops up, and then the"cancel"button is pressed, the window will become invisible without anything done to the file. If the"Exit"menu item is chosen instead, everything works just as fine.

From the"Edit"menu, you can add, delete, rename and search concepts and words. There is a bug here: when you rename a concept or word either by selecting the "Rename" menu item or clicking on the concept or word itself, then type in the new name and carriage return, an error message will pop out if the new name is an empty string or causes duplicate in the hierarchy.

After you press OK to get rid of the message, the concept or word is still being edited, if you press ESC, the bad name will be accepted. It's the user's responsibility not to deliberately introduce this kind of error into the file at the time being because the editor is not so stubborn as to give the same advice twice. The Drag-and-Drop feature has been added to the editor, making it easier to move a large portion of a hierarchy from one place to another. Note that only move is provided but not copy, even though by pressing CTRL when dragging a node, the cursor will have a"+"sign. The copy function is not provided because no duplicate concepts and words are allowed in a hierarchy.

SEMICONDUCTORS RAM MEMORIES

Memory is an essential element of today's electronics. Normally based around semiconductor technology, memory is used in any equipment that uses a processor of one form or another. Indeed as processors have become more popular and the number of microprocessor controlled items has increased so has the requirement for semiconductor memory.

An additional driver has been the fact that the software associated with the processors and computers has become more sophisticated and much larger, and this too has greatly increased the requirement for semiconductor memory. In addition to this new applications such as digital cameras, PDAs and many more applications have given rise to the need to memories. Accordingly it is not uncommon to see semiconductor memories of 4 Gbyte and more required for various applications.

With the rapid growth in the requirement for semiconductor memories there have been a number of technologies and types of memory that have emerged. Names such as ROM, RAM, EPROM, EEPROM, Flash memory, DRAM, SRAM, SDRAM, and the very new MRAM can now be seen in the electronics literature. Each one has its own advantages and area in which it may be used.

There is provided a semiconductor memory device for preventing an increase of a cell area of a Shadow RAM comprising a portion of an SRAM memory cell and a ferroelectric capacitor connected to a storage node of the portion of the SRAM memory cell and achieving high capacitance formation of a storage capacitor. The Shadow RAM is provided with a relay wiring layer between a wiring layer corresponding to the storage node and a lower electrode of the ferroelectric capacitor, a wiring corresponding to the storage node is connected to a relay wiring via a first and a second opening portion arranged at a first interval and the lower electrode of the ferroelectric capacitor is connected to a relay wiring via a third and a fourth opening portion arranged at a second interval narrower than the first interval.

Detailed Description it is an object of the invention to provide a semiconductor memory apparatus for preventing an increase in a cell area of a memory cell of a Shadow RAM and achieving high capacity formation of a storage capacitor. Further, it is an object of the invention to provide a semiconductor memory apparatus capable of designing a Shadow RAM by utilizing design data of a wiring layer of a transistor applied to an SRAM which has been generally used conventionally, as it is. Further, it is an object of the invention to provide a semiconductor memory apparatus achieving a reduction in a number of steps of design of a Shadow RAM and shortening of a design period of time and having a large storage capacity. A semiconductor memory apparatus according to the invention includes an SRAM memory cell and a Shadow RAM memory cell.

The Shadow RAM memory cell is provided with a ferroelectric capacitor at the SRAM memory cell and is constituted such that an area of the Shadow RAM memory cell is equal to an area of the memory cell of SRAM. Further, a semiconductor memory apparatus according to the invention at least includes a Shadow RAM having a ferroelectric capacitor at an SRAM memory cell, the Shadow RAM includes a relay wiring layer and two storage nodes of a portion of the SRAM memory cell is connected to the low electric capacitor respectively via a relay wiring of the relay wiring layer and an opening portion.

The respective storage nodes and the relay wiring of the relay wiring layer are connected via a first and a second opening portion and the relay wiring and a lower electrode of the ferroelectric capacitor are connected via a third and a fourth opening portion. The relay wiring is provided to make a distance between the third and the fourth opening portions narrower than the distance between the first and the second opening portions. That is, the relay wiring layer is provided, the relay wiring layer is formed with the relay wiring for connecting an upper layer wiring layer and a lower layer wiring layer in an arbitrary pattern shape and a position of an opening portion for connecting the upper layer wiring layer connected to the relay wiring and a position of an opening portion for connecting the lower layer wiring are set to different arbitrary positions

SEMICONDUCTOR MEMORY

Electronic semiconductor memory can be split into two main categories, according to the way in which they operate:

- RAM - Random Access Memory
- ROM - Read Only Memory

As the names suggest, the RAM or random access memory is used or reading and writing data in any order as required. It is used for such applications as the computer or processor memory where variables and other stored and are required on a random basis. Data is stored and read many times to and from this type of memory.

A ROM is a form of semiconductor memory to which data is written once and then not changed. In view of this technologies can be used that retain the data once the power is removed. As a result, this type of memory is widely used for storing programmes and data that must survive when a computer or processor is powered down.

For example the BIOS of a computer will be stored in ROM. As the name implies, data cannot be easily written to ROM. Depending on the technology used in the ROM, writing the data into the ROM initially may require special hardware. Although it is often possible to change the data, this gain requires special hardware to erase the data ready for new data to be written in.

OVERVIEW OF MEMORY TECHNOLOGIES

There is a large variety of types of ROM and RAM that are available. These arise from the variety of applications and also the number of technologies available. This means that there is a large number of abbreviations or acronyms and categories for memories ranging from Flash to MRAM, PROM to EEPROM, and many more:

Prom

This stands for Programmable Read Only Memory. It is a semiconductor memory which can only have data written to it once - the data written to it is permanent. These memories are bought in a blank format and they are programmed using a special PROM programmer. Typically a PROM will consist of an array of fuseable links some of which are"blown"during the programming process to provide the required data pattern.

Eprom

This is an Erasable Programmable Read Only Memory. This form of semiconductor memory can be programmed and then erased at a later time. This is normally achieved by exposing the silicon to ultraviolet light. To enable this to happen there is a circular window in the package of the EPROM to enable the light to reach the silicon of the chip. When the PROM is in use, this window is normally covered by a label, especially when the data may need to be preserved for an extended period.

The PROM stores its data as a charge on a capacitor. These is a charge storage capacitor for each cell and this can be read repeatedly as required. However it is found that after many years the charge may leak away and the data may be lost. Nevertheless, this type of semiconductor memory used to be widely used in applications where a form of ROM was required, but where the data needed to be changed periodically, as in a development environment, or where quantities were low.

Eeprom

This is an Electrically Erasable Programmable Read Only Memory. Data can be written to it and it can be erased using an electrical voltage. This is typically applied to an erase pin on the chip. Like other types of PROM, EEPROM retains the contents of the memory even when the power is turned off. Also like other types of ROM, EEPROM is not as fast as RAM.

Flash Memory

Flash memory may be considered as a development of EEPROM technology. Data can be written to it and it can be erased, although only in blocks, but data can be read on an individual cell basis.

To erase and re-programme areas of the chip, programming voltages at levels that are available within electronic equipment are used. It is also non-volatile, and this makes it particularly useful. As a result Flash memory is widely used in many applications including memory cards for digital cameras, mobile phones, computer memory sticks and many other applications.

Dram

Dynamic RAM is a form of random access memory. DRAM uses a capacitor to store each bit of data, and the level of charge on each capacitor determines whether that bit is a logical 1 or 0.

However these capacitors do not hold their charge indefinitely, and therefore the data needs to be refreshed periodically. As a result of this dynamic refreshing it gains its name of being a dynamic RAM. DRAM is the form of semiconductor memory that is often used in equipment including personal computers and workstations where it forms the main RAM for the computer.

Sram

Static Random Access Memory. This form of semiconductor memory gains its name from the fact that, unlike DRAM, the data does not need to be refreshed dynamically. It is able to support faster read and write times than DRAM (typically 10 ns against 60 ns for DRAM), and in addition its cycle time is much shorter because it does not need to pause between accesses. However it consumes more power, is less dense and more expensive than DRAM. As a result of this it is normally used for caches, while DRAM is used as the main semiconductor memory technology.

Sdram

Synchronous DRAM. This form of semiconductor memory can run at faster speeds than conventional DRAM. It is synchronised to the clock of the processor and is capable of keeping two sets of memory addresses open simultaneously. By transferring data alternately from one set of addresses, and then the other, SDRAM cuts down on the delays associated with non-synchronous RAM, which must close one address bank before opening the next.

MRAM

This is Magneto-resistive RAM, or Magnetic RAM. It is a non-volatile RAM memory technology that uses magnetic charges to store data instead of electric charges. Unlike technologies including DRAM, which require a constant flow of electricity to maintain the integrity of the data, MRAM retains data even when the power is removed. An additional advantage is that it only requires low power for active operation. As a result this technology could become a major player in the electronics industry now that production processes have been developed to enable it to be

Semiconductor memory technology is moving forward apace. Not only are the sizes of memories being increased, and the data densities improving, but new forms of semiconductor memory such as MRAM are being introduced. With the requirements for ever larger, faster and lower power memories always increasing, this area of technology will remain one of the most dynamic in the electronics industry.

READ-ONLY MEMORY (ROM)

DEFINITION

One major type of memory that is used in PCs is called read-only memory, or ROM for short. ROM is a type of memory that normally can only be read, as opposed to RAM which can be both read and written. There are two main reasons that read-only memory is used for certain functions within the PC:

PERMANENCE

The values stored in ROM are always there, whether the power is on or not. A ROM can be removed from the PC, stored for an indefinite period of time, and then replaced, and the data it contains will still be there. For this reason, it is called non-volatile storage. A hard disk is also non-volatile, for the same reason, but regular RAM is not.

SECURITY

The fact that ROM cannot easily be modified provides a measure of security against accidental (or malicious) changes to its contents. You are not going to find viruses infecting true ROMs, for example; it's just not possible. (It's technically possible with erasable EPROMs, though in practice never seen.) Read-only memory is most commonly used to store system-level programmes that we want to have available to the PC at all times.

The most common example is the system BIOS programme, which is stored in a ROM called (amazingly enough) the system BIOS ROM. Having this in a permanent ROM means it is available when the power is turned on so that the PC can use it to boot up the system. Remember that when you first turn on the PC the system memory is empty, so there has to be something for the PC to use when it starts up. this section for a description of the system BIOS ROM; see here for a description of the system boot sequence.

While the whole point of a ROM is supposed to be that the contents cannot be changed, there are times when being able to change the contents of a ROM can be very useful. There are several ROM variants that can be changed under certain circumstances; these can be thought of as"mostly read-only memory".:^) The following are the different types of ROMs with a description of their relative modifiability:

FEATURES

A regular ROM is constructed from hard-wired logic, encoded in the silicon itself, much the way that a processor is. It is designed to perform a specific function and cannot be changed. This is inflexible and so regular ROMs are only used generally for programmes that are static (not changing often) and mass-produced. This product is analagous to a commercial software CD-ROM that you purchase in a store.

PROGRAMMABLE ROM (PROM)

This is a type of ROM that can be programmed using special equipment; it can be written to, but only once. This is useful for companies that make their own ROMs from software they write, because when they change their code they can create new PROMs without requiring expensive equipment. This is similar to the way a CD-ROM recorder works by letting you"burn"programmes onto blanks once and then letting you read from them many times. In fact, programming a PROM is also called burning, just like burning a CD-R, and it is comparable in terms of its flexibility.

ERASABLE PROGRAMMABLE ROM (EPROM)

An EPROM is a ROM that can be erased and reprogrammed. A little glass window is installed in the top of the ROM package, through which you can actually see the chip that holds the memory. Ultraviolet light of a specific frequency can be shined through this window for a specified period of time, which will erase the EPROM and allow it to be reprogrammed again. Obviously this is much more useful than a regular PROM, but it does require the erasing light. Continuing the"CD"analogy, this technology is analogous to a reusable CD-RW.

ELECTRICALLY ERASABLE PROGRAMMABLE ROM (EEPROM)

The next level of erasability is the EEPROM, which can be erased under software control. This is the most flexible type of ROM, and is now commonly used for holding BIOS programmes. When you hear reference to a"flash BIOS"or doing a BIOS upgrade by"flashing", this refers to reprogramming the BIOS EEPROM with a special software programme.

Here we are blurring the line a bit between what"read-only"really means, but remember that this rewriting is done maybe once a year or so, compared to real read-write memory (RAM) where rewriting is done often many times per second!

NOTE

One thing that sometimes confuses people is that since RAM is the"opposite"of ROM (since RAM is read-write and ROM is read-only), and since RAM stands for"random access memory", they think that ROM is not random access. This is not true; any location can be read from ROM in any order, so it is random access as well, just not writeable. RAM gets its name because earlier read-write memories were sequential, and did not allow random access.

Finally, one other characteristic of ROM, compared to RAM, is that it is much slower, typically having double the access time of RAM or more. This is one reason why the code in the BIOS ROM is often shadowed to improve performance.

There is a type of memory that stores data without electrical current; it is the ROM (Read Only Memory) or is sometimes called non-volatile memory as it is not erased when the system is switched off.

This type of memory lets you stored the data needed to start up the computer. Indeed, this information cannot be stored on the hard disk since the disk parametres (vital for its initialisation) are part of these data which are essential for booting. Different ROM-type memories contain these essential start-up data, i.e.:

- The BIOS is a programme for controlling the system's main input-output interfaces, hence the nameBIOS ROM which is sometimes given to the read-only memory chip of the mother board which hosts it.
- *The bootstrap loader*: A programme for loading

(random access) memory into the operating system and launching it. This generally seeks the operating system on the floppy drive then on the hard disk, which allows the operating system to be launched from a system floppy disk in the event of malfunction of the system installed on the hard disk.

- The CMOS Setup is the screen displayed when the computer starts up and which is used to amend the system parametres (often wrongly referred to as BIOS).
- The Power-On Self Test (POST), a programme that runs automatically when the system is booted, thus allowing the system to be tested (this is why the system"counts"the RAM at start-up).

Given that ROM are much slower than RAM memories (access time for a ROM is around 150 ns whereas for SDRAM it is around 10 ns), the instructions given in the ROM are sometimes copied to the RAM at start-up; this is known as shadowing, though is usually referred to as shadow memory).

TYPES OF ROM

ROM memories have gradually evolved from fixed read-only memories to memories than can be programmed and then re-programmed.

ROM

The first ROMs were made using a procedure that directly writes the binary data in a silicon plate using a mask. This procedure is now obsolete.

PROM

PROM (Programmable Read Only Memory) memories were developed at the end of the 70s by a company called Texas Instruments. These memories are chips comprising thousands of fuses (or diodes) that can be"burnt"using a device called a"ROM programmer", applying high voltage (12V) to the memory boxes to be marked. The fuses thus burnt correspond to 0 and the others to 1.

EPROM

EPROM (Erasable Programmable Read Only Memory) memories are PROMs that can be deleted. These chips have a glass panel that lets ultra-violet rays through. When the chip is subjected to ultra-violet rays with a certain wavelength, the fuses are reconstituted, meaning that all the memory bits return to 1. This is why this type of PROM is called erasable.

EEPROM

EEPROM (Electrically Erasable Read Only Memory memories are also erasable PROMs, but unlike EPROMs, they can be erased by a simple electric current, meaning that they can be erased even when they are in position in the computer.

There is a variant of these memories known as flash memories (also Flash ROM or Flash EPROM). Unlike the classic EEPROMs that use 2 to 3 transistors for each bit to be memorised, the EPROM Flash uses only one transistor. Moreover, the EEPROM may be written and read word by word, while the Flash can be erased only in pages (the size of the pages decreases constantly). Lastly, the Flash memory is denser, meaning that chips containing several hundred mega octets can be produced. EEPROMs are thus used preferably to memorise configuration data and the Flash memory is used for programmable code (IT programmes).

CACHE MEMORIES

CACHE MEMORY

The cache is a small amount of high-speed memory, usually with a memory cycle time comparable to the time required by the CPU to fetch one instruction. The cache is usually filled from main memory when instructions or data are fetched into the CPU. Often the main memory will supply a wider data word to the cache than the CPU requires, to fill the cache more rapidly. The amount of information which is replaces at one time in the cache is called the line size for the cache. This is normally the width of the data bus between the cache memory and the main memory. A wide line size for the cache means that several instruction or data words are loaded into the cache at one time, providing a kind of pre fetching for instructions or data. Since the cache is small, the effectiveness of the cache relies on the following properties of most programmes:

Spatial Locality

Most programmes are highly sequential; the next instruction usually comes from the next memory location. Data is usually structured, and data in these structures normally are stored in contiguous memory locations.

- Short loops are a common programme structure, especially for the innermost sets of nested loops. This means that the same small set of instructions is used over and over.

Generally, several operations are performed on the same data values, or variables. When a cache is used, there must be some way in which the memory controller determines whether the value currently being addressed in memory is available from the cache. There are several ways that this can be accomplished. One possibility is to store both the address and the value from main memory in the cache, with the address stored in a type of memory called associative memory or, more descriptively, content addressable memory.

An associative memory, or content addressable memory, has the property that when a value is presented to the memory, the address of the value is returned if the value is stored in the memory, otherwise an indication that the value is not in the associative memory is returned.

All of the comparisons are done simultaneously, so the search is performed very quickly. This type of memory is very expensive, because each memory location must have both a comparator and a storage element. A cache memory can be implemented with a block of associative memory, together with a block of ``ordinary"memory. The associative memory would hold the address of the data stored in the cache, and the ordinary memory would contain the data at that address. Such a cache memory might be configured as shown in Figure..

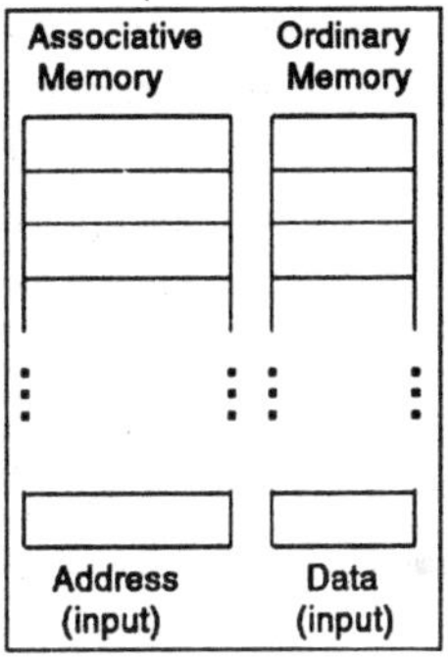

Fig. A Cache Implemented with Associative Memory.

If the address is not found in the associative memory, then the value is obtained from main memory. Associative memory is very expensive, because a comparator is required for every word in the memory, to perform all the comparisons in parallel. A cheaper way to implement a cache memory, without using expensive associative memory, is to use direct mapping. Here, part of the memory address (usually the low order digits of the address) is used to address a word in the cache. This part of the address is called the index. The remaining high-order bits in the address, called the tag, are stored in the cache memory along with the data. For example, if a processor has an 18 bit address for memory, and a cache of 1 K words of 2 bytes (16 bits) length, and the processor can address single bytes or 2 byte words, we might have the memory address field and cache.

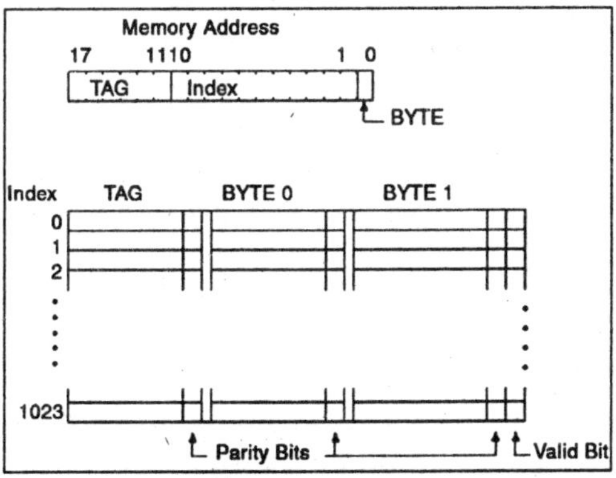

Fig. A Direct Mapped Cache Configuration.

This was, in fact, the way the cache is organized in the PDP-11/60. In the 11/60, however, there are 4 other bits used to ensure that the data in the cache is valid. 3 of these are parity bits; one for each byte and one for the tag. The parity bits are used to check that a single bit error has not occurred to the data while in the cache.

A fourth bit, called the valid bit is used to indicate whether or not a given location in cache is valid. In the PDP-11/60 and in many other processors, the cache is not updated if memory is altered by a device other than the CPU (for example when a disk stores new data in memory).

When such a memory operation occurs to a location which has its value stored in cache, the valid bit is reset to show that the data is ``stale"and does not correspond to the data in main memory. As well, the valid bit is reset when power is first applied to the processor or when the processor recovers from a power failure, because the data found in the cache at that time will be invalid.

In the PDP-11/60, the data path from memory to cache was the same size (16 bits) as from cache to the CPU. (In the PDP-11/70, a faster machine, the data path from the CPU to cache was 16 bits, while from memory to cache was 32 bits which means that the cache had effectively pre fetched the next instruction, approximately half of the time).

The amount of information (instructions or data) stored with each tag in the cache is called the line size of the cache. (It is usually the same size as the data path from main memory to the cache.) A large line size allows the prefetching of a number of instructions or data words. All items in a line of the cache are replaced in the cache simultaneously, however, resulting in a larger block of data being replaced for each cache miss.

The MIPS R2000/R3000 had a built-in cache controller which could control a cache up to 64K bytes. For a similar 2K word (or 8K byte) cache, the MIPS processor would typically have a cache configuration. Generally, the MIPS cache would be larger (64Kbytes would be typical, and line sizes of 1, 2 or 4 words would be typical).

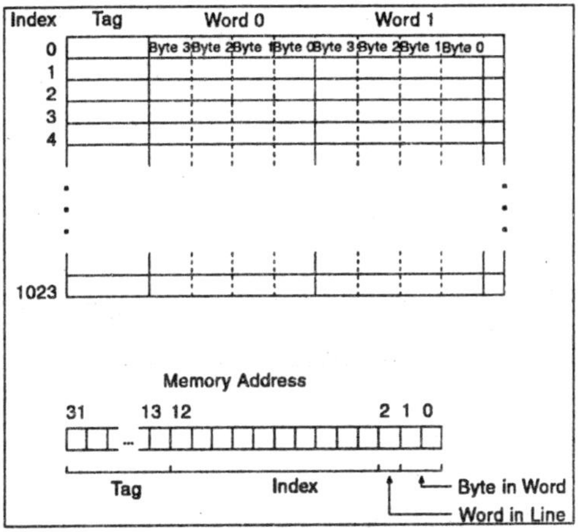

Fig. One Possible MIPS Cache Organization.

A characteristic of the direct mapped cache is that a particular memory address can be mapped into only one cache location. Many memory addresses are mapped to the same cache location (in fact, all addresses with the same index field are mapped to the same cache location.) Whenever a ``cache miss''occurs, the cache line will be replaced by a new line of information from main memory at an address with the same index but with a different tag.

Note that if the programme ``jumps around''in memory, this cache organization will likely not be effective because the index range is limited. Also, if both instructions and data are stored in cache, it may well happen that both map into the same area of cache, and may cause each other to be replaced very often. This could happen, for example, if the code for a matrix operation and the matrix data itself happened to have the same index values.

A more interesting configuration for a cache is the set associative cache, which uses a set associative mapping. In this cache organization, a given memory location can be mapped to more than one cache location. Here, each index corresponds to two or more data words, each with a corresponding tag. A set associative cache with n tag and data fields is called an ``n-way set associative cache''. Usually n = $^{2k}$, for k = 1, 2, 3 are chosen for a set associative cache (k = 0 corresponds to direct mapping). Such n-way set associative caches allow interesting tradeoff possibilities; cache performance can be improved by increasing the number of ``ways", or by increasing the line size, for a given total amount of memory. An example of a 2-way set associative cache, which shows a cache containing a total of 2K lines, or 1 K sets, each set being 2-way associative. (The sets correspond to the rows in the figure.)

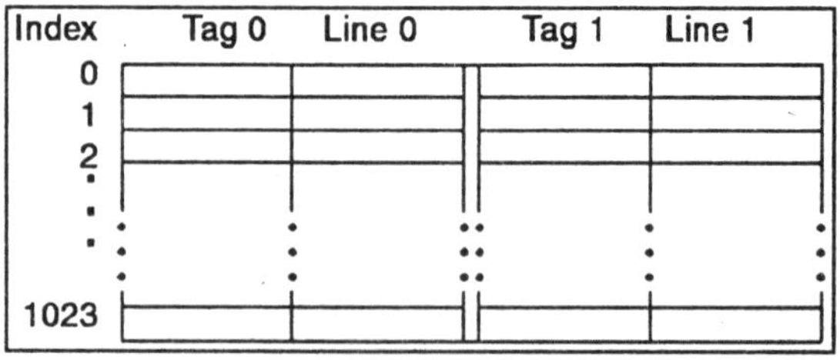

Fig. A Set-associative Cache Organization.

In a 2-way set associative cache, if one data word is empty for a read operation corresponding to a particular index, then it is filled. If both data words are filled, then one must be overwritten by the new data. Similarly, in an n-way set associative cache, if all n data and tag fields in a set are filled, then one value in the set must be overwritten, or replaced, in the cache by the new tag and data values. Note that an entire line must be replaced each time.

The most common replacement algorithms are:

- *Random*: The location for the value to be replaced is chosen at random from all n of the cache locations at that index position. In a 2-way set associative cache, this can be accomplished with a single modulo 2 random variable obtained, say, from an internal clock.
- *First in, first out (FIFO)*: Here the first value stored in the cache, at each index position, is the value to be replaced. For a 2-way set associative cache, this replacement strategy can be implemented by setting a pointer to the previously loaded word each time a new word is stored in the cache; this pointer need

only be a single bit. (For set sizes > 2, this algorithm can be implemented with a counter value stored for each ``line'', or index in the cache, and the cache can be filled in a ``round robin''fashion).

- *Least recently used (LRU)*: Here the value which was actually used least recently is replaced. In general, it is more likely that the most recently used value will be the one required in the near future. For a 2-way set associative cache, this is readily implemented by setting a special bit called the ``USED''bit for the other word when a value isaccessed while the corresponding bit for the word which was accessed is reset. The value to be replaced is then the value with the USED bit set. This replacement strategy can be implemented by adding a single USED bit to each cache location. The LRU strategy operates by setting a bit in the other word when a value is stored and resetting the corresponding bit for the new word. For an n-way set associative cache, this strategy can be implemented by storing a modulo n counter with each data word. (It is an interesting exercise to determine exactly what must be done in this case. The required circuitry may become somewhat complex, for large n.)

Cache memories normally allow one of two things to happen when data is written into a memory location for which there is a value stored in cache:

- *Write through cache*: Both the cache and main memory are updated at the same time. This may slow down the execution of instructions which write data to memory, because of the relatively longer write time to main memory. Buffering memory writes can help speed up memory writes if they are relatively infrequent, however.
- *Write back cache*: Here only the cache is updated directly by the CPU; the cache memory controller marks the value so that it can be written back into memory when the word is removed from the cache.

This method is used because a memory location may often be altered several times while it is still in cache without having to write the value into main memory. This method is often implemented using an ``ALTERED"bit in the cache. The ALTERED bit is set whenever a cache value is written into by the processor. Only if the ALTERED bit is set is it necessary to write the value back into main memory (i.e., only values which have been altered must be written back into main memory). The value should be written back immediately before the value is replaced in the cache.

The MIPS R2000/3000 processors used the write-through approach, with a buffer for the memory writes. (This was also the approach taken by the The VAX-11/780 processor) In practice, memory writes are less frequent than memory reads; typically for each memory write, an instruction must be fetched from main memory, and usually two operands fetched as well. Therefore we might expect about three times as many read operations as write operations. In fact, there are often many more memory read operations than memory write operations.

The behaviour (actually the miss ratio, which is equal to 1 - the hit ratio) for cache memories with various combinations of total cache memory capacity and line size. The results are from simulations of the behaviour of several ``typical"program mixes. Several interesting things can be seen from these figures; Figure shows that the miss ratio drops consistently with cache size.

Note, also, that increasing the line size is not always effective in increasing the throughput of the processor, although it does decrease the hit ratio, because of the additional time required to transfer large lines of data from the main memory to the cache.

WORKING OF CACHE MEMORY

The memory cache is high-speed memory available inside the CPU in order to speed up access to data and instructions stored in RAM memory. In this tutorial we will explain how this circuit works in an easy to follow language. A computer is completely useless if you don't tell the processor (i.e. the CPU) what to do. This is done thru a programme, which is a list of instructions telling the CPU what to do. The CPU fetches programmes from the RAM memory.

The problem with the RAM memory is that when it's power is cut, it's contents are lost - this classifies the RAM memory as a"volatile"medium. Thus programmes and data must be stored on non-volatile media (i.e. where the contents aren't lost after your turn your PC off) if you want to have them back after you turn off your PC, like hard disk drives and optical media like CDs and DVDs.

Data is Transferred to the CPU. The CPU can't fetch data directly from hard disk drives because they are too slow for it, even if you consider the fastest hard disk drive available. Just to give you some idea of what we are talking about, a SATA-300 hard disk drive - the fastest kind of hard disk drive available today for the regular user - has a maximum theoretical transfer rate of 300 MB/s. A CPU running internally at 2 GHz with 64-bit internal datapaths* will transfer data internally at 16 GB/s - over 50 times faster.

- *Translation*: The paths between the CPU internal circuits. This is rough math just to give you an idea, because CPUs have several different data paths inside the CPU, each one having different lengths. For example, on AMD processors the data path between the L2 memory cache and the L1 memory cache is 128-bit wide, while on current Intel CPUs this data path is 256-bit wide. If you got confused don't worry. This is just to explain that the number we published in the above paragraph isn't fixed, but the CPU is always a lot faster than hard disk drives.

The difference in speed comes from the fact that hard disk drives are mechanical systems, which are slower than pure electronics systems, as mechanical parts have to move for the data to be retrieved (which is far slower than moving electrons around). RAM memory, on the other hand, is 100% electronic, thus faster than hard disk drives and optimally as fast as the

CPU. And here is the problem. Even the fastest RAM memory isn't as fast as the CPU. If you take DDR2-800 memories, they transfer data at 6,400 MB/s - 12,800 MB/s if dual channel mode is used. Even though this number is somewhat close to the 16 GB/s from the previous example, as current CPUs are capable of fetching data from the L2 memory cache at 128- or 256-bit rate, we are talking about 32 GB/s or 64 GB/s if the CPU works internally at 2 GHz. Don't worry about what the heck"L2 memory cache"is right now, we will explain it later. All we want is that you get the idea that the RAM memory is slower than the CPU. By the way, transfer rates can be calculated using the following formula (on all examples so far"data per clock"is equal to"1"): Transfer rate = width (number of bits) x clock rate x data per clock/ 8. The problem is not only the transfer rate, i.e. the transfer speed, but also latency.

Latency (a.k.a."access time") is how much time the memory delays in giving back the data that the CPU asked for - this isn't instantaneous. When the CPU asks for an instruction (or data) that is stored at a given address, the memory delays a certain time to deliver this instruction (or data) back. On current memories, if it is labeled as having a CL (CAS Latency, which is the latency we are talking about) of 5, this means that the memory will deliver the asked data only after five memory clock cycles - meaning that the CPU will have to wait.

Waiting reduces the CPU performance. If the CPU has to wait five memory clock cycles to receive the instruction or data it asked for, its performance will be only 1/5 of the performance it would get if it were using a memory capable of delivering data immediately. In other words, when accessing a DDR2-800 memory with CL5, the performance the CPU gets is the same as a memory working at 160 MHz (800 MHz/ 5).

In the real world the performance decrease isn't that much because memories work under a mode called burst mode where from the second data on, data can be delivered immediately, if it is stored on a contiguous address (usually the instructions of a given programme are stored in sequential addresses). This is expressed as"x-1-1-1"(e.g."5-1-1-1"for the memory in our example), meaning that the first data is delivered after five clock cycles but from the second data on data can be delivered in just one clock cycle - if it is stored on a contiguous address, like we said.

It is interesting to plot the same data using log-log coordinates. Note that in this case. the graph is (very) roughly linear. The way size, or degree of associativity, of a cache also has an effect on the performance of a cache; the same reference determined that, for a fixed cache size, there was a roughly constant ratio between the performance of caches with a given set associativity and direct-mapped caches, independent of cache size.

VIRTUAL MEMORY

DEFINITION

Virtual Memory is a feature of an operating system that enables a process to use a memory (RAM) address space that is independent of other processes running in the same system, and use a space that is larger than the actual amount of RAM present, temporarily relegating some contents from RAM to a disk, with little or no overhead. In a system using virtual memory, the physical memory is divided into equally-sized pages. The memory addressed by a process is also divided into logical pages of the same size.

When a process references a memory address, the memory manager fetches from disk the page that includes the referenced address, and places it in a vacant physical page in the RAM. Subsequent references within that logical page are routed to the physical page. When the process references an address from another logical page, it too is fetched into a vacant physical page and becomes the target of subsequent similar references.

If the system does not have a free physical page, the memory manager swaps out a logical page into the swap area - usually a paging file on disk (in Windows XP: pagefile.sys), and copies (swaps in) the requested logical page into the now-vacant physical page. The page swapped out may belong to a different process. There are many strategies for choosing which page is to be swapped out. (One is LRU: the Least Recently Virtual memory enables each process to act as if it has the whole memory space to itself, since the addresses that it uses to reference memory are translated by the virtual memory mechanism into different addresses in physical memory. This allows different processes to use the same memory addresses - the memory manager will translate references to the same memory address by two different processes into different physical addresses. One process generally has no way of accessing the memory of another process. A process may use an address space larger than the available physical memory, and each reference to an address will be translated into an existing physical address. The bound on the amount of memory that a process may actually address is the size of the swap area, which may be smaller than the addressable space. (A process can have an address space of 4GB yet actually use only 2GB, and this can run on a machine with a pagefile of 2GB.)

The size of the virtual memory on a system is smaller than the sum of the physical RAM and the swap area, since pages that are swapped in are not erased from the swap area, and so take up two pages of the sum of sizes. Usually under Windows, the size of the swap area is 1.5 times the size of the RAM. *The virtual memory manager might issue the message*: "Your system is low on virtual memory. Windows is increasing the size of your virtual memory paging file."This happens if it is required to swap out a page from RAM to the pagefile while all pages in the pagefile are already taken. With that message, it will allocate more space to the pagefile and use the added space to store the newly- swapped-out page. One case that might cause the system to want to enlarge the pagefile is that too many processes are running.

In this case, only relatively little of each process'memory can fit in the RAM, and relatively many pages reside in the pagefile. In this case, the virtual memory system is required to hold too many pages - a"small"number of pages per process times"many"processes. In such a case it is also likely that the system will run slowly, since pages need to be swapped in and out more frequently. Another case that might cause the system to want to enlarge the pagefile is that a process has a memory leak. There, the process is occupying a lot of unused memory, which will likely be swapped away in the pagefile and never be swapped in.

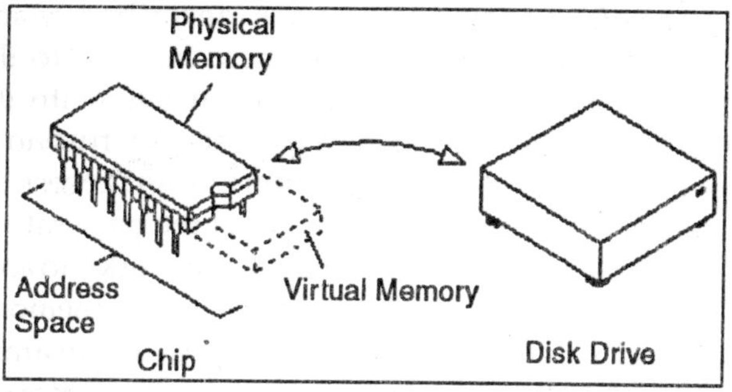

An imaginary memory area supported by some operating systems (for example, Windows but not DOS) in conjunction with the hardware. You can think of virtual memory as an alternate set of memory addresses. Programmes use these virtual addresses rather than real addresses to store instructions and data. When the programme is actually executed, the virtual addresses are converted into real memory addresses. The purpose of virtual memory is to enlarge the address space, the set of addresses a programme can utilize. For example, virtual memory might contain twice as many addresses as main memory. A programme using all of virtual memory, therefore, would not be able to fit in main memory all at once. Nevertheless, the computer could execute such a programme by copying into main memory those portions of the programme needed at any given point during execution. To facilitate copying virtual memory into real memory, the operating system divides virtual memory into pages, each of which contains a fixed number of addresses.

Each page is stored on a disk until it is needed. When the page is needed, the operating system copies it from disk to main memory, translating the virtual addresses into real addresses. The process of translating virtual addresses into real addresses is called mapping. The copying of virtual pages from disk to main memory is known as paging or swapping. The virtual memory subsystem of a processor implements the virtual address spaces provided to each process. This makes each process think it is alone in the system. The list of advantages of virtual memory are described in detail elsewhere so they will not be repeated here. Instead this section concentrates on the actual implementation details of the virtual memory subsystem and the associated costs. A virtual address space is implemented by the Memory Management Unit (MMU) of the CPU. The OS has to fill out the page table data structures, but most CPUs do the rest of the work themselves. This is actually a pretty complicated mechanism; the best way to understand it is to introduce the data structures used to describe the virtual address space. The input to the address translation performed by the MMU is a virtual address.

There are usually few-if any-restrictions on its value. Virtual addresses are 32-bit values on 32-bit systems, and 64-bit values on 64-bit systems. On some systems, for instance x86 and x86-64, the addresses used actually involve another level of indirection: these architectures use segments which simply cause an offset to be added to every logical address. We can ignore this part of address generation, it is trivial and not something that programmers have to care about with respect to performance of memory handling.

SIMPLEST ADDRESS TRANSLATION

The interesting part is the translation of the virtual address to a physical address. The MMU can remap addresses on a page-by-page basis. Just as when addressing cache lines, the virtual address is split into distinct parts. These parts are used to index into various tables which are used in the construction of the final physical address. For the simplest model we have only one level of tables.

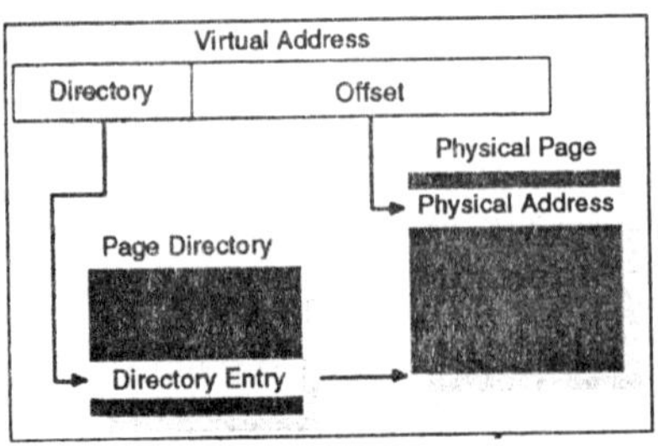

Fig. 1-Level Address Translation.

The different parts of the virtual address are used. A top part is used to select an entry in a Page Directory; each entry in that directory can be individually set by the OS. The page directory entry determines the address of a physical memory page; more than one entry in the page directory can point to the same physical address. The complete physical address of the memory cell is determined by combining the page address from the page directory with the low bits from the virtual address.

The data structure is stored in memory. The OS has to allocate contiguous physical memory and store the base address of this memory region in a special register. The appropriate bits of the virtual address are then used as an index into the page directory, which is actually an array of directory entries.

For a concrete example, this is the layout used for 4MB pages on x86 machines. The Offset part of the virtual address is 22 bits in size, enough to address every byte in a 4MB page. The remaining 10 bits of the virtual address select one of the 1024 entries in the page directory. Each entry contains a 10 bit base address of a 4MB page which is combined with the offset to form a complete 32 bit address.

MULTI-LEVEL PAGE TABLES

4MB pages are not the norm, they would waste a lot of memory since many operations an OS has to perform require alignment to memory pages. With 4kB pages (the norm on 32-bit machines and, still, often on 64-bit machines), the Offset part of the virtual address is only 12 bits in size. This leaves 20 bits as the selector of the page directory. A table with 2^{20} entries is not practical.

Even if each entry would be only 4 bytes the table would be 4MB in size. With each process potentially having its own distinct page directory much of the physical memory of the system would be tied up for these page directories. The solution is to use multiple levels of page tables. These can then represent a sparse huge page directory where regions which are not actually used do not require allocated memory. The representation is therefore much more compact, making it possible to have the tables for many processes in memory without impacting performance too much. Today the most complicated page table structures comprise four levels. Figure below shows the schematics of such an implementation.

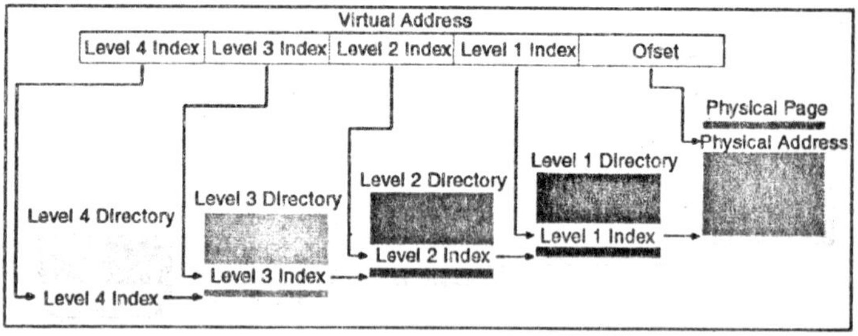

Fig. 4-Level Address Translation.

The virtual address is, in this example, split into at least five parts. Four of these parts are indexes into the various directories. The level 4 directory is referenced using a special-purpose register in the CPU. The content of the level 4 to level 2 directories is a reference to next lower level directory. If a directory entry is marked empty it obviously need not point to any lower directory. This way the page table tree can be sparse and compact. The entries of the level 1 directory are, just like in Figure, partial physical addresses, plus auxiliary data like access permissions.

To determine the physical address corresponding to a virtual address the processor first determines the address of the highest level directory. This address is usually stored in a register. Then the CPU takes the index part of the virtual address corresponding to this directory and uses that index to pick the appropriate entry. This entry is the address of the next directory, which is indexed using the next part of the virtual address. This process continues until it reaches the level 1 directory, at which point the value of the directory entry is the high part of the physical address. The physical address is completed by adding the page offset bits from the virtual address. This process is called page tree walking. Some processors (like x86 and x86-64) perform this operation in hardware, others need assistance from the OS. Each process running on the system might need its own page table tree. It is possible to partially share trees but this is rather the exception. It is therefore good for performance and scalability if the memory needed by the page table trees is as small as possible. The ideal case for this is to place the used memory close together in the virtual address space; the actual physical addresses used do not matter. A small programme might get by with using just one directory at each of levels 2, 3, and 4 and a few level 1 directories. On x86-64 with 4kB pages and 512 entries per directory this allows the addressing of 2MB with a total of 4 directories (one for each level). 1GB of contiguous memory can be addressed with one directory for levels 2 to 4 and 512 directories for level 1.

Assuming all memory can be allocated contiguously is too simplistic, though. For flexibility reasons the stack and the heap area of a process are, in most cases, allocated at pretty much opposite ends of the address space. This allows either area to grow as much as possible if needed. This means that there are most likely two level 2 directories needed and correspondingly more lower level directories.

But even this does not always match current practice. For security reasons the various parts of an executable (code, data, heap, stack, DSOs, aka shared libraries) are mapped at randomized addresses. The randomization extends to the relative position of the various parts; that implies that the various memory regions in use in a process are widespread throughout the virtual address space. By applying some limits to the number of bits of the address which are randomized the range can be restricted, but it certainly, in most cases, will not allow a process to run with just one or two directories for levels 2 and 3. If performance is really much more important than security, randomization can be turned off. The OS will then usually at least load all DSOs contiguously in virtual memory.

OPTIMIZING PAGE TABLE ACCESS

All the data structures for the page tables are kept in the main memory; this is where the OS constructs and updates the tables. Upon creation of a process or a change of a page table the CPU is notified. The page tables are used to resolve every virtual address into a physical address using the page table walk described above. More to the point: at least one directory for each level is used in the process of resolving a virtual address. This requires up to four memory accesses (for a single access by the running process) which is slow. It is possible to treat these directory table entries as normal data and cache them in L1d, L2, etc., but this would still be far too slow. From the earliest days of virtual memory, CPU designers have used a different optimization.

A simple computation can show that only keeping the directory table entries in the L1d and higher cache would lead to horrible performance. Each absolute address computation would require a number of L1d accesses corresponding to the page table depth. These accesses cannot be parallelized since they depend on the previous lookup's result. This alone would, on a machine with four page table levels, require at the very least 12 cycles. Add to that the probability of an L1d miss and the result is nothing the instruction pipeline can hide. The additional L1d accesses also steal precious bandwidth to the cache. So, instead of just caching the directory table entries, the complete computation of the address of the physical page is cached. For the same reason that code and data caches work, such a cached address computation is effective.

Since the page offset part of the virtual address does not play any part in the computation of the physical page address, only the rest of the virtual address is used as the tag for the cache. Depending on the page size this means hundreds or thousands of instructions or data objects share the same tag and therefore same physical address prefix.

The cache into which the computed values are stored is called the Translation Look-Aside Buffer (TLB). It is usually a small cache since it has to be extremely fast. Modern CPUs provide multi-level TLB caches, just as for the other caches; the higher-level caches are larger and slower. The small size of the L1TLB is often made up for by making the cache fully associative, with an LRU eviction policy. Recently, this cache has been growing in size and, in the process, was changed to be set associative. As a result, it might not be the oldest entry which gets evicted and replaced whenever a new entry has to be added. As noted above, the tag used to access the TLB is a part of the virtual address. If the tag has a match in the cache, the final physical address is computed by adding the page offset from the virtual address to the cached value. This is a very fast process; it has to be since the physical address must be available for every instruction using absolute addresses and, in some cases, for L2 look-ups which use the physical address as the key. If the TLB lookup misses the processor has to perform a page table walk; this can be quite costly.

Prefetching code or data through software or hardware could implicitly prefetch entries for the TLB if the address is on another page. This cannot be allowed for hardware prefetching because the hardware could initiate page table walks that are invalid. Programmers therefore cannot rely on hardware prefetching to prefetch TLB entries.

It has to be done explicitly using prefetch instructions. TLBs, just like data and instruction caches, can appear in multiple levels. Just as for the data cache, the TLB usually appears in two flavors: an instruction TLB (ITLB) and a data TLB (DTLB). Higher-level TLBs such as the L2TLB are usually unified, as is the case with the other caches.

CAVEATS OF USING A TLB

The TLB is a processor-core global resource. All threads and processes executed on the processor core use the same TLB. Since the translation of virtual to physical addresses depends on which page table tree is installed, the CPU cannot blindly reuse the cached entries if the page table is changed. Each process has a different page table tree (but not the threads in the same process) as does the kernel and the VMM (hypervisor) if present. It is also possible that the address space layout of a process changes.

There are two ways to deal with this problem:

- The TLB is flushed whenever the page table tree is changed.

- The tags for the TLB entries are extended to additionally and uniquely identify the page table tree they refer to.

In the first case the TLB is flushed whenever a context switch is performed. Since, in most OSes, a switch from one thread/process to another one requires executing some kernel code, TLB flushes are restricted to entering and leaving the kernel address space.

On virtualized systems it also happens when the kernel has to call the VMM and on the way back. If the kernel and/or VMM does not have to use virtual addresses, or can reuse the same virtual addresses as the process or kernel which made the system/VMM call, the TLB only has to be flushed if, upon leaving the kernel or VMM, the processor resumes execution of a different process or kernel.

Flushing the TLB is effective but expensive. When executing a system call, for instance, the kernel code might be restricted to a few thousand instructions which touch, perhaps, a handful of new pages (or one huge page, as is the case for Linux on some architectures). This work would replace only as many TLB entries as pages are touched. For Intel's Core2 architecture with its 128 ITLB and 256 DTLB entries, a full flush would mean that more than 100 and 200 entries (respectively) would be flushed unnecessarily.

When the system call returns to the same process, all those flushed TLB entries could be used again, but they will be gone. The same is true for often-used code in the kernel or VMM. On each entry into the kernel the TLB has to be filled from scratch even though the page tables for the kernel and VMM usually do not change and, therefore, TLB entries could, in theory, be preserved for a very long time. This also explains why the TLB caches in today's processors are not bigger: programmes most likely will not run long enough to fill all these entries.

This fact, of course, did not escape the CPU architects. One possibility to optimize the cache flushes is to individually invalidate TLB entries. For instance, if the kernel code and data falls into a specific address range, only the pages falling into this address range have to evicted from the TLB. This only requires comparing tags and, therefore, is not very expensive. This method is also useful in case a part of the address space is changed, for instance, through a call to munmap. A much better solution is to extend the tag used for the TLB access. If, in addition to the part of the virtual address, a unique identifier for each page table tree (i.e., a process's address space) is added, the TLB does not have to be completely flushed at all. The kernel, VMM, and the individual processes all can have unique identifiers.

The only issue with this scheme is that the number of bits available for the TLB tag is severely limited, while the number of address spaces is not. This means some identifier reuse is necessary. When this happens the TLB has to be partially flushed (if this is possible). All entries with the reused identifier must be flushed but this is, hopefully, a much smaller set. This extended TLB tagging is of general advantage when multiple processes are running on the system.

If the memory use (and hence TLB entry use) of each of the runnable processes is limited, there is a good chance the most recently used TLB entries for a process are still in the TLB when it gets scheduled again.

But there are two additional advantages:

- Special address spaces, such as those used by the kernel and VMM, are often only entered for a short time; afterward control is often returned to the address space which initiated the call. Without tags, two TLB flushes are performed. With tags the calling address space's cached translations are preserved and, since the kernel and VMM address space do not often change TLB entries at all, the translations from previous system calls, etc. can still be used.
- When switching between two threads of the same process no TLB flush is necessary at all. Without extended TLB tags the entry into the kernel destroys the first thread's TLB entries, though.

Some processors have, for some time, implemented these extended tags. AMD introduced a 1-bit tag extension with the

Pacifica virtualization extensions. This 1-bit Address Space ID (ASID) is, in the context of virtualization, used to distinguish the VMM's address space from that of the guest domains. This allows the OS to avoid flushing the guest's TLB entries every time the VMM is entered (for instance, to handle a page fault) or the VMM's TLB entries when control returns to the guest. The architecture will allow the use of more bits in the future. Other mainstream processors will likely follow suit and support this feature.

INFLUENCING TLB PERFORMANCE

There are a couple of factors which influence TLB performance. The first is the size of the pages. Obviously, the larger a page is, the more instructions or data objects will fit into it. So a larger page size reduces the overall number of address translations which are needed, meaning that fewer entries in the TLB cache are needed. Most architectures allow the use of multiple different page sizes; some sizes can be used concurrently. For instance, the x86/x86-64 processors have a normal page size of 4kB but they can also use 4MB and 2MB pages respectively. IA-64 and PowerPC allow sizes like 64kB as the base page size.

The use of large page sizes brings some problems with it, though. The memory regions used for the large pages must be contiguous in physical memory. If the unit size for the administration of physical memory is raised to the size of the virtual memory pages, the amount of wasted memory will grow. All kinds of memory operations (like loading executables) require alignment to page boundaries. This means, on average, that each mapping wastes half the page size in physical memory for each mapping. This waste can easily add up; it thus puts an upper limit on the reasonable unit size for physical memory allocation.

It is certainly not practical to increase the unit size to 2MB to accommodate large pages on x86-64. This is just too large a size. But this in turn means that each large page has to be comprised of many smaller pages. And these small pages have to be contiguous in physical memory. Allocating 2MB of contiguous physical memory with a unit page size of 4kB can be challenging. It requires finding a free area with 512 contiguous pages. This can be extremely difficult (or impossible) after the system runs for a while and physical memory becomes fragmented.

On Linux it is therefore necessary to pre-allocate these big pages at system start time using the special huget lbfs file system. A fixed number of physical pages are reserved for exclusive use as big virtual pages. This ties down resources which might not always be used. It also is a limited pool; increasing it normally means restarting the system. Still, huge pages are the way to go in situations where performance is a premium, resources are plenty, and cumbersome setup is not a big deterrent. Database servers are an example.

Increasing the minimum virtual page size (as opposed to optional big pages) has its problems, too. Memory mapping operations (loading applications, for example) must conform to these page sizes. No smaller mappings are possible. The location of the various parts of an executable have, for most architectures, a fixed relationship. If the page size is increased beyond what has been taken into account when the executable or DSO was built, the load operation cannot be performed. It is important to keep this limitation in mind. Figure shows how the alignment requirements of an ELF binary can be determined. It is encoded in the ELF programme header.

```
  $ eu-readelf -l/bin/ls
  Programme Headers:
    Type Offset VirtAddr PhysAddr
FileSiz MemSiz Flg
Align
  ...
    LOAD 0x000000 0x0000000000400000
  0x0000000000400000 0x0132ac 0x0132ac R E
0x200000
    LOAD 0x0132b0 0x00000000006132b0
0x00000000006132b0 0x001a71 0x001a71 RW
0x200000
```

In this example, an x86-64 binary, the value is 0x200000 = 2,097,152 = 2MB which corresponds to the maximum page size supported by the processor. There is a second effect of using larger page sizes: the number of levels of the page table tree is reduced. Since the part of the virtual address corresponding to the page offset increases, there are not that many bits left which need to be handled through page directories. This means that, in case of a TLB miss, the amount of work which has to be done is reduced.

Beyond using large page sizes, it is possible to reduce the number of TLB entries needed by moving data which is used at the same time to fewer pages. This is similar to some optimizations for cache use we talked about above. Only now the alignment required is large. Given that the number of TLB entries is quite small this can be an important optimization.

IMPACT OF VIRTUALIZATION

Virtualization of OS images will become more and more prevalent; this means another layer of memory handling is added to the picture. Virtualization of processes (basically jails) or OS containers do not fall into this category since only one OS is involved. Technologies like Xen or KVM enable-with or without help from the processor-the execution of independent OS images. In these situations there is one piece of software alone which directly controls access to the physical memory. In the case of Xen, the Xen VMM is that piece of software.

The VMM does not implement many of the other hardware controls itself, though. Unlike VMMs on other, earlier systems (and the first release of the Xen VMM) the hardware outside of memory and processors is controlled by the privileged Dom0 domain. Currently, this is basically the same kernel as the unprivileged DomU kernels and, as far as memory handling is concerned, they do not differ.

Important here is that the VMM hands out physical memory to the Dom0 and DomU kernels which, themselves, then implement the usual memory handling as if they were running directly on a processor. To implement the separation of the domains which is required for the virtualization to be complete, the memory handling in the Dom0 and DomU kernels does not have unrestricted access to physical memory. The VMM does not hand out memory by giving out individual physical pages and letting the guest OSes handle the addressing; this would not provide any protection against faulty or rogue guest domains. Instead, the VMM creates its own page table tree for each guest domain and hands out memory using these data structures. The good thing is that access to the administrative information of the page table tree can be controlled. If the code does not have appropriate privileges it cannot do anything.

This access control is exploited in the virtualization Xen provides, regardless of whether para- or hardware (aka full) virtualization is used. The guest domains construct their page table trees for each process in a way which is intentionally quite similar for para- and hardware virtualization. Whenever the guest OS modifies its page tables the VMM is invoked. 0

The VMM then uses the updated information in the guest domain to update its own shadow page tables. These are the page tables which are actually used by the hardware. Obviously, this process is quite expensive: each modification of the page table tree requires an invocation of the VMM. While changes to the memory mapping are not cheap without virtualization they become even more expensive now.

The additional costs can be really large, considering that the changes from the guest OS to the VMM and back themselves are already quite expensive. This is why the processors are starting to have additional functionality to avoid the creation of shadow page tables. This is good not only because of speed concerns but it also reduces memory consumption by the VMM.

Intel has Extended Page Tables (EPTs) and AMD calls it Nested Page Tables (NPTs). Basically both technologies have the page tables of the guest OSes produce virtual physical addresses. These addresses must then be further translated, using the per-domain EPT/NPT trees, into actual physical addresses. This will allow memory handling at almost the speed of the no-virtualization case since most VMM entries for memory handling are removed. It also reduces the memory use of the VMM since now only one page table tree for each domain (as opposed to process) has to be maintained. The results of the additional address translation steps are also stored in the TLB.

That means the TLB does not store the virtual physical address but, instead, the complete result of the lookup. It was already explained that AMD's Pacifica extension introduced the ASID to avoid TLB flushes on each entry. The number of bits for the ASID is one in the initial release of the processor extensions; this is just enough to differentiate VMM and guest OS. Intel has virtual processor IDs (VPIDs) which serve the same purpose, only there are more of them. But the VPID is fixed for each guest domain and therefore it cannot be used to mark separate processes and avoid TLB flushes at that level, too.

The amount of work needed for each address space modification is one problem with virtualized OSes. There is another problem inherent in VMM-based virtualization, though: there is no way around having two layers of memory handling. But memory handling is hard (especially when taking complications like NUMA into account. The Xen approach of using a separate VMM makes optimal (or even good) handling hard since all the complications of a memory management implementation, including"trivial"things like discovery of memory regions, must be duplicated in the VMM. The OSes have fully-fledged and optimized implementations; one really wants to avoid duplicating them.

This is why carrying the VMM/Dom0 model to its conclusion is such an attractive alternative. Figure above shows how the KVM Linux kernel extensions try to solve the problem. There is no separate VMM running directly on the hardware and controlling all the guests; instead, a normal Linux kernel kernel is used to manage the memory of the system. Guest domains run alongside the normal user-level processes in what the creators call"guest mode". The virtualization functionality, para- or full virtualization, is controlled by another user-level process, the KVM VMM. This is just another process which happens to control a guest domain using the special KVM device the kernel implements. The benefit of this model over the separate VMM of the Xen model is that, even though there are still two memory handlers at work when guest OSes are used, there only needs to be one implementation, that in the Linux kernel. It is not necessary to duplicate the same functionality in another piece of code like the Xen VMM.

This leads to less work, fewer bugs, and, perhaps, less friction where the two memory handlers touch since the memory handler in a Linux guest makes the same assumptions as the memory handler in the outer Linux kernel which runs on the bare hardware. Overall, programmers must be aware that, with virtualization used, the cost of memory operations is even higher than without virtualization. Any optimization which reduces this work will pay off even more in virtualized environments. Processor designers will, over time, reduce the difference more and more through technologies like EPT and NPT but it will never completely go away.

Chapter 8

Storage Devices

INTRODUCTION

COMPUTER STORAGE DEVICES

A device capable of storing data. The term usually refers to mass storage devices, such as disk and tape drives. In a computer, storage is the place where data is held in an electromagnetic or optical form for access by a computer processor.

Computer data storage; often called storage or memory refer to computer components, devices and recording media that retain digital data used for computing for some interval of time.

Knowing what kinds of storage devices are available can keep you from using up too much space on your computer's hard drive. They can also help keep your computer's hard drive from crashing, along with keeping it running at top speed.

As we see in modern day computers, storage devices can be found in many forms. Storage devices can be classified based on many criterions. Of them, the very basic is as we learned in schools ie; Primary storage and Secondary storage. Storage devices can be further classified based on the memory technology that they use, based on its data volatility etc...

The following list gives a few classifications of memory devices:

- Primary and Secondary and Tertiary Storage
- Volatile and non-volatile storage
- Read only and Writable storage

- Random Access and Sequential Access storage
- Magnetic storage
- Optical storage
- Semiconductor storage

Let us see in detail about each type of storage devices.

Primary and Secondary and Tertiary Storage

In simple words, primary storage is the storage device that is directly connected to the CPU and store data temporarily during execution. i.e. CPU can directly access primary storage and stores instruction and data for execution/processing. The most popular example of this kind of memory is the RAM (Random Access Memory) that we use in modern day computers.

CPU registers, Caches and other memories connected to the CPU local bus falls in this category. Primary storage devices are comparatively faster than all other kinds of memory types. Usually primary storage devices are considered to be directly connected to the processor.

But in reality, modern computers employ components like Virtual Memory Manager, DRAM controllers etc.. in between processor and the memory but the notion of 'Direct connection' is still valid since these components are transparent to the processor. Volatile memories are usually used as primary storage. On the contrary, Secondary storage may not be directly accessible by the processor.

And is usually used for more permenent storage of data. This requires secondary storage devices to be non-volatile. Secondary storage devices are connected to storage controllers and the CPU is required to talk to the controllers in order to access information from secondary devices. The most popular example of secondary device is the Hard disk.

CD ROM, DVD ROM, USB mass storage devices, Floppy etc.. are also falls in this category. Secondary storage devices are also called Mass Storage Devices since the capacity of these devices are comparatively large. The picture below illustrates the classification of different types of Storage Devices as described above.

Primary Storage		
Directly accessible from CPU		
Ram	Regster	Cache
Secondary Storage		
Accessible through special hardware		
Hard disk	Flash	Floppy
Tertiary Storage		
Accessible through mechanical means		
Tape libraries	Optical jukebox	

Volatile and Non-volatile Storage

As the name implies, volatile memory looses its contents when power supply is withdrawn. So usually Volatile memories are used for temporary storage of data. In some exceptional cases, volatile memory devices are used along with long life batteries to make semi-permenent storage devices. Compared with non-volatile storage, Volatile storage devices are faster while both reading and writing data. This makes these kinds of memories very suitable to be used as main memories of computers. In fact, the memories we use in computers (RAM) are volatile devices.

Volatile Storage		
Data is lost when power is withdrawn		
Ram	Register	Cache
Non-Volatile Storage		
Maintains data even after power cycle		
Hard disk	Flash	Floppy

Non-volatile storage devices retain the contents even in absence of active power source. This makes non-volatile devices suitable for long term permenent data storage. Non-volatile devices usually available in large capacities. Hard Disks, CD ROM, Floppy disks, Flash, ROM etc.. are examples of non-volatile memory devices. Non-volatile storage devices are slower when compared to volatile storage devices. But some non-volatile can faster during read operation and slower during write operation. Semiconductor non-volatile memory devices fall in this category.

Read only and Writable Storage

Read only storage devices only allows contents to be read from and doesn't allow the contents to be modified. Meanwhile, Writable storage devices allow both content retrieval as well as content modification. Read only devices are usually used for long term permanent storage where modification of data is not necessary. CD ROM, DVD etc are examples of Read Only Storage devices. Some Read Only Storage devices comes with factory programmed data which you can only read but not modify. There is another class of devices called Write Once Read Multiple (WORM) devices which allows us to write data to it one and only one time and allows any number of subsequent reads. CD-R and DVD-R are technically comes under this category.

Read only Storage		
Data can't be written to the Device		
Rom	CD-R	EEPROM
Read/write storage		
Data can be written to the Device		
Hard disk	Flash	Ram

Random Access and Sequential Access storage

Random Access storage devices allow retrieval of content from any location in the same amount of time. i.e. Latency (The time taken to access a particular location in storage) is independent of content's location. RAM used in computers is an example of Random Access Memory. In sequential access storage devices, data can be accessed in sequential manner only. And the time taken to read from a particular location will be dependant on the location last accessed. Example of a sequential access device is the Tape storage device. Sequential access devices are usually used for backup purpose only, where frequent access of information is not required.

Random access storage		
Access any location randomly		
Ram	Flash	EEPROM
Sequential access storage		
Access data sequentially		
Tape		

Magnetic Storage

Magnetic storage devices store information in the form of magnetic field on magnetically coated surface. Magnetic storage devices fall in the category of non-volatile devices. This makes magnetic storage devices to be useful for long term data storage. Hard disks, Floppy disks and tape devices are examples of magnetic storage devices. Data is written to magnetic media with the help of electromagnetic heads. The same head is usually used also for retrieval of data. Though magnetic storage medias can hold large amount of data, these are considered to be bulky and not usable for mobile applications. But technological advancements made it possible to create large capacity magnetic storage devices with small size. An example for this is Apple's ipod classic which is available with a built in hard disk with a capacity as large as 160 GB for music/video storage.

Magnetic storage	
Data is recorded on magnetic media	
Hard disk	Floppy

Optical Storage

Optical storage devices store data on reflective polycarbonate discs in the form of pits and bumps. Data is recorded on the disc by pointing modulated laser beam on to the rotating disc. This makes a series of tiny pits which doesn't reflect light and bumps that reflect light. For reading the data, a low power laser beam is focused to the track and the reflected beam is directed to a photo diode.

Optical storage	
Data is recorded on optical media	
CD	DVD

Semiconductor Storage

Semiconductor storage devices store data in tiny memory cells made of very small transistors and capacitors made of semiconductor materials such as silicon. Each cell can hold one bit of information and an array of cells stores large chunk of information. Semiconductor storage devices can be volatile and non-volatile. RAM is an example of volatile semiconductor storage device. EEPROM and FASH are examples of non-volatile semiconductor storage devices. FLASH devices are gaining popularity over conventional secondary storage devices like hard disks. There are a large number of products in the market now which uses FLASH devices exclusively as secondary storage (Eg. MP3 players, Mobile Phones etc...)

Random access storage		
Access any location randomly		
Ram	Flash	Eprom

Part1 of this series of articles end here. This article is expected to give you very basic information of storage device classifications and technologies.

COMMON STORAGE DEVICES

- Floppy Disks
- Zip Disks
- CD + RW
- CD + R
- DVD + RW
- DVD + R
- Removable Hard Drive
- Internet Hard Drive
- Flash
- PC Cards
- Smart Cards

- Storage Tapes
- Memory Sticks
- Smart Media

Floppy Disk

They are plastic square disks, usually with a silver or black sliding piece going across the top. These disks come in a variety of colours and they hold about 144 million bytes. (Bytes are characters, symbols and letters).

Zip Disk

They look like a floppy disk, but they are a little thicker. This disk also comes in a variety of colours and holds about 200 MB of data.

CD + RW Disc (Compact Disc Rewriteable)

This disc looks like a regular CD. The only difference is that you can write on this disc and erase it as many times as you want. It works just like a floppy disk or a zip disk. A CD + RW disc holds about 650 MB.

CD + R Disc (Compact Disc Recordable)

This one is a CD that you can record on. It's mostly used to record audio and once it's been written on, you cannot rewrite or erase anything off of it. This compact disc comes in different sizes, but they are usually silver in colour. (Some CDs are black in colour and they actually don't get as many scratches on them as the silver ones do. They are also a lot less fragile).

A DVD – R Disc (Digital Video Recordable)

These discs hold the space of about 4.7 GB and are used to record movies on.

Removable Hard Drive

This is a disk drive in which a plastic or metal case surrounds the hard drive. It can be inserted and removed just like a floppy disk. It holds about 2 GB of data.

Internet Hard Drive

This one is a service on the Internet that provides storage space to computer users. This service offers about 25 MB of space, but it could be more, depending on the service type.

Flash Drive

This a storage device that comes in many colours and has a stick shape to it.

They are very small in size, but they can hold anywhere between 256 MB and 3 GB of material on them.

PC Card

This is a thin credit card size device that fits into a PC card slot, usually on a notebook computer. This card simply adds storage to most notebooks.

Smart Cards

These are the size of an ATM card. When inserted into a smart card reader, they can read and update data for you.

Storage Tape

This one is a magnetically coated ribbon of plastic, capable of storing large amounts of data at a very low cost. Usually, storage tapes are a little bigger than audio tapes. Older computers used tape and tape drives, but even today, some people still back their systems up with storage tape.

These tapes hold between 20 GB to about 110 GB of data. An external tape drive can be purchased separately as well, but those are even harder to find.

Miniature Mobile Storage Media

This is used mostly with handheld computers and digital cameras.

Memory Stick

This is a rectangular shaped disk that is used mostly with digital cameras and notebook computers. They hold approximately 128 MB as well.

Micro Drive

This is a square disk that has 1 GB of space and is used with digital cameras and handheld computers.

Smart Media Disc

This is a square disk that has 2 MB to about 128 MB of space on it. It's used with digital cameras, handheld computers and photo printers.

INPUT UNITS

OVERVIEW

The aim of the Input Unit is to provide an efficient service regarding crime and accident recording. The Unit provides advice and support to Police Officers regarding the creation, update and amendment of our crime reporting system and also the creation of accident reports.. Input staff has responsibility for the initial investigation into minor, historic, and non-urgent crime complaints.

INPUT: GETTING DATA FROM THE USER TO THE COMPUTER

Some input data can go directly to the computer for processing. Input in this category includes bar codes, speech that enters the computer through a microphone, and data entered by means of a device that converts motions to on-screen action. Some input data, however, goes through a good deal of intermediate handling, such as when it is copied from a source document and translated to a medium that a machine can read, such as a magnetic disk. In either case the task is to gather data to be processed by the computer ‹sometimes called raw data and convert it into some form the computer can understand.

Keyboard

A keyboard is usually part of a personal computer or part of a terminal that is connected to a computer somewhere else.

Alphanumeric keypad: It consists of keys for English alphabets, 0 to 9 numbers, and special characters like +/* () etc.

Function Keys: There are twelve function keys labeled F1, F2, F3, ..., F12. The functions assigned to these keys differ from one software package to another. These keys are also user programmable keys.

Special-function keys: These keys have special functions assigned to them and can be used only for those specific purposes. Functions of some of the important keys are defined below.

Enter: It is similar to the 'return' key of the typewriter and is used to execute a command or programme.

Spacebar: It is used to enter a space at the current cursor location.

Backspace: This key is used to move the cursor one position to the left and also delete the character in that position.

Delete: It is used to delete the character at the cursor position.

Insert: Insert key is used to toggle between insert and overwrite mode during data entry.

Shift: This key is used to type capital letters when pressed along with an alphabet key. Also used to type the special characters located on the upper-side of a key that has two characters defined on the same key.

Caps lock: Cap Lock is used to toggle between the capital lock feature. When 'on', it locks the alphanumeric keypad for capital letters input only.

Tab: Tab is used to move the cursor to the next tab position defined in the document. Also, it is used to insert indentation into a document.

Ctrl: Control key is used in conjunction with other keys to provide additional functionality on the keyboard.

Alt: Also like the control key, Alt key is always used in combination with other keys to perform specific tasks.

Esc: This key is usually used to negate a command. Also used to cancel or abort executing programmes.

Numeric keypad: Numeric keypad is located on the right side of the keyboard and consists of keys having numbers (0 to 9) and mathematical operators (+ - */) defined on them. This keypad is provided to support quick entry for numeric data.

Cursor movement keys: These are arrow keys and are used to move the cursor in the direction indicated by the arrow (up, down, left, right).

Mouse

A mouse is an input device with a ball on its underside that is rolled on a flat surface, usually the desk on which the computer sits. The rolling movement causes a corresponding movement on the screen. Moving the mouse allows you to reposition the pointer, or cursor, an indicator on the screen that shows where the next interaction with the computer can take place. The cursor can also be moved by pressing various keyboard keys.

Mouse Actions

Left click: Used to select an item.

Double click: Used to start a programme or open a file.

Right click: Usually used to display a set of commands.

Drag and drop: It allows you to select and move an item from one location to another. To achieve this place the cursor over an item on the screen, click the left mouse button and while holding the button down move the cursor to where you want to place the item, and then release it.

Trackball

A variation on the mouse is the trackball. You may have used a trackball to play a video game. The trackball is like an upside-down mouse-you roll the ball directly with your hand. The popularity of the trackball surged with the advent of laptop computers, when traveling users found them- selves without a flat surface on which to roll the traditional mouse.

Source Data Automation: Collecting Data Where It Starts

Efficient data input means reducing the number of intermediate steps required between the origination of data and its processing. This is best accomplished by source data automation ‹the use of special equipment to collect data at the source, as a by-product of the activity that generates the data, and send it directly to the computer. Recall, for example, the supermarket bar code, which can be used to send data about the product directly to the computer.

Magnetic-Ink Character Recognition

Abbreviated MICR, magnetic-ink character recognition is a method of machine-reading characters made of magnetized particles. The most common example of magnetic characters is the array of numbers across the bottom of your personal check. Most magnetic-ink characters are preprinted on your check. If you compare a check you wrote that has been cashed and cleared by the bank with those that are still unused in your checkbook, you will note that the amount of the cashed check has been reproduced in magnetic characters in the lower-right corner. These characters were added by a person at the bank by using a MICR inscriber.

Scanner

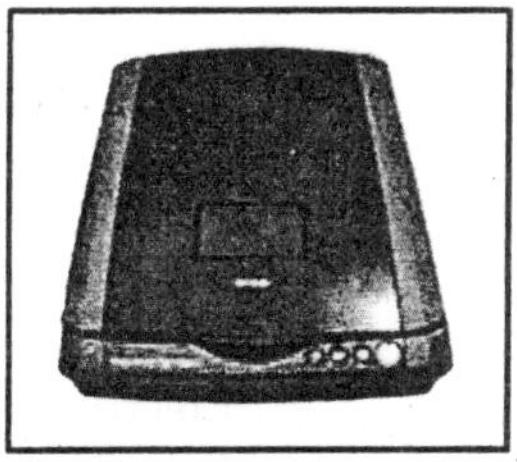

Fig. Flatbed Scanner

An inexpensive way to get entire documents, pictures, and anything on a flat Surface into a computer is by using a scanner. Scanners use optical recognition systems that have a light beam to scan input data to convert it into electrical signals, which are sent to the computer for processing. Optical recognition is by far the most common type of source input, appearing in a variety of ways: optical marks, optical characters, bar codes, handwritten characters, and images. Scanners use *Optical Character Recognition* software, to translate text on scanned documents into text that is suitable for word processors and other computer applications.

Index

A

Accumulators 184
Aircraft-warning 35
Algorithms 22, 72, 95, 105, 120, 121, 124, 131, 139, 148, 158, 169, 178, 239, 247, 266
Analog Computers 30, 31
Arbitrary Graphs 22
Arithmetical 84, 87
Assembly Languages 36, 61

B

Bayes Rule 22
Berry Computers 47
Bit Strings 23, 24, 25

C

Circuits 14, 37, 38, 39, 40, 57, 71, 72, 184, 192, 196, 197, 203, 204, 247
Colossus Computer 46
Correcting Codes 13, 14, 15, 21, 22, 23

D

Decimal Point 2, 5, 6, 121, 168, 170
Decoder 14, 16, 17, 18, 19, 171, 172, 175, 179, 181, 183
Demonstration 31
Denormalized 103, 126, 131, 132, 133, 134
Desktop Computers 49
Digital 1, 5, 14, 15, 30, 31, 33, 34, 40, 46, 47, 49, 51, 53, 54, 113, 184, 188, 195, 196, 199, 206, 229, 233, 266, 272, 275, 276
Digital Computers 30, 31
Dimensionalities 24

E

Electronic pen 49, 50
Encoder 14, 16, 21
Equivalently 28
Error Detecting 23

F

Floating Point 6, 10, 12, 186, 187

G

Generation 30, 33, 34, 36, 37, 38, 39, 40, 41, 43, 200, 217, 252

Graphical Models 22, 23
Group Floating-Point 11

H

Hammed Byte 26, 27, 28
Handheld Computer 49, 50, 273, 274
Harvard Mark 34, 46
Hierarchy 225, 226, 227, 228, 229
HyperCard 43
Hypercube 23, 24
Hypertext 43

I

Integer 1, 2, 3, 4, 6, 8, 9, 12, 64, 66, 67, 68, 92, 101, 115, 116, 121, 122, 123, 124, 137, 138, 142, 143, 144, 168, 173, 185, 187, 214, 217
Integrated Circuits 14, 40

L

Linear Codes 14, 21
Logarithm 2, 3, 136, 137, 161, 203, 212, 220, 221, 223, 224

M

Magnetic Disk 36, 37, 54, 226, 274
Magnetic Drum 37
Mainframes 44, 47, 48
Manchester 34, 70
Mantissa 6, 8, 9, 10, 11, 12, 13, 168, 169, 170, 214, 215
Microcomputers 40, 42, 47, 48
Microprocessor 41, 171, 173, 184, 191, 195, 199, 229
Miniaturized 38
Minicomputer 40, 45, 47
Multi-tasking units 47

N

N-tuples 15, 16, 18, 19, 20
Nano Computer 53
Nibble 26, 27
Notebook Computers 50, 273

P

Parity 13, 25, 27, 28, 29, 242
PDA 49, 50, 53, 229
Perfect Codes 19
Personal Computer 31, 42, 45, 47, 52, 233, 274
Pocket Pc 49
Probability Distribution 22
Probability Estimations 22

S

Semiconductor Memory 229, 230, 231, 232, 233, 234
Semiconductors 229
Sequence 15, 16, 61, 86, 94, 95, 113, 130, 145, 176, 178, 180, 191, 192, 197, 199,
Signed Binary Fractions 6
Signed Numbers 4, 67, 68, 122
Single-bit Error 24, 25
Single-precision 10, 11, 12, 13, 144
Super Computer 44, 50, 51

T

Tablet Pc 49
Toggling 3
Turbo Codes 14, 21, 23

Two-bit Error 25, 26
Two's Complement 12, 66, 67, 73, 75, 84, 122

U

Ultra Mobile Pc 50

V

Vertices 24, 25
Voltage 1, 31, 33, 181, 232, 233, 238

W

Web Browser 43
Word Processor 277

Z

Z_3 Computers 46